THE POLITICS OF PEA
POST-COLD

THE CASS SERIES ON PEACEKEEPING
ISSN 1367–9880
General Editor: Michael Pugh

This series examines all aspects of peacekeeping, from the political, operational and legal dimensions to the developmental and humanitarian issues that must be dealt with by all those involved with peacekeeping in the world today.

THE POLITICS OF PEACEKEEPING IN THE POST-COLD WAR ERA

Editors David S. Sorenson and
Pia Christina Wood

FRANK CASS
London and New York

First published 2005 in Great Britain by
Frank Cass
2 Park Square, Milton Park, Abingdon, Oxfordshire, OX14 4RN

Simultaneously published in the USA and Canada by
Frank Cass
270 Madison Ave., New York, NY 10016

Frank Cass is an imprint of the Taylor & Francis Group

Typeset in Great Britain by Keyword Publishing Services Ltd
Printed and bound in Great Britain by
TJ International Ltd., Padstow, Cornwall

British Library Cataloguing in Publication Data
A catalogue record for this book is available from the British Library

Library of Congress Cataloging in Publication Data
A catalog record for this book has been requested

ISBN 0-7146-8488-0 (Hb)
ISBN 0-7146-5596-1 (Pb)

Contents

Contributors

Alan James Bullion has a Ph.D. in International Relations from the University of Southampton; and is currently Associate Lecturer/Research Associate in Politics, The Open University, UK (1992–). His current research interests include Sri Lanka, India, UN peacekeeping, Tamil nationalism, and Asian agriculture.

Mary N. Hampton is an Associate Professor of Political Science from the University of Utah, and was in residence at Air War College during 2000–2003 as a visiting professor in the International Security Studies Department. Her areas of research and teaching include international relations theory, international security issues, German/European foreign and security policy, and US foreign and security policy. She has published numerous articles and written or co-edited two books. Her most recent publications include 'Eagle in the Field of Blackbirds: U.S. Military Lessons Learned and Applied in Bosnia and Kosovo', a chapter in Lily Gardner-Feldman (ed.), *Cooperation or Competition?*; ' "The Past, Present, and the Perhaps": Is Germany a "Normal" Power?', in *Security Studies* (winter 2000); and 'Kosovo: Boom or Bust for the trans-Atlantic Relationship?', co-authored with Heiko Borchert in *Orbis* (spring 2002).

Herbert M. Howe is Research Professor of African Studies at the Edmund A. Walsh School of Foreign Service, Georgetown University. He is the author of *Ambiguous Order: Military Forces in African States* (Lynne Rienner Publishers, 2001), as well as articles on African militaries in such journals as *The Journal of Modern African Studies* and *International Security*.

Alexander Ramsbotham heads the UN and Conflict Unit at United Nations Association-UK. He previously edited the *International*

Peacekeeping News and its successor the *Conflict Resolution Monitor*, publications produced by the Department of Peace Studies, University of Bradford, and continues to edit the 'Digest' and 'Documentation' sections of the Frank Cass journal *International Peacekeeping*. He is co-author, with David J. Francis, Mohammed Faal and John Kabia, of *The Dangers of Co-deployment: UN Co-operative Peacekeeping in Africa* (Ashgate, forthcoming) and regularly comments on UN and related affairs in the British media.

David Rudd served in the Canadian military between 1985 and 1990. He holds a graduate degree in international relations from Dalhousie University in Halifax, Nova Scotia, and has been the Executive Director of the Canadian Institute of Strategic Studies (CISS) since 1998. He is a regular contributor to print and electronic media analyses of Canadian defence and security issues.

Erwin A. Schmidl is head of the Section of Contemporary History at the Austrian Defence Academy in Vienna (Institute of Strategy and Security Policy). He has worked and published on various aspects of peace operations for the past 12 years. Also, he has served as desk officer for peacekeeping in the Foreign Ministry's UN Department in 1991–92, and was UN observer in South Africa in 1994.

Hugh Smith is Associate Professor in the School of Politics, University College, University of New South Wales, at the Australian Defence Force Academy in Canberra and was Founding Director of the Australian Defence Studies Centre at the College from 1987 to 1991. He has edited several books on peacekeeping and has published widely on armed forces and society, including topics such as officer education, conscientious objection, recruitment, women in combat, and reserve service. His most recent publication is an edited collection entitled *The Strategists*, published by the Australian Defence Studies Centre.

David S. Sorenson is Professor of International Security Studies at the US Air War College. He previously served on the faculty at Denison University, and was Senior Research Associate at the Mershon Center at Ohio State University. He has a Ph.D. from the Graduate School of International Studies, University of Denver, and has published books and articles on American national security issues.

Cynthia A. Watson is Associate Dean for Curriculum and Faculty Development at the National War College, Washington, DC, where she has been a faculty member since 1992. She writes extensively on militaries and security issues in the former 'Third World', focusing particularly on Argentina, China, and Colombia. She is on the Editorial Board of *Third World Quarterly*, and is currently completing a book on the collapse of Colombia. She has an MA in Latin America Studies and Economic History from the London School of Economics and earned her Ph.D. in International Studies from the University of Notre Dame.

Pia Christina Wood is Director of International Studies and Associate Professor of Political Science at Wake Forest University. She has published articles and book chapters on French foreign policy, the politics of the European Union, and Franco–German relations. Her forthcoming book is entitled *French Foreign Policy toward the Arab–Israeli Conflict from Charles de Gaulle to Jacques Chirac: The Search for Influence*.

Tom Woodhouse holds the Adam Curle Chair in Conflict Resolution at the Department of Peace Studies, University of Bradford, UK. He was the founding director of the department's Centre for Conflict Resolution and has written widely on conflict analysis and conflict resolution. He edited the special issue of the journal *International Peacekeeping*, entitled *Peacekeeping and Conflict Resolution*, published by Frank Cass (spring 2000). He has recently completed a report on conflict prevention and the war on terror, entitled 'Building the Democratic Peace' (IDEA, Stockholm).

Abbreviations

ADF	Australian Defence Force
AFRC	Armed Forces Revolutionary Council (Nigeria)
ALP	Australian Labour Party
ASEAN	Association of Southeast Asian Nations
BMATT	British Military Advisory and Training Team
CAECOPAZ	Argentinian Joint Training Center for Blue Helmets
CENCAMEX	Training Center for Members of Peace Missions Abroad
CENCOOP	Central European Nations Cooperation in Peace Support
CENTCOM	Central Command (US)
CFSP	Common Foreign and Security Policy (Europe)
CINC	Commander-in-Chief
CJTF	Combined Joint Task Force (US)
COIN	counter-insurgency
CPE	complex-political emergency
C2W	Command and Control Warfare (UK)
DCI	Defense Capabilities Initiative (NATO)
DFAT	Department of Foreign Affairs and Trade (Australia)
DFID	Department for International Development (UK)
DPKO	Department of Peace Keeping Operations (New York)
ECMM	European Community Monitor Mission (Balkans)
ECOMOG	Ecomomic Community of West African States Military Observer Group
ECOWAS	Economic Community of West African States
EIPC	Enhanced International Peace Capabilities
ESDP	European Security and Defence Policy
EUMM	European Union Monitor Mission (Balkans)
EW	electronic warfare (UK)
FAR	Rwandan Armed Forces
FCO	Foreign and Commonwealth Office (UK)
FUNCINPEC	National United Front for an Independent, Neutral, Peaceful and Cooperative Cambodia

IAEA	International Atomic Energy Agency
ICSS	International Common State Sovereign (Canada)
IFOP	Institut Français d'Opinion Publique
INTERFET	International Force in East Timor
ISAF	International Security Assistance Force (Afghanistan)
JDCC	Joint Doctrine and Concepts Centre
JWP	Joint Warfare Publication (UK)
KFOR	Kosovo Force (NATO)
KPNLF	Khmer People's National Liberation Front
KVM	Kosovo Verification Mission
MFO	Multinational Force and Observers
MINUGUA	UN Mission in Guatemala
MINURSO	UN Mission for the Referendum in Western Sahara
MIPONUH	UN Civilian Police Mission in Haiti
MOD	Ministry of Defence (UK)
MOMEP	Military Observer Mission in Ecuador and Peru
MONUA	UN Mission in Angola
MONUC	UN Mission in the Congo
NAFTA	North Atlantic Free Trade Agreement
NATO	North Atlantic Treaty Organization
NPFL	National Patriotic Front of Liberia
OAU	Organization for African Unity
OPEC	Organization of Petroleum Exporting Countries
OPSEC	operational security (UK)
OSCE	Organization for Security and Cooperation in Europe
PKO	peace-keeping operation
PND	Department of National Defence (Canada)
PNG	Papua New Guinea
PRK	People's Republic of Kampuchea
PSO	peace support operation
PSTC	Peace Support Training Centre (Canada)
PSYOPS	psychological operations
RPF	Rwandan Patriotic Front
RPR	Rassemblement pour la République
RUF	Revolutionary United Front (Liberia)
SACEUR	Supreme Allied Commander Europe
SDR	Strategic Defence Review (UK)
SFOR	Stabilization Force in Bosnia and Herzegovina (NATO)
SHIRBRIG	Stand-by High Readiness Brigade
SIRPA	Armed Forces Information and Public Relations Service (France)

TCC	troop-contributing country
UNAMET	UN Assistance Mission in East Timor
UNAMIC	UN Advanced Mission in Cambodia
UNAMIR	UN Assistance Mission in Rwanda
UNAMSIL	UN Assistance Mission in Sierra Leone
UNDOF	UN Disengagement Observer Force
UNEF	UN Emergency Force
UNFICYP	UN Force in Cyprus
UNHCR	UN High Commissioner for Refugees
UNIDO	UN Industrial Development Organization
UNIFIL	UN Interim Force in Lebanon
UNIIMOG	UN Iran–Iraq Military Observer Group
UNIKOM	UN Iraq–Kuwait Observation Mission
UNITAF	United Task Force (Somalia)
UNMIBH	UN Mission in Bosnia and Herzegovina
UNMIH	UN Mission in Haiti
UNMIK	UN Mission in Kosovo
UNMOGIP	UN Military Observer Group in India and Pakistan
UNPROFOR	UN Protection Force
UNSCOM	UN Special Commission
UNTAC	UN Transitional Authority in Cambodia
UNTAET	UN Transitional Administration in East Timor
UNTAG	UN Transitional Assistance Group
UNTEA	UN Temporary Executive Authority
UNTSO	UN Supervision Organization
ZHS	Safe Humanitarian Zone

Introduction

Pia Christina Wood and David S. Sorenson

BACKGROUND

It is virtually impossible to say when the first peacekeeping mission went into action, but the use of military force to maintain peace between potential combatants probably pre-dates the Romans. Still, for much of human history, the most common application of military force was in war, and peacekeeping missions were relatively rare until after World War II. In the nuclear era, though, the chances of even a small war escalating to an atomic conflagration gave peacekeeping a new impetus. The newly created United Nations found itself sending forces to the Middle East in the wake of the Israeli–Arab war of 1948, setting a precedent for many missions to follow.

The evolution of United Nations (UN) peacekeeping can be divided into at least three major time periods: the end of World War II and the formation of the United Nations until the mid-1980s, the mid-1980s until the end of the Cold War, and the post-Cold War period.[1] It is important to note that the Charter of the United Nations identifies the organization's principal role as the maintenance of international peace and security but does not contain any direct provisions for peacekeeping. Instead, peacekeeping emerged as a response to the Cold War hostility between the superpowers, and its principles and practices were established and defined as peacekeeping operations (PKOs) were mounted.

During the first time period, the conceptualization of peacekeeping evolved and peacekeeping operations were generally non-coercive, impartial, supported by the UN Security Council, accepted by the parties involved, and deployed after a cessation of hostilities had occurred to separate warring parties. The United Nations Operation in the Congo (UNOC) in 1960 was an exception as its mandate evolved to include restoring the territorial integrity of the country after the province of Katanga declared its independence. A further element of these 'first-generation' peacekeeping operations was the general exclusion of troops from the five permanent members based on the desire for an impartial, independent UN force without any 'special interest' in the conflict. This practice was ignored, on occasion, as witnessed by France's participation in UNIFIL (United Nations Interim Force in Lebanon) in 1978. Other countries, including Canada, Ireland, Austria, Holland, the Nordic countries, Fiji, and Nepal, however, considered participation in UN peacekeeping operations to be an important component of their foreign policy and provided troops on a regular basis. National motivations varied, from Canada's desire to justify its military and distance itself from the United States to the Nordic countries' efforts to increase their international influence and reduce the possibility of superpower confrontation to Fiji, where PKOs served as opportunities for both added income and military training of its forces.[2]

By the mid-1980s, cooperation replaced confrontation, and stalemate in the UN Security Council began to wane. Supported by a growing consensus among the permanent members, the UN launched peacekeeping operations in various countries including Afghanistan, Namibia, Angola, and Nicaragua. In Namibia, in particular, UN troops performed a variety of jobs outside the boundaries of traditional peacekeeping, making UNTAG (United Nations Transition Assistance Group) the first of the second-generation PKOs.[3] During this 'transition' period, the member states, including the permanent members of the Security Council, began to accord greater credence to the United Nations and its role in mediating conflicts.

The collapse of the Soviet Union and end of the Cold War had a dramatic impact on the United Nations and its peacekeeping operations. In this third period, the Security Council, no longer immobilized by the veto of the five permanent members, approved UN observer and peacekeeping missions to conflict-ridden states in growing numbers. Between 1988 and 1991, the UN created ten observer missions and PKOs, a number which almost equals the 13 observer missions and PKOs mounted between 1948 and 1988. By mid-1994, some 80,000 military troops and civilians were taking part in PKOs around the world. In addition, the definition of peacekeeping expanded as the nature of PKOs changed in several important ways. First, the permanent members of the Security Council began to send troops to participate in UN PKOs. In particular, France and the UK became very active in and major contributors to PKOs. Second, the UN initiated PKOs increasingly as a response to interstate rather than intrastate conflicts. Third, the Security Council began to approve PKOs under Chapter VII of the UN Charter, which allows for the use of force. Fourth, the right to intervene for humanitarian purposes was accepted as a new justification for UN PKOs.

This expansion of UN peacekeeping activity has created numerous difficulties for the United Nations as an organization and for the member states participating in the PKOs. In the post-Cold War world, the UN was increasingly called on to respond to 'challenges of a different kind, with no peace to keep and humanitarian concerns raising demands for intervention with no clear guide-lines on how to proceed'.[4] The concept of peace-keeping expanded to include peacemaking, peace building, and peace enforcement operations – often designated 'second-generation' PKOs because they include military, political, social and humanitarian aspects seldom present in traditional PKOs. Moreover, as the number, complexity, and objectives of these PKOs increased, the terminology used to define them remained unclear. As a result, 'peacekeeping' is widely used as a generic term that encompasses all variations of first-generation and second-generation peacekeeping operations and includes UN-controlled or -sponsored PKOs and UN-mandated PKOs (controlled by a coalition of states with authorization by the UN Security Council).

With these new types of PKOs, success has often proved elusive, as demonstrated by events in Somalia, Rwanda, and Bosnia. Bosnia, in particular, pointed out the weaknesses of UN-controlled peacekeeping operations as UNPROFOR (United Nations Protection Force) proved incapable of keeping a non-existent peace or halting the violence and widespread ethnic cleansing. The perceived impotence of UNPROFOR eventually led to the creation of IFOR (Implementation Force) and, one year later, SFOR (Stabilization Force). Both were NATO-led multi-national forces with a UN Security Council authorization. In the wake of UNPROFOR, governments shifted away from UN-controlled PKOs for difficult situations, opting instead for PKOs controlled by a regional organization (NATO) or an ad-hoc coalition with a mandate from the UN Security Council. KFOR (Kosovo Force) and ISAF (International Security Assistance Force) in Afghanistan are two recent examples of this approach. At the time of writing (2002), it appears that peacekeeping has undergone a retrenchment as nations are less willing to commit troops.

THE DESIGN OF THE BOOK

A substantial number of works analyzing and explaining PKOs have appeared in response to the dramatic increase and complexity of peacekeeping operations in the post-Cold War era. The majority of these studies have concentrated on the operational aspects of PKOs, specific PKOs and lessons learned, and/or discussions of broader themes such as Humanitarian Intervention.[5] Largely missing in the literature on PKOs in the post-Cold War era are analyses of states' motivations for participating in PKOs and the roles played by domestic political actors (executive, legislature, military, media, public opinion) in the decision-making process. This edited volume was designed to address this gap.

The editors chose ten countries to represent a wide range of participants in PKOs. They are three countries (Australia, Germany, Argentina) whose participation in PKOs dramatically increased in the post-Cold War period, three permanent members (France, the UK, the United States) of the UN Security Council, two countries with long-standing experience in PKOs (Austria, Canada), and two regional powers (Nigeria, India). Using the broad generic definition of peacekeeping outlined above, the editors asked each contributor to focus on the national-level explanations for each country's participation in PKOs in the post-Cold War period. These motivations not only differed depending on the peacekeeping operation, but participation often rested on a combination of interests. Examples include increasing their international status and prestige, gaining regional influence, safeguarding or securing a permanent seat on the UN Security Council, access to training and weapons, containing regional instability, and humanitarian concerns. In addition, they were asked to analyze the role, position, and influence of the domestic political players in the decision-making process. Questions to be addressed included: who were the major political participants in the debate? What interaction occurred between the executive and legislature? What was the position of the military and how much influence did it wield? When and to what extent were the media and public opinion influential?

THE INDIVIDUAL CHAPTERS

The first three chapters represent countries whose commitment to peacekeeping expanded substantially in the context of the post-Cold War order. Hugh Smith attributes Australia's greater activism and participation in PKOs in Cambodia, Somalia, and East Timor to a mixture of motivations. They include the prevention of regional instability, which supports Australia's security interests, the expansion of Australia's influence, cooperation with neighboring states and allies, and a response to humanitarian concerns. While there is general agreement and support for PKOs in Australia, different perspectives and debates have arisen over broad policy questions, including the appropriate level of support for PKOs and whether PKOs detract from Australia's national defense readiness. Germany's participation in PKOs can be attributed directly to the end of the Cold War. Mary Hampton explains that Germany has replaced its long-standing reluctance to participate in any military activities that might appear threatening with a willingness to project soft power or 'power lite' capabilities. Following a favorable ruling by the German constitutional court in 1994, the way was cleared for German participation in PKOs, and German troops participated in PKOs in Bosnia, Macedonia, Kosovo, and Afghanistan among other countries. German participation in these PKOs has met with broad domestic support largely because the operations were aimed at defending humanitarian and democratic values and German troops were part of a larger coalition. Cynthia Watson argues that economic imperatives largely drive Argentina's peacekeeping activism in the post-Cold War period. Elected president in 1989, Carlos Saúl Menem was faced with difficult economic choices and the question of how to justify the large Argentine military without any communist threat. Participation in peacekeeping provided the answer and, in 2000, Argentina had the seventh largest contingent of UN peacekeepers. For Menem, participation in UN peacekeeping was beneficial for several reasons, including enhancing Argentina's international prestige, justifying the role and size of the military, garnering economic compensation to pay its troops, and improving Argentina's reputation, which had suffered from its 1982 conflict with the UK over Las Malvinas/the Falkland Islands.

Chapters Four, Five, and Six provide analyses of peacekeeping participation for three of the five permanent members of the UN Security Council. In the post-Cold War period, both France and the UK have been highly active and engaged participants in UN PKOs. Using four PKOs (Cambodia, Rwanda, Kosovo, and Afghanistan) as examples, Pia Wood outlines France's motivations for its strong support of the UN and peacekeeping. France views its participation in UN PKOs as a justification for its permanent seat on the UN Security Council and a method to protect its international 'rank' and assert its influence on the world stage. Additional reasons include the protection of economic interests, the maintenance of influence in countries formerly part of its empire, the prevention of regional instability, and political and humanitarian considerations. Internally, there has been little fundamental disagreement over France's participation in PKOs, a trend that has continued even during periods of cohabitation.

Tom Woodhouse and Alexander Ramsbotham argue that British peacekeeping evolved slowly from Britain's post-colonial experience, shifting from the military emphasis on conflict termination to political consent building among the parties to the conflict. British peacekeeping adopted this goal partly to seek a more permanent end to local conflict and partly to avoid crossing the so-called 'Mogadishu line' from peacekeeping into war. Humanitarian groups like Oxfam have also influenced British peacekeeping in responding more to social crises, particularly in sub-Saharan Africa, which has also led to more inter-governmental coordination between the Ministry of Defence and other ministries such as the Department of International Development. One consequence of these changes was the successful British rescue of the failing UNAMSIL (United Nations Assistance Mission in Sierra Leone), which although successful has not apparently prevented the increased politicization of peacekeeping in British politics. Instead, divisions have widened between those who view British peacekeeping as idealistic and those who claim that it is the first step back towards neo-imperialism.

David Sorenson finds the United States to be a reluctant contributor to UN-operated PKOs, favoring missions that advanced US national interests over missions designed to promote collective interests. After disappointing results in Haiti and the tragedy of Somalia, both the US military and a majority in the US Congress called for limits on US peacekeeping participation. The Clinton Administration developed PDD-25 in response, making the US role in PKOs more selective and multilateral. The George W. Bush Administration has not entered into any new UN-operated PKOs, and instead moved to scale back current operations and threatened to veto US participation in future UN operations unless the US peacekeepers received immunity from possible International Criminal Court prosecution.

Austria and Canada are both countries with long-standing experience in peacekeeping. Erwin Schmidl explains that in the post-Cold War era participation in peacekeeping operations has become the prime task of the Austrian Armed Forces and is an important aspect of Austria's foreign policy. In 1999, the Austrian government strengthened its support of peacekeeping efforts with the creation of the new Austrian International Peace Support Command. Canada, perhaps more than Austria, has made peacekeeping an important cornerstone of its foreign policy. David Rudd explains that Canada's reasons for its active participation in PKOs include national interests and the promotion of Canadian values such as the peaceful resolution of disputes, the promotion of liberal democracy, the alleviation of suffering, and the enhancement of human security. As is the case for the UK and France, a general internal consensus exists in favor of supporting Canada's activism in peacekeeping. The parliamentary system and the power of the Prime Minister have served to limit debate on the issue and public opinion remains generally supportive.

Nigeria and India are both regional powers and active in peacekeeping operations. Herb Howe explains that Nigeria's ambition to be the regional leader led it to create ECOMOG (Economic Community of West African States Military Observer Group) and assume most of the responsibilities of this peacekeeping force. Nigeria's stated motives in support of ECOMOG's deployment to Liberia and Sierra Leone included preventing the spillover of the conflict to other states in the region, helping foreign nationals in Liberia, and preventing more civilian deaths from continued civil strife. Critics, however, contended that anglophone–francophone rivalries were at the root of Nigeria's support of ECOMOG. Recently, Nigeria's military and peacekeeping capabilities have been seriously weakened by corruption and successive rulers' deliberate undermining of the armed forces. India's participation in PKOs since the end of the Cold War has been extensive. Alan Bullion analyzes India's motivations for its activism in peacekeeping, which include the promotion of regional stability, solidarity with non-aligned countries, training experiences for Indian troops, greater international recognition of India as a major power, and the desire to gain a permanent seat on the UN Security Council. Bullion argues that India's negative experience with the PKO to Sierra Leone (UNAMSIL) will not fundamentally undermine its traditional support for peacekeeping but may lead Indian leaders to carefully evaluate future participation in PKOs.

NOTES

1. The exact dates for the different stages of UN peacekeeping vary depending on the author. Some authors further divide the three time periods. See for example: K. A. Mingst and M. P. Karns, *The United Nations in the Post-Cold War Era* (Boulder, CO: Westview Press, 1995), Chapter 6; J. Tercinet, 'Les politiques nationals en matière de la paix', *Arès*, Vol. XVII, No. 41 (October 1998), pp. 25–35; S. M. Hill and S. P. Malik, *Peacekeeping and the United Nations* (Aldershot: Dartmouth Publishing Company, 1996).
2. Tercinet, 'Les politiques nationals en matière de la paix', pp. 29–30.
3. Mingst and Karns, *The United Nations in the Post-Cold War Era*, p. 83.
4. Ibid., p. 92.
5. A prodigious number of works exist on this topic. See for example: K. Allard, *Somalia Operations: Lessons Learned* (Washington, DC: National Defense University Press, 1995); D. Carment and P. James (eds), *The International Politics of Ethnic Conflict:*

P. C. Wood and D. S. Sorenson

Policy and Peacekeeping, Vol. II (Pittsburgh, PA: Pittsburgh University Press, 1995); T. Findlay, *Cambodia: The Legacy and Lessons of UNTAC* (Oxford: SIPRI/Oxford University Press, 1995); M. Pugh, 'Humanitarianism and Peacekeeping', *Global Society*, Vol. 10, No. 3 (September 1996), pp. 205–24; S. R. Ratner, *The New UN Peacekeeping* (New York: St Martin's Press, 1995); Bruce D. Jones, *Peacemaking in Rwanda: the Dynamics of Failure* (Boulder, CO: Lynne Rienner Publishers, Inc., 2001); N. MacQueen, 'Peacekeeping by Attrition: The United Nations in Angola', *The Journal of Modern African Studies*, Vol. 36 (September 1998); Michael W. Doyle, 'Peacebuilding in Cambodia, Legitimacy and Power', in Elizabeth M. Cousens and Chetan Kumar (eds), *Peacebuilding as Politics* (Boulder, CO: Lynne Rienner Publishers, 2001), pp. 89–112; Janet E. Heininger, *Peacekeeping in Transition: the United Nations in Cambodia* (New York: The Twentieth Century Fund Press, 1994).

ONE

————◄○►————

Australia

Hugh Smith

INTRODUCTION

Australia has long prided itself on being a supporter of the United Nations and international cooperation – in short, a 'good international citizen'. In the negotiations to establish the UN, Australian diplomats played an active role. With the 'enthusiasm of an idealist and the satisfaction of a creator', the left-wing Labor government saw the organization as a means of reducing international tensions and an opportunity for middle and small powers to influence the great.[1] Australia served on the Security Council in 1946–47 and its Foreign Minister, Dr H. V. Evatt, became President of the General Assembly in 1948. Soon after the first peace-monitoring operations began in the Middle East in 1948 and India–Pakistan in 1949, Australia contributed a small contingent to the latter in 1950.

The Australian government did not look to the UN alone for security. Traditional ties with Britain and links with the United States forged in World War II were seen as the bedrock of the nation's defenses. The right-wing Liberal government under Prime Minister Menzies that took office from December 1949 was particularly concerned with what it saw as a rising tide of communism throughout the world and in Asia in particular. The Korean War, to which Australia promptly dispatched ground, naval, and air forces in 1950 to fight under the UN flag, confirmed this gloomy assessment. The ANZUS treaty signed by Australia, New Zealand, and the US in 1951 provided much-needed reassurance that a 'great and powerful friend' would underwrite Australian defense. The Cold War rather than the UN had come to dominate Australian thinking on peace and security.

This set the pattern for the next twenty years or so. Australia fought against communism alongside the United States in Korea (1950–53) and in

Vietnam (1962–72), and alongside the UK in Malaya (1950–60) and Borneo (1963–66). This left few resources with which to support UN peacekeeping even if Australia had wished to contribute more. Australia contemplated participation in the UN Emergency Force in 1956 – a move supported by the Department of External Affairs but viewed very reluctantly by the Department of Defence which anticipated logistic support problems in any major commitment so far from Australia. However, Prime Minister Menzies' outspoken support for Britain's use of force in the Suez crisis (which caused tensions with the United States and Canada) led Egypt to make clear its objection to any Australian presence.[2] By way of compensation, perhaps, a small number of military observers was sent to the UN Truce Supervision Organization from 1956 onwards. The only other commitments before the 1970s were medical activities for UNTEA (UN Temporary Executive Authority) in West New Guinea in 1962 and a police contribution to UNFICYP (UN Force in Cyprus) in Cyprus from 1964.

The years from 1972, when Australia withdrew its troops from Vietnam and Australia's voters elected a reformist Labor government under Prime Minister Whitlam, Labor, after spending 23 years in opposition, saw greater willingness to take part in peacekeeping operations. The new government was anxious to reduce the military orientation of Australia's foreign policy, offering 500 personnel to UNEF (UN Emergency Force) II in the Middle East in 1973 and 200 infantry to UNFICYP in 1974. The UN rejected both proposals, which preferred countries such as Australia to provide more sophisticated (and more expensive) capabilities – a policy well known to the government. Critics suggested that Australia preferred to make offers that the UN was likely to refuse.[3] One genuine constraint on Australian participation was uncertainty over its defense strategy. President Nixon's Guam Doctrine of 1969 had called on America's allies to do more for their own security while withdrawal from Vietnam in 1972 signified the end of the doctrine of 'forward defense' whereby Australia sought a military presence in Asia in cooperation with the US as the first line of defense.

While Australia was re-thinking its defense policy, involvement in UN peacekeeping remained at low levels under the Liberal government elected in 1975: a helicopter detachment in UNEF II from 1976 to 1979 and military observers in UNIIMOG (UN Iran–Iraq Military Observer Group) from 1988 to 1990. The British connection helped persuade Australia to send about 150 troops to Rhodesia/Zimbabwe to help the Commonwealth Monitoring Force oversee the hand-over of power from a white minority regime to majority rule in 1979–80. The US connection likewise encouraged Australia to participate in the MFO (Multinational Force and Observers) from 1982, mainly with air transport. The Labor government that came to office in 1983 continued this linkage. In 1985, however, participation in UNMOGIP (UN Military Observer Group in India and Pakistan) in Kashmir was discontinued on the grounds that Australia was over-committed. In 1988 Foreign Minister Evans could describe Australia as 'a traditional supporter of the UN's peacekeeping activities'.[4] But it was far from being a substantial contributor. Two principal factors helped change this situation.

In the course of 1986–87, defense policy finally focused on the capacity to protect Australian territory as the prime determinant of force structure and capabilities.[5] Given this priority, the 1987 White Paper noted, Australia might 'usefully contribute to peacekeeping operations ... on a scale appropriate to our circumstances'.[6] Moreover, since no direct threat to the country could be foreseen for many years, apart from minor incursions, something was needed to demonstrate the value of the military to the community and to sustain morale. Both the government and the military thought peacekeeping a worthwhile task that would also gain popular support. In 1989–90 Australia made its largest contribution up to this time (304 personnel) to UNTAG (UN Transitional Assistance Group) in Namibia, making good an offer it had first put forward in 1979. The success of this operation (another with substantial British involvement) reinforced Australia's readiness to undertake more peacekeeping tasks.

The other significant factor in encouraging Australia to expand its peacekeeping commitments in the course of the 1990s was the end of the Cold War which allowed the UN to take a far more active role in promoting peace, especially through peacekeeping operations. The end of the Cold War also helped in some cases to produce unstable situations where peacekeeping was needed and in other cases raised the prospect of a settlement previously off the agenda. An important example of the latter was the series of negotiations leading to the resolution of the conflict in Cambodia and the creation of UNTAC (UN Transitional Authority in Cambodia) in 1992. Australia had been proactive in the diplomatic settlement and was expected to provide a substantial commitment. Though not the largest contributor, Australia sent over 500 personnel to support field communications for the force (plus air transport at a later stage) as well as providing the force commander, Major-General John Sanderson.

The Australian government was also ready to participate more substantially in peacekeeping further afield, sending a communications unit to MINURSO (UN Mission for the Referendum in Western Sahara) in 1991, movement control personnel to UNOSOM (UN Operation in Somalia) in 1992, and a medical team to UNAMIR (UN Assistance Mission in Rwanda) in 1994. The steady progress of UNTAC in creating a degree of stability in the lead-up to the election of May 1993 provided further encouragement. A request from the US to take part in the US-led Unified Task Force (UNITAF) in Somalia from 1992 to 1993 was also agreed to, even though it overlapped with the Cambodian commitment and meant that some 1,800 ADF (Australian Defence Force) personnel were involved in peacekeeping of one kind or another out of a trained force of about 62,000 regulars.

This level of contribution created some concerns in Australia about the costs and disadvantages of participation in peacekeeping (to be discussed below). In the event, Australia's commitment declined to a low level once more after the Cambodian and Somali operations were completed and a contingent of 300 personnel had returned from Rwanda in 1994. Any attempts to contain peacekeeping activities at a minimal level, however, were soon frustrated by events much closer to Australia and in areas where the nation's interests were far more directly involved, notably Papua New Guinea (PNG) and East Timor. The Liberal government elected in 1996 was to engage Australia more deeply and more dangerously in peace-keeping than any of its predecessors.

Australia had granted independence to PNG in 1975 and continued to provide major support to the government and the Defence Force in an attempt to maintain stability and national unity. The island province of Bougainville, however, had from the beginning been dissatisfied with its place in PNG and by 1988 began armed resistance with a view to gaining independence. After several years of inconclusive military and diplomatic efforts to effect a resolution, the parties brokered a truce in 1997, followed by a peace settlement of sorts.[7] This led to extensive Australian and New Zealand military involvement in monitoring the arrangements. The UN Security Council agreed to send a five-person Observer Mission in June 1998 to assist and support the settlement. It remains unclear when and whether the Australian and New Zealand military personnel will be withdrawn.

Far more substantial was Australian involvement in East Timor following the vote for independence from Indonesia in August 1999 and the subsequent violence by militia forces against the civilian population. An international crisis led to the UN authorizing the dispatch of an international force of about 11,000 to East Timor (INTERFET – International Force in East Timor) to which Australia made the largest contribution (5,700, including about 700 naval and air force personnel).

The Force Commander was an Australian, Major-General Peter Cosgrove. In February 2000 INTERFET handed over security responsibilities to UNTAET (UN Transitional Administration in East Timor), with Australia maintaining a contribution of some 1,600 military personnel out of about 7,500.

The Australian Defence Force has experienced the full gamut of peacekeeping operations from military observation to counter-insurgency operations, from humanitarian tasks such as food relief and medical assistance, to support for electoral processes and maintaining law and order. It has provided technical specialists, infantry soldiers, engineers, force commanders, and many other types of personnel; while the Army has provided by far the greatest numbers, air force and navy personnel have also participated.

Fortunately, the one major operation for which Australia had full responsibility, INTERFET, proved successful in a short period and did not become entangled in a large-scale internal conflict. Fortunately, too, only four military personnel have been killed while on peacekeeping duty (none from direct hostile action). However, the risks and costs involved, the level of ADF participation, and the value of peacekeeping itself have all caused questions to be raised as to why Australians should be so deeply engaged in conflicts and disasters not of their making.

AUSTRALIAN INTERESTS AND PEACEKEEPING

Governments of different persuasions since 1945 have justified Australia's contributions to peacekeeping on various grounds. At times a general obligation to support the UN in promoting the cause of peace or simple humanitarian concerns has been stressed, particularly in the case of operations remote from Australia. In other cases, national interest in settling particular disputes has been more evident, especially in Cambodia, Papua New Guinea, and East Timor. The benefits of political stability and the desirability of cooperation with neighboring states have underpinned support for peacekeeping in Australia's region. Other benefits have been emphasized, ranging from the ideological (assisting democratic transition) to the military (training and motivational value of peacekeeping). The risks and disadvantages of peacekeeping have not been overlooked though governments have naturally played them down. Occasionally, too, party politics have intruded. To illustrate some of the play of interests involved, three case studies will be outlined.

Multinational Force and Observers

The first is a non–UN operation, the Multinational Force and Observers (MFO) in the Sinai, which became an issue in Australia in March 1981, following a US request for Australian participation.[8] The fact that the UN did not endorse the operation helped drive a wedge between the Liberal government and the Labor Party opposition although other factors were also at work.

The Australian Labor Party (ALP) argued that the force was more part of Cold War maneuvering than a genuine contribution to peace.[9] It could well aggravate tensions in the Middle East due to US involvement and might encourage the Israeli government to move northwards against Lebanon once its southern borders were secure. Australia might also be seen as a pawn of the US, and thereby risk losing not only the good will of the majority of Arab states (which opposed the MFO and were important trading partners of Australia) but also its good standing with Third World countries in general. These problems would be avoided, the ALP claimed, if the operation could be brought under the UN umbrella. It was clear, however, that making support for the operation contingent on UN authorization was a convenient strategy to cover up differences within the party over the alliance with the US and over support for the Israeli or the Arab cause.[10]

The issue created considerable debate within Australia. Newspaper editorials were divided, with the *Canberra Times* consistently arguing that the US and Israel should accept a UN operation and the *Australian* claiming that the prospect of furthering peace in the Middle East justified the risks involved.[11] Also influential were two important pressure groups: the Jewish lobby which strongly supported Australian participation and the farm lobby which was concerned about endangering trade in primary produce with Arab states. It was this that led the Deputy Prime Minister, a member of the Country Party in coalition with the Liberals, to express initial doubts about participation in a non–UN operation.[12] Public opinion was also cautious. One poll reported 72 percent opposed to sending troops, 25 percent in favor.[13]

The Liberal government recognized the difficulties and risks but came down in favor of participation. In his speech announcing Australia's commitment, Prime Minister Malcolm Fraser emphasized the importance of the peace process in the Middle East – a region that posed 'probably the most serious threat to world peace'.[14] In his view the absence of UN endorsement was due to obstruction on the part of the Soviet Union, which had opposed the Camp David accords from the outset. It would, in fact, be unwise to embark on a UN operation that would be subject to the Soviet veto at any point. The Prime Minister made clear that Australian involvement was not unconditional, being predicated on West European participation and on a clear distinction between the MFO and the Rapid Deployment Force which the US was in the process of creating for military operations in the Middle East. The decision to participate had been taken only after extended debate and, as the Prime Minister acknowledged, it was 'more finely balanced than others'.

The MFO commitment revealed a mix of international and internal political factors and relatively rare party differences over peacekeeping. Other issues raised in the debate included the risk to troops, potential loss of national control over forces, and the financial burden. When the opposition won government in 1983, it recognized the valuable work done by the MFO but decided that the commitment should not be 'open-ended' and Australia scheduled their withdrawal by 1986. The withdrawal took place as planned but the issue did not disappear. In 1988–89 the government declined an approach by the US to return to the MFO and provide a commander, a decision criticized by the Liberal opposition.[15] By 1992, however, it was finally persuaded of the merits of resuming participation. The Minister for Defence stated that Australia wished to assist in the Middle East peace process, which was once more revitalized; he also referred to a formal request from the MFO itself.[16] The US no doubt welcomed Australia's modest contribution, which Australia resumed in 1993, remaining in place to this day.

UN Transitional Authority in Cambodia (UNTAC)

Where political controversy surrounded the MFO commitment, Australia's involvement in UNTAC took place amid broad consensus.[17] The peace settlement was a long time in the making. Cambodia had suffered under the genocidal regime of Pol Pot in the 1970s and had been occupied by Vietnam since December 1978. In the late 1980s a number of Southeast Asian and other countries began discussions with a view to a political settlement. When Vietnam announced its intention in January 1989 to withdraw later in the year, negotiations began in earnest. The parties included the four political factions in Cambodia, the six members of ASEAN, Vietnam, the permanent members of the UN Security Council, and Australia. When negotiations stalled, Australia launched a major initiative and the Security Council endorsed a plan for Cambodia in September 1990.

Some took it for granted that Australia would make a significant contribution to the UN operation. The reasons for this were the same as those for Australia's involvement in the negotiated settlement – a mixture of pragmatic and humanitarian considerations.[18] The situation in Cambodia, especially after Vietnamese withdrawal, was likely to be unstable as long as the Khmer Rouge retained influence; in turn, this was likely to create tensions between the nations of Southeast Asia and to draw in the great powers, notably China, Russia, and the United States. Australia thus had a natural interest in resolving a long-standing conflict in its own region. It would also demonstrate its good faith and diplomatic skills to states in the region with which it was seeking to engage more fully. At the same time the tragedy of genocide and civil war in Cambodia together with continuing refugee problems struck a genuine humanitarian chord in Australian policy-makers. The Foreign Minister, Senator Gareth Evans, also acknowledged a personal interest in Cambodia because of travel there as a young student.[19]

The initial contribution of some 535 personnel, spread throughout the country to provide communications for UNTAC, was the largest Australian peacekeeping commitment to date.[20] At a time when the military priorities of the Cold War were no longer relevant and Australia was looking to enhance relations with its neighbor, the Cambodian operation filled the bill. In announcing the commitment Prime Minister Keating referred to the great suffering of the Cambodian people and the need for international action; he recognized that Australian service personnel would be at risk but reassured the public that they would not be engaging in hostilities.[21] In the event the operation met little or no opposition at home and was supported by editorials with headings such as 'Playing our part in ending a nightmare'.[22] A popular Sunday newspaper, the *Sun Herald*, ran a series of letters from Cambodia by an Australian Army captain. The appointment of an Australian, Major-General John Sanderson, as Force Commander signified international recognition of Australia's peacekeeping capabilities while reassuring the public that the operation was in safe hands.

East Timor: INTERFET and UNTAET

Australia's peacekeeping role in East Timor from 1999 onwards differed again in kind and extent from earlier involvements. A Portuguese colony until 1974, an independent East Timor proved unstable and was forcibly taken over by Indonesia in December 1975. The Australian government, in the midst of a constitutional crisis, believed there was no alternative but to acquiesce in this. One of the few countries to recognize Indonesia's incorporation of the territory, Australia under both Labor and Liberal governments maintained the view that good relations with its large and powerful neighbor were a high priority. An ongoing resistance movement against Indonesian forces, however, accompanied by an effective international diplomatic campaign, won considerable sympathy within Australia and other parts of the world, including the UN.[23]

Events came to a head in 1998–99 when Indonesian President Habibie, a much weaker figure than his predecessor Suharto, agreed to hold a referendum on the future of East Timor, a move made in part under pressure from Australia.[24] A UN Assistance Mission in East Timor (UNAMET) was established to organize and monitor the ballot but Indonesia insisted on retaining responsibility for security in its province. Contrary to Indonesian expectations, the people of East Timor voted on 30 August 1999 overwhelmingly (78.5 percent) for independence from, rather than autonomy within, Indonesia. In response militia forces in East Timor, supported and assisted by elements in the Indonesian military, launched violent attacks against the civilian population, raping women, killing perhaps 1,000–2,000 people, destroying up to 80 percent of the country's buildings and causing an outflow of refugees into Indonesian West Timor in excess of 200,000 out of a population of some 750,000.

Rapid action was needed to restore order and relieve suffering. Previously reluctant to push for a peacekeeping force over Indonesian reluctance, Australia now argued strongly for the UN to authorize such a mission, offering to make 2,000 troops available within 48 to 72 hours.[25] Only Australia was in a position to act immediately, having initiated plans for such an eventuality earlier in the year. Under pressure from the US, Indonesia agreed to the presence of an International Force in East Timor (INTERFET) which arrived in the capital Dili on 20 September. Led by Australia, which provided 5,700 out of 11,000 personnel, the force included several Southeast Asian nations with whom Australia had developed close military ties over a long period.[26] Substantial contingents came from Thailand (1,603) and the Philippines (597) as well as New Zealand (770), Jordan (707), Italy (518), Canada (470), and the Republic of Korea (436). Important to all contributors was endorsement by the UN.

The UN authorized the operation on 15 September under Chapter VII of the Charter. INTERFET was permitted to take 'all necessary measures' in order 'to restore peace and security in East Timor'.[27] In the event, militia resistance to the peacekeeping force was minimal, thanks in part to determined action by Australian and other forces. Some problems arose over the Australian military's 'can-do' attitudes and war-like approach to the perceived threat, including explicit criticism to this effect by the Prime

Minister of Malaysia.[28] Relations between the Malaysian and Australian governments had been delicate for some time, but countries such as Thailand and the Philippines were genuinely concerned that the activities of INTERFET not give offense to Indonesia, a fellow member of the Association of Southeast Asian Nations (ASEAN). However, the rapid restoration of stability and the establishment of a working relationship with Indonesian military and civilian authorities ensured that tensions remained limited.

Australia's largest, most complex and potentially most dangerous peacekeeping mission created little controversy at home. Public opinion supported the commitment and seemed prepared to pay the price, including a proposed special levy on income tax (though this was not imposed in the event). An opinion poll taken on 12 September 1999 showed 77 percent in favor of Australia sending troops, with only 15 percent against.[29] Widespread sympathy for the East Timorese, together with memories of East Timorese help for Australian forces against the Japanese during World War II, ensured much support, as did pride in the behavior and achievements of Australian soldiers. The commander of INTERFET, Major-General Cosgrove, was subsequently promoted to head the Australian Army and named Australian of the Year in 2001.[30]

Australia's commitment – despite considerable nervousness on the part of the government about Indonesian reactions, the prospect of casualties, the evident limits on Australian capabilities, and the risk of entanglement in protracted violence – was almost inevitable. Having pushed for the ballot on self-determination, Australia could hardly turn its back on the result while the world was watching. Besides, INTERFET was a valuable exercise in cooperation with Australia's regional friends. The same was true when INTERFET handed over to the UN Transitional Administration in East Timor (UNTAET) in February 2000. Established under Security Council Resolution 1272 on 25 October 1999, UNTAET retained a Chapter VII mandate. The Australian contribution to the military component was still the largest – 1,600 out of 7,500 personnel – but for reasons of diplomacy the Force Commander came from the Philippines (later Thailand). Australia retained the position of Deputy Commander.

What caused greatest controversy in Australia was not the military commitment as such but the Liberal government's diplomacy surrounding the independence of East Timor. Accusations were made by commentators, editorialists, and academics that Australia under both Liberal and Labor governments had appeased Indonesia for too long and had failed to put greater pressure on its government to agree to a peacekeeping force to provide security in East Timor before the election.[31] It was also reported that the Australian government knew – or should have known – from intelligence predictions that widespread slaughter would result if the August referendum were lost.[32] The government vigorously rejected suggestions that it should therefore accept some responsibility for the violence that occurred. This at times bitter controversy, however, did not diminish bipartisan and popular support for the role of the ADF.

Looking at Australia's participation in peacekeeping and at these three commitments in particular, certain patterns are evident. During the Cold War, Australia was primarily concerned with its place in the Western bloc. Peacekeeping was for the most part a minor activity; larger commitments had to be seen within the context of relations with the United States (or in some cases Britain) and maintaining good relations with the rest of the world. As the Cold War ended, Australia felt able to make larger and more independent commitments.

Where UN operations involved Australia's own region, moreover, there were strong reasons for active involvement in both diplomatic activities designed to promote settlements and in ensuing peacekeeping operations. By contrast, Australia has shown far less interest in peacekeeping in Latin America or Europe. A number of individuals have served on attachment in the former Yugoslavia, for example, but no unit was committed – in contrast to New Zealand, which provided a company. Engagement in African peacekeeping has reflected both humanitarian concerns and readiness to serve alongside the United States.

In sum, Australia's participation in peacekeeping reflects a mixture of self-interest, enlightened or otherwise, and genuine concern for international peace and humanitarian goals. By and large, the Australian people and political parties have found little wrong with this approach. Where criticism has arisen, it has mostly been directed against broader foreign policy lines or against essentially tactical matters such as the conditions of service for peacekeepers, the support provided for families, rates of pay, the award of medals, or inadequacies in equipment and logistics. Once Australia dispatches troops overseas, moreover, calls to bring them home have been rare. Australia's contribution to peacekeeping and the exemplary performance of its personnel has been a source of pride among the general population.

PARTICIPANTS – INTERESTS AND MOTIVATIONS

While general support for peacekeeping by Australia has been strong, this is not to say that controversy has been absent or that different perspectives have not been put forward. Debate, particularly in the course of the 1990s, has focused on broad policy questions. Does Australia do too much or too little in support of peacekeeping? Is this activity detracting from Australia's capacity to provide for its own defense? Should the Defence Force be more structured and equipped for peacekeeping than for war fighting? Is continual participation in peacekeeping likely to undermine the ADF's military ethos?

Various participants in the debate can be identified: the ADF itself, the Department of Defence, the Department of Foreign Affairs and Trade, the government and parliament, certain interest groups and public opinion. These will be considered in turn, though it should be noted that no one organization or group has held a single, unified view and in each case positions have been nuanced rather than dogmatic. Nor has there been a clear and unequivocal policy laid down by government. Indeed, the failure of the attempt to establish such a policy in 1993 is itself instructive.

From 1989 to 1993 Australia had undertaken several major commitments – UNTAG, UNTAC, and UNITAF – as well as making a number of minor contributions. With further demands for Australian participation likely, the government was concerned that peacekeeping might distort defense priorities. It was one thing to make small contributions for extended periods or even large contributions for short periods. This could be done based on the ADF's existing force structure and capability. However, it would be another matter to maintain a high level of participation indefinitely. Equipment, training, doctrine, organization, and levels of readiness might all be affected by an enhanced and continuing commitment to peacekeeping. Calls from the UN for the earmarking of national forces were also a cause of concern.

For some years successive policy statements prepared by the Department of Defence had emphasized that defense of Australia was the priority task for the ADF. *Defence of Australia 1987* noted in a single paragraph that Australia could contribute to peacekeeping from the force-in-being 'on a scale appropriate to our circumstances'.[33] The *Force Structure Review 1991* stated that peacekeeping tasks could be conducted within current and planned force structure, though it also noted that Australia's small overall force levels would impose limits on future commitments.[34] A small ADF Peacekeeping Centre was established in 1993 to develop doctrine and run training courses for Australian and overseas military and civilian personnel. But by this time the government felt the need to draw some boundaries – quantitative and qualitative – around what might be expected of Australia in terms of peacekeeping.

A document issued in mid-1993 by the Minister for Defence entitled *Peacekeeping Policy: The Future Australian Defence Force Role* acknowledged that a strong case could be made for Australia to increase its commitments significantly above Cold War levels. This would help fulfill Australia's international obligations and secure its reputation without requiring major change in the Defence Force. It was proposed that an appropriate level of participation would be an average minimum commitment of some 200 personnel at any one time. This was well above the Cold War average (about 20–25 at any one time) but well below what many thought necessary and reasonable for a wealthy country facing no immediate security threat. The idea was that peacekeeping should remain 'a supplementary activity' for the ADF.[35] This was also signaled by the Chief of the General Staff who 'firmly rejected' any suggestion that the Army or Defence Force be structured to reflect peacekeeping commitments.[36]

Peacekeeping Policy also proposed qualitative criteria for determining which operations Australia should support and under what conditions. Relevant factors mentioned included location and duration of the commitment, objectives of the operation, extent of international and regional support, security of personnel, costs of participation, and adverse effects on training.[37] The *Strategic Review 1993* issued in December also emphasized the need for any operation to have 'clear objectives that are achievable within a well-defined and acceptable time-frame'.[38] Again, in 1994, the Minister for Defence spelled out eight broad criteria that would guide any Australian decision to participate in peacekeeping.[39] All this can be read as a series of cautions from Defence's perspective, as possible reasons to limit or even abstain from contributions to particular operations.

Limitations were also suggested by according priority to operations within Australia's region – by implication those beyond Southeast Asia were in principle less deserving of Australian participation. This also tied in with the policy of defense cooperation with regional states. But *Peacekeeping Policy* noted that apart from Cambodia there were 'limited prospects for . . . peacekeeping in our region'.[40] In similar vein the Minister for Defence observed that the UN had not always been up to the mark and warned that 'there may be a need to dampen down expectations of what the UN can achieve in terms of peacekeeping'.[41]

The official statement of defense policy in November 1994, *Defending Australia*, was only a little less negative. It recognized the value of peacekeeping in terms of enhanced standing for Australia both globally and regionally and of community expectations; indeed, Australia would 'seek every opportunity to participate in operations that meet our case-by-case criteria'.[42] But there would be no earmarking of forces, no minimum number of personnel and no requirement to structure the ADF for peacekeeping 'other than at the margins'; the versatility of a force dedicated to defense of Australia would suffice to meet peacekeeping obligations.[43] The message was clear. The Department of Defence and the ADF did not oppose peacekeeping and recognized its benefits; but they were concerned to ensure that peacekeeping did not undercut what they saw as their main task – defense of Australia – and to restrain undue expectations of what the ADF might be expected to do. The message was there for anyone to hear – whether the Department of Foreign Affairs and Trade (DFAT), parliament, or the general public.

Certainly, DFAT took a more global view than Defence. Since 1988 under the leadership of an energetic and internationalist minister, Senator Gareth Evans, the Department had paid great attention to the role that the United Nations and regional organizations could play in promoting international security. In a speech to the General Assembly in October 1989 Evans had expressed an interest in earmarking forces for UN service.[44] In 1993 he published a book written with the assistance of his Department that examined ways of building international peace.[45] The end of the Cold War, Evans believed, opened up new opportunities for small and middle powers such as Australia to contribute to peace – as it had in Cambodia. Peacekeeping could be an important means of exercising and expanding Australian influence. At this time, too, Evans did not push for earmarking forces but supported the listing of capabilities that might be made available to the UN rather than nominating specific units for peacekeeping (as Australia had done since 1990).[46]

Two parliamentary inquiries in the 1990s reflected this debate about Australia's peacekeeping policies, in particular the question whether the ADF should be structured in some measure for peacekeeping. *United Nations Peacekeeping and Australia*, a report by the Senate Standing Committee on Foreign Affairs, Defence and Trade in May 1991, expressed broad support for Australian participation in peacekeeping and proposed it as an explicit 'objective' of the Defence Force. However, each decision should be taken on its merits, bearing in mind a wide range of factors and carefully spelling out the nation's purposes in taking part.[47] As to any impact on the ADF, the Committee concluded that peacekeeping tasks should be met from existing capabilities, stating quite unequivocally that peacekeeping should 'play no role in determining force structure'.[48]

A report by the Joint Standing Committee on Foreign Affairs, Defence and Trade in December 1994 went a little further. Again, the attitude was supportive of Australian involvement provided that each decision took into account a wide range of factors. This report, however, suggested that 'there is scope at the margins of force structure decision-making for specifically accommodating peacekeeping requirements' in particular cases. Since peacekeeping was likely to be a major activity of the ADF in future, it could not be sidelined altogether and should therefore be 'taken into consideration in force structure deliberations'. This, the Committee argued, would be possible 'without significantly affecting the ability of the ADF to perform its primary task'; that is, defense of Australia.[49] The Report also referred to the differing perspectives of the Department of Defence and Foreign Affairs on peacekeeping and recommended closer collaboration and coordination.[50]

Governments of both left and right in the 1990s continued to wrestle with the challenge of maintaining Australia's defense capabilities with a more or less static defense budget. No policy-makers or parliamentarians advocated abstention from peacekeeping, nor did they actively seek more extensive commitments. The unavoidable upsurge in commitments at the end of the decade, however, pushed official policy a little further. A new defense White Paper in 2000 acknowledged that military tasks other than conventional war were becoming more common and that this required a greater capacity to deploy more substantial forces more quickly than before.[51] Tasks might range from humanitarian assistance at one end of the spectrum to more dangerous and forceful peacekeeping operations at the other. The ADF had to be prepared for such activities and this would be done with 'forces built primarily to defend Australia'.[52] The word 'primarily' suggested that the door had opened slightly.

Public support for Australian peacekeeping has been strong in recent years and remains so despite the very large and potentially risky commitment to East Timor from 1999 onwards. Opinion polls, letters to newspapers, and editorials indicate broad and continuing support with frequent expressions of pride in the performance of the ADF. An extensive community consultation conducted in July–September 2000 preparatory to the White Paper later in the year also reported that 'participation in peacekeeping operations, particularly in the region, is strongly supported as being in Australia's interests'.[53] What seems to be the case is that public opinion is wary in advance of committing forces overseas but generally supports participation in operations that are in the national interest or to the benefit of the international community.[54] Bipartisan political endorsement virtually ensures popular backing.

Few quibbles have been heard about the cost of peacekeeping; indeed, the Australian public supported a proposal to impose an extra levy on taxation to pay for the East Timor operation (not implemented in the event). Some individuals and organizations have expressed disappointment that Australia has not done more or structured its forces for peace-keeping.[55] Most public criticism, however, has been directed at failures to provide good conditions of service for military personnel and shortcomings in logistics, transport, and communications.

One reason for popular support is clearly that peacekeeping which promotes stability in Australia's region is widely seen as contributing to Australia's regional interests and hence directly and indirectly to national security. It is the sort of activity that Australia might have had to undertake even if the UN and peacekeeping had not been invented. The fact that costs have been bearable and the total loss of life remains in single figures (far lower than many other nations) reinforces this assessment. Widespread international praise for the performance of Australian peacekeepers also helps maintain popularity. Critical, too, is the fact that most peacekeeping, particularly in association with the UN, has support across the party-political spectrum. Differences of emphasis only can be perceived and there seems no reason to expect any radical changes in the policy of the major parties towards peacekeeping.

THE FUTURE

While broad consensus marks public and official attitudes towards peacekeeping, some uncertainties can be discerned in the next few years. First, peacekeeping may lead Australia into commitments that tie down Australian forces for indefinite periods. It is likely, for example, that the ADF will remain in East Timor for several years after independence (as it did in PNG after 1975) in order to assist the new state to provide for its internal and external security. While there are national-interest reasons for this, a long-drawn-out and costly commitment might be blamed on the initial peacekeeping action and resolutions made to avoid similar 'mistakes' in future. Australia's current involvements in Bougainville and in the Solomon Islands may reinforce such a view. Reactions of this kind are not necessarily rational but could help make future peacekeeping commitments into a domestic political issue.

Second, the popular focus on peacekeeping in Australia's region may lead to greater unwillingness – coupled to some extent perhaps with inability – to contribute to operations further afield. The government may decline requests from the UN for Australian involvement because it is already heavily involved in its own region. The public may also see the UN as too demanding. Yet some actors in Australia, notably the Department of

Foreign Affairs and various non-government organizations, may be anxious to fulfill what they see as the wider obligations as part of being 'a good international citizen'. Certain tensions could result though a radical division of opinion seems unlikely.

Finally, the capabilities of the ADF itself must be considered. Force structure and the priority given to different types of mission may come to be a focus of disagreement. If the ADF is continually and heavily engaged in peacekeeping, there will be strong arguments to acquire equipment, organize logistics, develop transport capabilities, train personnel, and develop doctrine that is oriented more towards peacekeeping than defense of Australia against conventional attack. Major budget increases have been foreshadowed over the next 10 years, which would ease these tensions, but because of previous experience, there can be no guarantee that funds will in fact be forthcoming.

If finance and force structure are problematic, so too are personnel matters. Peacekeeping can be very personnel-intensive for the ADF, and recruiting and retaining sufficient numbers is likely to remain a continuing challenge for a great variety of reasons found in virtually all Western countries.[56] Reserves may help fill some gaps, and the Australian government passed legislation in 2001 which extends the situations in which reserve forces can be called to serve to include peacekeeping. At the same time, peacekeeping itself can contribute to attrition among personnel. Australians who have taken part in operations often report an immense satisfaction and sense of achievement but also a degree of disillusionment on return to the routine of peacetime training and administration. Many feel that the job they did while peacekeeping was the best they ever had and that they are unlikely to have such a satisfying posting again. Yet if the opportunity arose, few would probably want to become 'permanent peacekeepers' with all the disruption to family and personal life this entails.

Whether the demands on Australia will become too great for comfort depends on many things. Money and personnel are important but the critical factor will be the stability of Australia's region, especially the future of Indonesia and its potential to dissolve into a number of provinces seeking independence. There are real prospects for civil wars and for humanitarian crises such as mass killings, refugee flows, starvation and disease that may call for peacekeeping forces of one kind or another. With its present capabilities and force structure Australia would be very hard pressed to handle a second substantial operation in addition to that in East Timor but it may well be expected to do so by some combination of the United Nations, the United States and the Australian public. This would provide a true test of Australia's commitment to peacekeeping among the government and community alike.

NOTES

1. T. B. Millar, *Australia in Peace and War* (Canberra: Australian National University Press, 1978), p. 386.
2. W. J. Hudson, *Blind Loyalty: Australia and the Suez Crisis, 1956* (Melbourne: Melbourne University Press, 1989), pp. 134–5.
3. Millar, *Australia in Peace and War*, p. 409, n. 6.
4. Department of Foreign Affairs and Trade, *Australian Foreign Affairs Record* (October 1988), p. 394.
5. *Review of Australia's defence capabilities*, Report to the Minister for Defence by Mr Paul Dibb (Canberra: Australian Government Publishing Service, 1986); Department of Defence, *The Defence of Australia 1987* (Canberra: Australian Government Publishing Service, 1987).
6. Department of Defence, *The Defence of Australia 1987*, pp. 8–9.
7. For details see the Department of Foreign Affairs and Trade website at http:// www.dfat.gov.au/geo/png/bougainville/peace_process_chron.html.
8. Hugh Smith, 'The Politics of Peacekeeping in Australia', in Smith (ed.), *Australia and Peacekeeping* (Canberra: Australian Defence Studies Centre, UNSW, Australian Defence Force Academy, 1990), pp. 30–32; see also Rodney Gouttman, *Bondi in the Sinai: Australia, the MFO, and the Politics of Participation* (Lanham, MD: University Press of America, 1986).
9. For a full account of these arguments see the statements by ALP members in *Commonwealth Parliamentary Debates*, House of Representatives (22 October 1981), pp. 2417–22, 2424–27, 2434–36.
10. Smith, 'The Politics of Peacekeeping in Australia', p. 32.
11. *Canberra Times* (25 November 1981); *Australian* (2 February 1982).
12. Gouttman, *Bondi in the Sinai*, pp. 76, 100.
13. *Melbourne Age* (21 September 1981), p. 4.
14. *Commonwealth Parliamentary Debates*, House of Representatives (22 October 1981), pp. 2412–17.
15. *Commonwealth Parliamentary Debates*, Senate (26 May 1989), p. 2878.
16. Ministerial Statement, Department of Defence, MIN 235/92 (21 October 1992).
17. For more details on the UN in Cambodia see Trevor Findlay, *Cambodia: The Legacy and Lessons of UNTAC* (Oxford: Oxford University Press for the Stockholm International Peace Research Institute, 1999); and Hugh Smith (ed.), *International Peacekeeping: Building on the Cambodian Experience* (Canberra: Australian Defence Studies Centre, UNSW, Australian Defence Force Academy, 1994).
18. For an explanation of Australian thinking see the chapter by Foreign Minister Gareth Evans, 'The Comprehensive Political Settlement to the Cambodia Conflict: An Exercise in Cooperating for Peace', in Smith (ed.), *International Peacekeeping*.
19. Ibid., p. 9.
20. For Australian assessments of UNTAC see Lieutenant Colonel Steve Ayling, 'UNTAC: The Ambitious Mission', in Hugh Smith (ed.), *Peacekeeping: Challenges*

for the Future (Canberra: Australian Defence Studies Centre, UNSW, Australian Defence Force Academy, 1993); Lieutenant General John Sanderson, 'UNTAC: Successes and Failures', in Smith (ed.), *International Peacekeeping*.

21. *Commonwealth Parliamentary Debates*, House of Representatives (1 April 1992), pp. 1593–7.
22. *Australian* (25 September 1991).
23. For a range of views on Australia's historical relationship with East Timor see James Cotton (ed.), *East Timor and Australia* (Canberra: Australian Defence Studies Centre, UNSW, Australian Defence Force Academy, 1999).
24. For an official account of events leading up to the UN's involvement in 1999 see *East Timor in Transition 1998–2000: An Australian Policy Challenge* (Canberra: Department of Foreign Affairs and Trade, 2001). For a range of critical and supportive views of Australian policy in this period see *East Timor, Report of the Senate Foreign Affairs, Defence and Trade References Committee* (Canberra: Commonwealth Parliament, December 2000), especially chapters 6 and 7 (also available at http://www.aph. gov.au/senate/committee/fadt_ctte/East%20Timor/index.htm).
25. Cotton (ed.), *East Timor in Transition 1998–2000*, pp. 133–4.
26. On Australia's negotiations with regional countries to set up INTERFET see Alan Ryan, *'Primary Responsibilities and Primary Risks': Australian Defence Force Participation in the International Force East Timor* (Canberra: Land Warfare Studies Centre, 2000), pp. 45–54.
27. Security Council Resolution 1264 (15 September 1999).
28. Ryan, *'Primary Responsibilities and Primary Risks'*, pp. 89–102.
29. *Australian* Newspoll, http://www.theaustralian.news.com.au.
30. The latter is most unusual for a serving military officer. On the enormous popularity and myth-making surrounding General Cosgrove see Jenelle Bonnor, *The Politics of Defence in Australia*, Working Paper no. 68 (Canberra: Australian Defence Studies Centre, UNSW, Australian Defence Force Academy, 2001), pp. 10–11. Available at http://idun.itsc.adfa.edu.au/ADSC/WP%2068.pdf.
31. See, for example, William Maley, 'Australia and the East Timor Crisis: Some Critical Comments', *Australian Journal of International Affairs*, Vol. 54, No. 2 (July 2000).
32. Cotton (ed.), *East Timor in Transition 1998–2000*, pp. 183–90.
33. Department of Defence, *The Defence of Australia 1987*, p. 9.
34. Department of Defence, *Force Structure Review 1991* (Canberra: DPUBS 35/91, 1991), p. 2.
35. Minister for Defence, *Peacekeeping Policy: The Future Australian Defence Force Role* (Canberra: DPUBS 2092/93, June 1993), p. 3.
36. Lieutenant General John Grey, 'The Australian Army View', *Asia-Pacific Defence Reporter* (June–July 1993), p. 8. Grey also discusses some of the costs and benefits to the Army of participation in peacekeeping.
37. Minister for Defence, *Peacekeeping Policy*, Annex B, pp. 12–13.
38. Minister for Defence, *Strategic Review 1993* (Canberra: DPUBS 8009/93, December 1993), p. 16.
39. Senator the Honorable Robert Ray, 'International Peacekeeping: Australian and Regional Perspectives', in Smith (ed.), *International Peacekeeping*, pp. 102–3.
40. Minister for Defence, *Peacekeeping Policy*, p. 3.
41. Senator the Honorable Robert Ray, 'Peacekeeping and Peacemaking – the Challenge for the Future', in Smith (ed.), *Peacekeeping: Challenges for the Future*.

42. Minister for Defence, *Defending Australia: Defence White Paper 1994* (Canberra: DPUBS 12065/94, November 1994), pp. 104–5.
43. Minister for Defence, *Defending Australia*, p. 106.
44. Cited in Graeme Cheeseman, *Structuring the ADF for UN Operations: Change and Resistance*, Working Paper no. 34 (Canberra: Australian Defence Studies Centre, UNSW, Australian Defence Force Academy, 1995), p. 5.
45. Gareth Evans, *Cooperating for Peace: The Global Agenda for the 1990s and Beyond* (Sydney: Allen & Unwin, 1993).
46. Gareth Evans, 'Opening Address', in Kevin Clements and Christine Wilson (eds), *UN Peacekeeping at the Crossroads* (Canberra: Peace Research Centre, Australian National University, 1994), p. 20.
47. *United Nations Peacekeeping and Australia*, Senate Standing Committee on Foreign Affairs, Defence and Trade (Canberra: Commonwealth Parliament, May 1991), Recommendation 18, §§7.5–7.14.
48. *United Nations Peacekeeping and Australia*, Recommendation 16, §§6.40–6.42.
49. *Australia's Participation in Peacekeeping*, Joint Standing Committee on Foreign Affairs, Defence and Trade (Canberra: Commonwealth Parliament, December 1994), §§5.28–5.31 and Recommendation 27.
50. *Australia's Participation in Peacekeeping*, §§4.74–4.77 and Recommendation 23.
51. Minister for Defence, *Defence 2000: Our Future Defence Force* (Canberra: Defence Publishing Service, October 2000), §§2.6–2.12.
52. Minister for Defence, *Defence 2000: Our Future Defence Force*, §6.2.
53. *Australian Perspectives on Defence: Report of the Community Consultation Team* (Canberra: Commonwealth of Australia, Defence Review 2000, September 2000), p. 10. Though there are questions about the process of consultation, this judgement accords with other indicators of community views. See G. Cheeseman and H. Smith, 'Public consultation or political choreography? The Howard Government's quest for community views on defence policy', *Australian Journal of International Affairs*, Vol. 55, No. 1 (April 2001).
54. For this argument in relation to all military intervention overseas, including wars, see G. Cheeseman and I. McAllister, 'Popular and Élite Support in Australia for Overseas Military Intervention', *Australian Journal of International Affairs*, Vol. 48, No. 2 (November 1994).
55. For a range of arguments see Cheeseman, *Structuring the ADF for UN Operations*, p. 56. For an outline of the problem see Department of Defence, *Submission to the Inquiry into Recruitment and Retention of Australian Defence Force Personnel*, Senate. For an outline of the problem see Department of Defence, Submission to the Inquiry into Recruitment and Retention of Australian Defence Force Personnel, Senate.
56. For an outline of the problem see Department of Defence, Submission to the Inquiry into Recruitment and Retention of Australian Defence Force Personnel, Senate.

TWO

Germany[1]

Mary N. Hampton

INTRODUCTION

Since unification, Germany has exhibited both change and continuity in its domestic and foreign policies. While continuity has been the watchword for foreign policy under the Kohl and Schroeder governments, important changes have occurred in German military/security policy. One need only think back to the German posture struck during the outbreak and conduct of the US-led Gulf War in 1991 to recognize the rapidity and magnitude of change in the German orientation toward military intervention and power projection. At that time, the German political leadership and the public were unwilling to contribute militarily in the conflict, and there was wide-ranging debate inside Germany as to the justification of the use of force in that instance. Both analysts and participants in German politics viewed the phenomenon as being exemplary of the German culture of reticence that had evolved since the end of World War II. However, little more than a decade later, Germany participated in peacekeeping missions in the Balkans, was fully engaged in Operation Allied Force, peacekeeping, and contributed substantially to the US-led war on terrorism in Afghanistan.

The purpose of this chapter is twofold. First, it examines the seemingly drastic shift in German attitudes and willingness to eschew past reticence and intervene militarily in any number of instances alongside NATO and EU allies. Second, it explores how participation in peacekeeping reveals the emerging German security identity and approach to crisis and conflict situations. The chapter argues that Germany has moved away from its long-standing culture of reticence in military-security affairs, long identified with semi-sovereign West Germany. Instead, through a process of gradually projecting its power abroad, Germany is beginning to assume a role of nuanced leadership in the EU's security governance approach to conflict prevention and resolution. In so doing, Germany has taken advantage of the opportunities afforded it in its foreign policy, yet continues to be uniquely constrained in pursuing its interests.

German power has reemerged since unification, but has assumed a unique form. The current German tendency to be assertive in projecting soft power capabilities and to pursue leadership in peacekeeping operations reflects sensitivity to the threat perceptions of others and historical lessons learned based on the misuse of power in Germany's past.[2] In this way, Germany remains a non-traditional power, since peacekeeping missions are less threatening and less overtly self-interested than other military intervention forms.[3] The resulting German brand of interventionism therefore seeks to establish what has been dubbed *security governance* as the center-piece of international order; that is, that security objectives are best achieved by deliberately employing a mix of non-military means, and turning to military tools only as a last resort. This projection of 'power lite' not only coalesces neatly with the emerging European order in which German power is embedded and plays a key role; it increasingly establishes Germany as a lead state for constructing alternative security futures in the international order.

Germany has now assumed a critical role among Western powers in debating and redefining the proper mix of soft and hard power in asserting power preferences abroad. Where the US increasingly views the use of its military in peacekeeping and soft power operations as counterproductive to American strategic interests, European states, and Germany in particular, view such interventions as central components to security governance.

FROM RETICENCE TO READINESS: EN ROUTE TO GERMAN INTERVENTIONISM

It had become the norm by the 1980s to speak of West Germany's domestic proclivity to reject the notion of West German military intervention or military power projection. The anti-militaristic streak among West Germans emerged at the end of World War II and found expression in the 1950s, especially with the 'ohne mich' (without me) movement during the debate about West German rearmament. The position was one informed by the legacy of and the collective internalization of lessons learned in World War II and the Holocaust. This orientation produced a strong domestic political consensus that held for over forty years. West Germans vowed 'never again war' and 'never again Auschwitz'; never again to intervene militarily beyond the national borders, especially in regions harmed in the past by German military adventurism, and never again to allow itself to be counted on the side of anti-democratic forces in the world.[4]

Hence, according to the West German constitution the West German military could only be used in the case of direct attack on the homeland and/or in conjunction with the NATO alliance. Increasingly, Germans perceived themselves as representing a 'civilian power' in the world. This position was further underpinned by the subservience of the West German military to NATO. West German dependence on NATO, and especially on the US military and nuclear guarantees, allowed the 'never again war' cultural norm to flourish. Clearly, West Germany would not be asked, expected, nor did it want, to intervene beyond its borders in light of the US role as protector. Consequently, on the increasing number of occasions when Germany was asked to participate in UN peacekeeping operations in the 1980s, the requests were turned down. As Thorsten Stein observes, the Federal government argued that it was 'too early to deploy German Armed Forces abroad (outside the framework of NATO), let alone in areas where the specter of World War II still lingered. These may have been sound political concerns, but they were not valid legal arguments.'[5] In short, the domestic political consensus and the international environment continued to constrain German perceptions of and opportunities for projecting power abroad.

Most analysts assumed this German culture of reticence to be resilient and stable well into the future, and but for the collapse of the Cold War system and the unification of the two Germanys, perhaps it would have been. However, the systemic shudders of 1989–90 radically altered the domestic and international environments for Germany. While the culture of reticence held on through the Gulf War of 1991, it was the last expression of the domestic consensus in that form. Other countries openly and widely criticized the German government for its hesitation to act in solidarity with its allies.[6]

The Kohl government therefore challenged the domestic consensus politically by agreeing to German participation in UN peacekeeping operations (UN PKO) in the early 1990s. The Free Democratic Party (FDP) and the opposition Social Democratic Party (SPD) then put the agreement to the test by submitting a query regarding German military intervention to the German Constitutional Court.[7]

The constitutional finding of 1994 made room for German military deployment outside the national borders in the pursuit of 'safeguarding peace', as long as German military forces were part of 'peacekeeping troops. Moreover, the constitutional finding required that peace-securing measures' be within the context of the UN system of collective security, and in conjunction with its allies. The court went no further in defining other ways and venues in which German military power could be projected, and no one has yet pressed the court to do so. What the ruling did was to clear the way for German participation in peacekeeping operations under the aegis of international institutions and multilateralism. Specifically, the ruling reinforced existing constitutional law as being a 'sufficient constitutional basis for Germany's participation in military operations led or authorized by the UN, and that no other provision in the Basic Law ... could be interpreted as forbidding such participation.'[8] The ruling further legitimized German participation in multilateral operations through international organizations other than the UN, as long as such operations are conducted according to the strictures of the 'system of mutual security', and 'within the framework' of that system.[9]

The constitutional ruling helped a new political will to emerge that was ready to answer the demands of a changing international environment. The way was paved for German PKO and peace enforcement contributions in Somalia, Bosnia, Macedonia, Afghanistan, and many other areas in the world. Interestingly, Germany's peace enforcement participation in Kosovo in 1999 was executed without a UN mandate, and yet drew no political challenge from the left or from the opposition Christian Democratic Union/Christian Social Union (CDU/CSU) parties. This fact reflects the emerging domestic consensus that permits German military involvement abroad under specified and limited circumstances.

In short, the German domestic consensus moved away from the 'never again war' response to German military intervention beyond its borders. What has emerged since the constitutional court gave the green light to German military intervention beyond homeland defense is a new consensus of 'never on our own'. What Somalia, Bosnia, Kosovo, Macedonia, and Afghanistan have in common regarding German military participation and domestic support is that they have all been conducted 'in solidarity' with Germany's allies, and have all included critical components of defending humanitarian and democratic values against the encroachment of would-be and proven violators of those values. It means that Germany can intervene abroad and will participate in fighting the forces of anti-democracy only under special circumstances and only alongside its democratic allies.[10] John Duffield notes that the German impulse to assert itself militarily remains tempered by 'the imperative to be a reliable, predictable, dependable partner'. In short, the new consensus requires Germany to act with its allies and partners in the name of human rights and democratic values.

'POWER PROJECTION LITE'

To distinguish current German military power projection abroad from a more traditionalist understanding, the German variant may be referred to as 'power projection lite'. First, power projection lite means that German military security policy still must be seen as non-threatening. German operations began in the early 1990s as relatively risk-free operations and graduated to more militarily muscular interventions. The gradual escalation of German risk-taking and the scope of its interventions assuaged external and internal hesitations alike.[11] Second, German power projection lite has meant that narrowly defined national interests are still not permissible as the basis upon which to set the guidelines for German security policy preferences. The potential for a German *Sonderweg* is thereby precluded.[12] Thus, power projection lite is based on a very restricted understanding of the uses of force beyond national borders. Further, it is a policy based on German incremental change and adaptation to the changed environment and demands of the post-Cold War world.[13]

GERMAN MILITARY INTERVENTION AND THE DOMESTIC RIGHT–LEFT DIVIDE

In German domestic politics, the long-lasting consensus based on reticence and self-restraint was viewed differently on the right and left. For many on the right and center-right, it was recognized that West Germany was a semi-sovereign state, and that necessarily constrained national options. It was also recognized that history would play a critical and continuing role in constraining postwar German policy. Finally, for many, but especially for Konrad Adenauer and his political heir, Helmut Kohl, the past must act as a compass in directing German foreign policy and national identity permanently embedded in a greater European configuration.

After unification, some analysts and policy-makers on the center and center-right began to advise Bonn/Berlin to seek 'normalization' in its foreign policy, to begin to reassess its interests and pursue them as sovereign states do, with regard to self-interest.[14] For example, German scholar Christian Hacke has argued that sovereign Germany ought to behave differently than the semi-sovereign West Germany, and ought to forego the former's tendencies to pursue foreign policy that is based on too much timidity and self-restraint.[15] While Hacke advocates the continuation of European integration as a key German objective, he argues that even integration policy needs to be weighed according to German interests, not

German timidity. In short, many in the center and center-right reflect realist proclivities, believing that sovereign Germany ought to behave as other sovereign states do. That said, most of those analysts continue to acknowledge the singularity of Germany's twentieth-century history, and therefore end up promoting a foreign policy that is pursued multilaterally and in close coordination with Germany's allies. However, many on the center-right would be willing to step from behind the constraints of power projection lite that tie German military intervention to PKO-type missions only. Edmund Stoiber, the CSU candidate for German Chancellor in 2002, promoted on occasion a potentially much more muscular German military projection policy, calling on Germany to assume its place alongside the US as the leading European ally acting more readily in the name of German national interests. Further, while multilateralism is acknowledged as the framework through which German power projection will likely be pursued, some on the center-right advocate more national assertiveness where and when necessary.

Some occupants of Germany's center-left political configurations share the above positions as well. However, many on the left and center-left advocated the 'never again war' and 'never again Auschwitz' as immutable moral directives, with the historical onus on postwar Germany to represent a peaceful 'civilian' power in the world. For this group, Germany had a moral responsibility to resist war-like and intemperate behavior and to present itself as a unique example of the first pacifistic, post-national state. The center-left also argued that Germany must resist pursuing power politics and support for military adventurism in the world. Based on this perception, many on the left saw the US and NATO as antagonistic to their future vision for Europe, and many advocated a winding down for NATO and promoted the ascendancy of a Europe-wide security framework like the OSCE (Organization for Security and Cooperation in Europe), one free from the bipolar US–Soviet strategic antagonisms. Many members of the current 'red–green' coalition were of this persuasion, and it is among this group that most change has occurred since unification.

Ludger Volmer, a Green member of the German Bundestag, and an advisor on foreign policy to Foreign Minister Joschka Fischer, catalogues succinctly the change among many in this group. He argues that the pacifism of the German left in the 1950s and 1960s ('ohne mich'), 1970s (anti-Vietnam policies of the US), and the 1980s (anti-nuclear terror of bipolar deterrence) were all well founded, but also that each was unique, derived from the real threats to peace of the time. Volmer avers that much changed with the end of the Cold War and bipolarity, and that circumstances since have made German participation in military interventions sometimes necessary. For example, he argues that Germany had to participate in the military intervention in Kosovo against Serb leadership because the moral imperative of 'never again Auschwitz' outweighed that of 'never again war'. He posits further that sovereign Germany owes it to its democratic allies and the rest of the world to participate in military actions that are morally justified and multilaterally pursued, especially since such interventions no longer serve the purposes of one bloc against the other, but of greater international interests. Otherwise, were Germany not to participate, it might be perceived that the Germans 'want to hide behind their history and let others carry the burdens'.[16] Finally, Volmer insists that terrorism is a real threat to Germany and the rest of the world, and that Germany's participation in the US-led coalition against international terrorism was not a flight into militaristic adventurism, but a necessary component of a multi-pronged international effort to fight terrorism and the political conditions that give rise to it.

The domestic elements of Germany's emerging consensus are important to sort out and analyze for a number of reasons. First, it is important to understand the basis for change among the different political players and how each came to view the conditions that led to change. Second, it should raise a warning flag that the current incarnation of German power projection lite may change to something more traditional in the near future. If and when that possibility becomes reality, a new domestic fight will break out over Germany's proper place among military powers. Already, the Schroeder government has faced and will continue to face some stiff opposition from his governing coalition over various German military interventions, even of the 'soft' kind. The voices of doubt have been growing throughout 2002 over the issues of military over-extension and underfunding, and concerning the nature of the cases in which the Schroeder government now inserts the military. It is quite possible that the left could be headed for another internal battle over means and ends concerning military power, not unlike that which ruptured Helmut Schmidt's hold on his ruling party, the SPD, and the SPD's hold on power in the early 1980s which led to the 16-year-long tenure of the Kohl-led CDU/CSU/FDP coalition government.

The newly emerged consensus may therefore be shallow, short-lived, and already undergoing revision. Some argue that the Schroeder government and the sentiments expressed by his competitor in the 2002 national elections, Stoiber, foreshadow a more assertive, nationally oriented German foreign and security policy. Clearly, the German military is suddenly omnipresent, with German troops present around the globe as peacekeepers and enforcers. Germans also hold the Deputy

SACEUR (Supreme Allied Commander Europe) position at NATO and the General Directorship of the EU military staff, under Generals Dieter Stoeckmann and Rainer Schuwirth respectively. As noted, continued evolution in this direction could provoke domestic political conflict, especially from the left.

GERMAN POWER PROJECTION LITE: MATURING WITHIN THE ESDP

The German focus on soft power projection reflects what Peter Katzenstein has called the internationalization of German interests.[17] German participation in peacekeeping reflects the increased attention being given to the European Common Foreign and Security Policy (CFSP). The CFSP is evolving within the context of the European Security and Defence Policy (ESDP), and the general commitment to an autonomous European security structure and identity, which ESDP advocates, has been growing since the British and French agreement at St-Malo in 1998. While the Germans were initially hesitant, or at least rather silent on the autonomy issue, they have become active supporters since the EU Nice summit of 2000, where it was eventually agreed that ESDP would theoretically complement NATO, thus leaving NATO as the security institution of first choice in Europe.

The most important developments in the ESDP revolve around the Headline Goals that were articulated at the EU summit in Helsinki in 1999. The goals include having 50,000 to 60,000 EU troops available for deployment within 60 days and for up to 100 days. Germany is projected to be the largest contributor and has committed a contingent of 30,000 troops. The EU troops are to be deployable in a number of situations that were spelled out as the Petersberg Tasks in 1997 in Amsterdam. The tasks are to include humanitarian assistance, PKO, crisis management and prevention, and peace enforcement operations. The tasks also clearly advocate that any military component must be pursued as a last resort, and only then as one piece of a broader approach to security that includes political, economic, and environmental concerns. This approach has been called security governance. It is clear that the emphasis is on the softer side of power projection, and is a direct manifestation of the emerging European multilateral approach to security. In this sense, Katzenstein's claim that the EU has taken on the features of a German approach to the internationalization of national interests is confirmed, where the tools of security governance are first political, economic, and diplomatic and are military only as a last resort. To a large extent, European, and especially German, notions of security governance characterize the collective security approach to international relations.

To the extent that the EU continues to pursue core objectives through security governance and crisis management, Germany's soft power approach, or its power projection lite, will be the engine of the European approach to security, and increasingly redefine what a 'normal' military security policy looks like. German Chancellor Gerhard Schroeder reflected the new approach succinctly in an April 2001 interview with the German weekly, *Die Zeit*: 'Military skills and strength are featuring less and less prominently in 21st century European security programs.' He further averred: 'The question of security cannot be left to the military.'[18] In a similar fashion, Egon Bahr, the main architect of the SPD's former Chancellor Willi Brandt's path-breaking foreign policy, *Ostpolitik*, argues: 'To create stability through binding relationships, in which the power of the military plays an increasingly smaller role, that is the European way.'[19]

That said, it should be remembered that a number of European states, France and the UK in particular, retain their traditional security policy approaches as well as the new European approach. Both are willing to project military power unilaterally, bilaterally, or multilaterally. This fact sets them apart from Germany and in this way, German power projection lite remains singular. One question for the future of European security policy, therefore, will be whether British and French policies evolve in a way that becomes more commensurate with the German approach, or whether this bifurcation in European approaches to security issues leads Germany to emulate the other two.

If the British and French retain their traditional power projection capabilities and willingness, will Germany in fact at some point follow suit and evolve beyond its current emphasis on projecting military power multilaterally and mainly through PKO? After all, it was practically inconceivable just a decade ago that Germany would shuck off its almost fifty-year 'ohne mich' approach to military power projection beyond its national borders. The change, once it came, was relatively rapid and seemingly widely accepted among the public and elite class. There is evidence that Germany is enhancing its military visibility and status on all fronts, and recently included an example of traditional military power projection when it assumed the naval command for the previously US-led anti-terrorism operations around the Horn of Africa. Working from their base in Djibouti, where about 1,200 German Navy personnel are stationed, this is Germany's largest naval deployment since World War II. The Germans will likely hold the command spot until October 2002.[20]

Further, it is worth considering the impact that the European security governance approach has on trans-Atlantic relations. While many in the Pentagon, Congress, and Washington elite circles, particularly those of the Bush Administration, have come to view peacekeeping as a drain on US resources and military readiness, many in Europe, especially Germany, have decided that PKO should be a central component of Western security strategy. The widening chasm over the purposefulness of PKO and who should be participating in them has already caused friction in trans-Atlantic security relations. This rift became particularly clear regarding PKO in Kosovo, and was a hot issue during the 2000 presidential election, when Condoleezza Rice made her now famous comment about US troops escorting children to kindergarten.[21] One of the effects has been a greater boost to the Europeans in moving forward on ESDP.

Finally, the German and European proclivity to favor PKO as a central component of Western military policy also reflects diverging trans-Atlantic perceptions of the usefulness of the UN. For Germany and other European states, the fact that NATO's war in Kosovo was executed without a UN mandate was highly problematic. In fact, in Germany, many read the 1994 constitutional court ruling as making UN mandates necessary ingredients for Germany's participation in PKO and other collective security policies. While the worry revealed more political sensibilities than constitutional directives, German leaders have since repeatedly made clear their demand that Germany only participate in PKO and other missions that have a UN mandate.

For the US, on the other hand, the lack of a UN-mandate was seen by many as a positive development. Since the 1993 Somalia intervention, the Clinton Administration, and certainly the current Bush Administration, have resisted participating in UN-mandated PKO. In fact, Presidential Directive 25 was issued during the Clinton Administration after the Somalia débâcle. It rejected US participation under a wide array of conditions and set stringent conditions for US participation. The guidelines it set were used to justify US lack of involvement in the Rwandan humanitarian débâcle of 1994.[22] Related, the Republican-dominated American Congress withheld overdue US funds for the UN until agreement was reached to reduce US dues and to curtail the UN peacekeeping budget from 30 percent to 27 percent.[23] In contrast, UN Secretary-General Kofi Annan recently discussed the possibility of having the EU's emerging rapid reaction force available for UN PKO.[24]

The Europeans, and especially the Germans, have been eager to tie the US to previous and ongoing peacekeeping commitments. In the Balkans and Afghanistan, the Germans have been insistent that US Secretary of

State Colin Powell's phrase of 'in together, out together' be upheld. The Germans recently revisited that concept in attempting to keep the US directly involved in postwar peacekeeping and institution-building efforts in Afghanistan. In December of 2001, the German government created a short-term row between itself and the British and Americans by insisting successfully that the UN security forces and mission in Afghanistan be kept separate from the ongoing US military campaign, and then that the US remain after its military campaign wound down.[25]

In short, just as Germany and Europe were coalescing around a new consensus based on multilateralism and the empowerment of international institutions like the UN, the US was back tracking from such a position and re-emphasizing a more narrowly defined concept of national interest.[26]

SPECIFIC EXAMPLES OF GERMAN PEACEKEEPING

Germany is engaged globally today in a number of peacekeeping, peace enforcement, and crisis management and/or prevention operations, and is vying to become the leader of the EU as the advocate of security governance.[27] Between 1991 and today, there has been some form of German participation in diplomatic, humanitarian missions, PKO, observer, or peace enforcement operations in Cambodia, Georgia, Somalia, Bosnia, Kosovo, Macedonia, and East Timor. Among the operations were those that included very minor participation by the Germans, such as the 150 soldiers assigned to a medical unit between 1992 and 1993 in Cambodia. There have also been cases of intense German involvement.[28] As examples, Germany led the way after Operation Allied Force in proposing and executing the Stability Pact for former Yugoslavia, and Berlin has now assumed the lead role for NATO and the EU in Macedonia. The real turning point in German involvement abroad came with the political change in 1998, when the red–green coalition government of Schroeder replaced the 16-year-old coalition government of Helmut Kohl. In 1998, the Bundeswehr's engagement abroad was minimal. At that time, there were about 2,000 German soldiers in Bosnia and scarcely a dozen with the UN mission in Georgia. Today that figure has gone up substantially.[29] In total, Germany currently has 9,995 troops deployed in PKO and peace-related multilateral operations. There are 11 German troops in Georgia as UN observers, 92 commando special unit soldiers in Kandahar, 126 soldiers in Uzbekistan, 238 nuclear–biological–chemical (ABC) troops in Kuwait, 586 soldiers in Macedonia, 876 soldiers with the international security forces of International Security Assistance Force (ISAF) in Kabul, 1,278 Navy troops in the Horn of Africa,

1,719 supporting Joint Force in Bosnia (SFOR – Stabilization Force), and 4,705 in Joint Guardian in Kosovo (KFOR – Kosovo Force).[30] I will focus below on German participation in the Kosovo, Macedonia, and Afghanistan operations. All reveal clearly an emerging pattern in German behavior. Through PKO and power projection lite, Germany is asserting its leadership in Europe through the EU, NATO, and the UN, and is also beginning to do so outside of Europe, in countries like Afghanistan.

Kosovo

In many ways, the ongoing NATO intervention in Kosovo has really been a watershed in the evolution of German and European security identities. For example, between 1998 and 2000 in Kosovo, the EU provided the bulk of the peacekeeping troops and the bulk of financial aid; the EU spent 3.1 billion euros compared to the 900 million dollars spent by the US. As of 2002, the EU provided 80 percent of the troops in Bosnia and Kosovo, to the Americans' 17 percent. Also, the intervention in Kosovo has gone a long way to instill confidence in the EU that it can successfully carry out a collective security policy over a sustained period of time. As of May 2002, the EU had raised the possibility of taking over the policing operations in Bosnia and perhaps Kosovo. Already, the EU's overall policy to Southeastern Europe has been viewed by most as a success in its multi-pronged approach. More specifically, Germany experienced the Kosovo intervention as the first truly successful example of its power projection lite. In 1999, for the first time in postwar history, majorities of the German Parliament, from left to right, were voting in favor of Germany military intervention beyond national borders. The fact that the 'red–green' coalition government under Schroeder's leadership was in power may well have been fortuitous. As many have noted, if the CDU/CSU had still been in power at the time the Kosovo crisis reached its head, there would not have been the broad left-to-right consensus for intervention.[31] Also striking was the sustained support of the German public, which had previously been loath to see Germany intervene militarily abroad. While there was much less support in former East Germany than in the West for the interventions, overall public opinion remained positive. An Emnid public opinion survey revealed at the end of June 1999 that 73 percent of German respondents believed that Germany's military contribution was constructive in helping to end the Kosovo conflict.[32]

The reasons for the broad-based support are many. First, as noted above, the newly emerging domestic consensus of 'never on our own' fit the parameters of the Kosovo intervention well. Wolfgang Ischinger, who is currently (2004) the German Ambassador to the US and a former top cabinet member in the Kohl government, argues that the Kosovo intervention represented a break with past European wars that were based on geopolitical power struggles. He observes that the multilateral intervention in Kosovo was based on 'the need to avert a humanitarian catastrophe. Instead of national interests, the international community pursued the goal of implementing the basic principles of law and humanity.'[33] Thus, Allied Force and the follow-on peacekeeping mission contained all the ingredients that validated the new German approach to international power projection: it was multilateral; it was clearly in aid of a set of collective security goals; it was proof positive to the world that Germany was willing to take its place among the other responsible democracies to stop ethnic cleansing and punish the perpetrator; it was carried out within NATO, the trans-Atlantic security organization that has been directly tied to German democratic identity.[34]

In the context of the emerging consensus regarding a common EU security governance approach to international relations, and Germany's place therein, Kosovo was path-breaking. Consistent with its adherence to the EU's Petersberg Tasks, Germany's ongoing mission in Kosovo has included economic, political, humanitarian, and military components. Germany has been involved since 1998 in all NATO, OSCE, and UN missions in Kosovo, including the Air Verification Mission, the OSCE Verification Mission, the Extraction Force, Operation Allied Force, and KFOR. Not only has Germany participated in KFOR, but also the commander of those NATO forces since 1999 has been German General Klaus Reinhardt. At the end of 1999, Germany had provided 4,870 of the 41,350 troops in KFOR. Of the 5,800 troops deployed in that period, Germany was the third largest troop provider behind Italy and the US. Germany had the second largest police contingent. In total, Germany provided 10 percent of overall UN/NATO costs.

In May of 2002, NATO decided to downsize its peacekeeping missions in Bosnia and Kosovo. The allies agreed to cut the Bosnia mission by 20–30 percent and to streamline the Kosovo mission as well. While this move is clearly reflective of the increased American proclivity to disengage from Europe, it will enhance the role of the EU and Germany in maintaining the commitments in Southeastern Europe. As noted above, the EU has already assumed the leadership for police missions in Bosnia and will likely follow suit in Kosovo. Further, the role of Germany has increased in all EU and NATO missions.

Macedonia

After the Albanian insurgency threatened to bring Macedonia to civil war in August 2001, NATO helped broker a peace deal on 13 August that included broader rights for the Albanians. Part of the deal was the deployment of around 4,500 NATO troops to the country for thirty days, 600 of which were German. Led by the British, NATO's Task Force Harvest mission was to collect weapons surrendered by insurgent ethnic Albanians.[35]

A follow-on NATO mission was unanimously approved by the UN Security Council and executed to protect 120 civilian peace monitors from the EU and OSCE. On 27 September 2001, the German Parliament agreed to deploy forces for Task Force 'Amber Fox', which took the place of Harvest. Berlin suggested that Germany become the lead state in this second phase of engagement in Macedonia, a suggestion that was welcomed and finally accepted by NATO and the Macedonian government. The operation came under the leadership of German Brigadier-General Heinz-Georg Keerl, its duration was not specified, and the Germans have contributed the lion's share of troops: 586 out of the 750–1,000-strong force.[36] In response to the request from the Macedonian President, the North Atlantic Council (NAC) agreed in February 2002 to extend the Fox mission until 26 June 2002. The mission remained the same and, after some hesitation, Germany decided to continue its leadership role until June. The German Parliament approved the three-month extension in March of 2002. The large majority of the German Parliament, and a significant portion of the red–green coalition, was supportive of the extension: 470 voted for the extension, 34 against. These numbers were similar to those received in the first extension vote three months earlier and were a welcome contrast for the Schroeder government when compared to the bare majority received in September 2001 for the initial mandate.[37]

The mission in Macedonia is an interesting example of Germany's emerging commitment and leadership inclination in PKO. It is also an arena for muted discord between NATO and the EU. The mission in Macedonia conforms neatly to the EU's Headline Goals commitments, and has been successfully executed to date. Crisis prevention and assisting in the democratization process are at the heart of both the Macedonia operations and the Headline Goals. In discussing the extension of Germany's leadership role, Foreign Minister Joschka Fischer noted that the mission in Macedonia represented 'a successful example of conflict prevention'.[38]

Because of the nice fit between the Macedonia mission and the EU's ESDP objectives, a row broke out early in 2002 over whether or not the

EU should take over responsibility for the mission from NATO. It would represent an early test case of ESDP and, while no American troops are now involved in Fox anyway, it would provide proof that the EU can operate such a mission without NATO or the US. The Spanish government and the EU High Commissioner for foreign policy, Javier Solana, first raised the issue at an EU foreign ministers' summit in February.

A leaked British internal document then revealed a division within the UK government over whether the Blair Administration should further support the mission under the EU's aegis. In the document, the nay-sayers in the UK government, represented by Defence Secretary Geoffrey Hoon in the leaked document, held that 'UK troops would be at risk because the EU's defence arm was not ready for such a dangerous mission'.[39] Many NATO officials echoed this position, believing that the EU 'was ill-prepared for such an operation'.[40]

Supporters of the switch in the UK government were weak in their support of the mission going to the EU, but argued that if it did, the UK should be present. Elsewhere supporters argued that the EU already possessed an initial operating capability established for the ESDP, even though those capabilities were not due to be finalized and operational until 2003. To the supporters it was seen as very important '"to plant the EU rapid deployment force flag somewhere" to prove it is ready to take on military tasks in place of NATO'.[41] As of early May 2002, the operation had been extended to June as a NATO mission, with no clearly articulated determination after that.[42] There were indications that the German government was willing to sign up for yet a third tour of duty as the lead state.[43]

Afghanistan

As in the cases of Kosovo and Macedonia, German participation in US-led but UN-sponsored operations in Afghanistan fits the pattern of German power projection lite. The Schroeder government has supported military and non-military actions in Afghanistan to subdue terrorists and to help reconstruct war-torn Afghanistan. As in the former two cases of German involvement, the moral objectives of humanitarian assistance and upholding democratic values have been the policy center-piece. The German government has been particularly supportive of UN efforts to reconstruct Afghanistan and of the independent UN security assistance forces sent into that country, going so far as hosting the UN talks on postwar reconstruction of Afghanistan at the Petersberg Hotel near Bonn.

Germany's participation in the non-military multilateral international efforts to reconstruct Afghanistan is substantial. Germany provided 22 million euros in 2001 for emergency humanitarian aid, contributed to developmental assistance in multiple forms, and promoted the development of civil societal tasks such as education. Apropos the Petersberg Agreement that emphasizes the importance of helping to establish the rule of law, Germany is also getting involved in developing such a training program. Berlin contributed 2 million euros to the UN's Afghan Interim Administration Fund, and 18 million euros to the World Bank's reconstruction efforts. Germany is also supporting the many UN-related activities in Afghanistan including UN programs for refugee and displaced persons programs, for education and culture restoration, for counseling trauma victims, for controlling small arms, for mine clearing, combating drugs, and for food security.[44]

On the military side, the German Parliament approved German participation for the PKO in Afghanistan on 21 December 2001, following the UN's adoption of Security Council Resolution 1386. Schroeder pledged 3,900 troops for the anti-terror campaign centered in, but not limited to, Afghanistan.[45] Again, as part of this collective security activity and in coalition with its democratic allies, Germany decided to participate in such peacekeeping activities as helping to establish a democratic government, training new security and armed forces, and in guaranteeing peaceful and safe conditions for UN personnel on the ground. Members of German élite forces, the Kommando Spezialkräfte (KSK), have also been engaged in Afghanistan.[46]

Schroeder called for the Europeanization of the security assistance force that Chapter VII of the UN Charter mandated, whereby the soldiers are granted 'an appropriate measure of security for themselves and for the fulfillment of their mission'.[47] The German government was invited by the UN Security Council to take over command of the UN forces when British leadership devolved after 30 April 2002. While the Schroeder government seriously contemplated the request, it finally decided that Germany was already stretched thin with leadership responsibilities in Macedonia and Bundeswehr participation in the places discussed above.[48] That said, Berlin did agree to take a lead role in building up the new police force in Afghanistan.

A number of factors distinguish Germany's Afghanistan mission from Macedonia and Kosovo. First, the terrorist threat is seen as a direct threat to German national security. Thus, while humanitarian objectives remain in the forefront, German leaders do talk of traditional national security goals when discussing German participation in the war on terrorism. For example, Fischer stated in an interview that the attacks of 11 September represented 'an attack on the open society'.[49] While he was adamant in arguing that the war on terrorism must be waged with non–military means against the political problems that cause deep–going modernization crises in the developing world, he was also clear that the attacks represented a war on the West in general. That said, the Schroeder government, like many others in the EU, has balked, however subtly, at extending the war against terrorism to Iraq or Iran, two of the states named by US President George Bush in his 'axis of evil' reference. Interestingly, the trans–Atlantic lack of consensus on this issue is largely due to the EU's, and especially Berlin's, preference for a multi–pronged approach to terrorism and other security threats, reflecting a preference for the military tool only as a last resort.

Second, unlike the other examples of German power projection lite, the Afghanistan mission is out of area; that is, out of Europe. This fact is significant in revealing the increasingly global nature of German power projection lite. As raised above, whether these differences fuel the domestic debate over increased German military commitments and power intentions remains to be seen.

THE FUTURE OF GERMAN PKO AND POWER PROJECTION LITE

As argued throughout this chapter, German participation in multilateral PKO has evolved quickly and has become widespread. However, for some time questions have been raised about 'the overtaxed army', and German over-extension.[50] Now questions are also being raised about the nature of and reasons for German military intervention abroad. For example, the question was recently posed in *Der Spiegel*: 'Why the hasty change to an intervention army that now numbers ten thousand and is pursuing all imaginable enemies in ten different countries?' Further, 'Does Germany really want to become a warring country again ...?'[51] In other words, echoes of the half-century-long culture of reticence can be heard, and will likely grow louder. This will be especially true if the German government continues to expand quietly its military reach and missions, which have already now gone somewhat beyond the confines of PKO.

Concerning over-extension, a number of reasons account for the increasing skepticism concerning German military commitments. First, the fact that this proliferation of German activity happened so quickly has raised doubts. Second, the number of operations in which German troops are involved leads to questions of over-extension. Third, the disconnect is palpable between these proliferating missions and the inability of the current government to carry through needed military reforms and raise the funds necessary to maintain current German operations into the future. Fourth, it is an election year and, while domestic issues will dominate the political agenda, Stoiber raised certain foreign and security policies as wedge issues in the campaign. Fifth, and finally, the left–center coalition is already fracturing over the extent and number of military operations being led by the Schroeder government.

Concerning funding issues, a disjuncture has existed between military reform and military projection goals and funding realities since the assumption of power by the Schroeder government in 1998. Beginning with the EU's stated Headline Goals in 1998, the German government has attempted to have Germany assume its share of responsibilities in participating in multilateral EU missions. In fact, the Schroeder government keeps putting Germany forward as a leader in many such missions. As such, recent and current military reforms have aimed at moving the German military posture away from territorial defense, reflecting Cold War realities, and toward increased mobility and flexibility as appropriate to the EU's rapid deployment force scheme and as spelled out in NATO's 1999 Defense Capabilities Initiative (DCI).[52] Defense Minister Rudolf Scharping's set of reforms has included a reduction in the overall size of the Bundeswehr and a reorientation 'away from territorial defense and towards crisis management and crisis prevention operations outside of Germany'.[53] Yet, at each step the government's ambitions are beset by under-funding problems and continued defense budget cuts. There has been a precipitous drop over the last decade in the defense budget. For example, in 1990, the outlay for the defense budget was 57.5 DM. In 2002, it is 46.7 DM.[54] Most affected in these drops is the investment money needed for research and development if Germany is to deliver on its expanded role and responsibilities in NATO, the EU, and the UN. In short, the German government's ambitions are far larger than its capability to deliver, and that shortcoming became a campaign issue in the 2002 election cycle.

Along that latter track, the 2002 campaign revealed Edmund Stoiber's willingness to move even further out from behind the shadows of the reticent German past than Shroeder. He focused his message not just on increasing the defense budget (criticizing the Schroeder government for its inability to do so); he also argued that Germany needed to become more assertive in pursuing specifically defined German interests abroad, and could thereby focus less on European interests when needed. In this regard, Stoiber encouraged a closer working relationship between Germany and the US in waging war internationally against terrorism.

He accused Schroeder of damaging Germany's key role with the US, and promoted 'Germany's traditional role as Washington's linchpin ally on the continent'.[55] Whether Stoiber would actually try to free Germany more from its multilateral shackles and encourage bilateralism and/or more strategic flexibility once in power is another question.[56] It is clear that he picked a theme that the Schroeder government itself has been much more willing to pursue than the previous Kohl regime: to speak of German self-interest in various foreign policy domains.[57]

Having said that, and as noted above, the left-of-center coalition began to show signs of disharmony during 2002 over military-security issues. The left wings of the SPD and Greens grew particularly uncomfortable with the pace and depth of the Schroeder–Fischer policy of projecting German military policy abroad. Demonstrations accompanying US President Bush's summer visit to Germany in 2002 were reflective of that growing dissension in the party ranks.

Finally, the advent of unified Germany's power projection lite presents a theoretical and practical puzzle. I have argued, along with many others, that the transition from the consensus around the culture of reticence, which emphasized German self-restraint and non-military power projection, to its current consensus of projecting power, but lightly, has been incremental and adaptational. However, it is also possible that the current phase of German power projection, one that emphasizes PKO and non-military means of intervention, is just another benchmark along the way to a German return to the traditional pursuit of national self-interest and the military power projection that goes along with it. If this is to be the case, then the post-Cold War changes in German security policy will be viewed as a radical break with its post-1945 past. In that context, PKO will have become just another tool in Germany's emerging military security kit.

If not, and if the recent consensus holds, then PKO will remain the symbol of German power projection lite and become even more central to the EU's security governance approach to international relations. In this scenario, the bifurcation in European military security policies will be tested. So too will the half-century trans-Atlantic security consensus.

NOTES

1. See Mary N. Hampton, '"The Past, Present, and the Perhaps": Is Germany a "Normal" Power?', *Security Studies*, Vol. 10, No. 2 (winter 2000/2001), pp. 179–202.
2. For their helpful suggestions, I would like to thank Peter Gehrhardt, Matthew Rhodes, and the editors, David Sorenson and Pia Wood.

3. I am especially grateful to Lily Gardner-Feldman for inviting me to participate in a workshop on 'Is Germany a Traditional Power?' at the American Institute for Contemporary German Studies (AICGS), Washington DC (February 2002). Participants included Drs Ulrich Klotz, Christian Tuschhoff; Dr Lily Gardner-Feldman was the discussant; Dr Jeffrey Anderson was the chair.

4. For works that examine Germany's culture of reticence, see John Duffield, *World Power Forsaken; Political Culture, International Institutions, and German Security Policy After Unification* (Stanford, CA: Stanford University Press, 1998), Thomas Banchoff, *The German Problem Transformed* (Ann Arbor, MI: The University of Michigan Press, 1999), Thomas Berger, *Cultures of Anti-Militarism: National Security in Germany and Japan* (Baltimore, MD: Johns Hopkins University Press, 1998), and Hampton, '"The Past, Present, and the Perhaps"', pp. 179–202. On 'never again war' and 'never again Auschwitz', see Ludger Volmer, 'Was bleibt vom Pazifismus – Ueberlegungen zu einer neuen Weltinnenpolitik', *Frankfurter Rundschau* (January 2002), p. 7; *Homepage des Auswaertiges Amt.*

5. Thorsten Stein, 'Germany's Constitution and Participation in International Peacekeeping Operations', *Asia Pacific Review*, Vol. 7, No. 2 (2000), pp. 33–40; quotation on p. 35.

6. Collective security is basically defined as the multilateral pursuit of security objectives that include community interests and values, as opposed to national security, where traditional narrow national interests are pursued. Today's usage of collective security largely reflects its Wilsonian heritage in combination with the regional security dynamics that have emerged in Europe, especially since the end of the Cold War. For a discussion of current uses of the term, see David S. Yost, *NATO Transformed: The Alliance's New Role in International Security* (Washington, DC: US Institute of Peace, 1998), esp. Chapters 1, 2 and 5. For an in-depth discussion of traditional understandings of collective security, see the classic by Inis Claude, Jr, *Power and International Relations* (New York: Random House, 1962), especially Chapter 4.

7. See Stein, 'Germany's Constitution', p. 36.

8. Ibid., p. 37. See also Ralph Thiele, 'Winning War and Peace', in Lily Gardner-Feldman (ed.), *Cooperation or Conflict? American, European Union and German Policies in the Balkans* (Washington, DC: American Institute for Contemporary German Studies, 2001), pp. 238–73.

9. Stein, 'Germany's Constitution', p. 37.

10. Ulrich Krotz used this phrase and helped clarify it during his presentation at the American Institute for Contemporary German Studies, Washington, DC, and April, 2002.

11. See *Redefining German Security: Prospects for Bundeswehr Reform.* German Issues No. 25 (Washington, DC: American Institute for Contemporary German Studies, 2001).

12. Historically, the concept of a German *Sonderweg* bequeathed to Germany a unique history that left Germany destined to play powerful and singular roles in European affairs. German nationalists often used the concept to justify German primacy, which translated into aggressive foreign policy.

13. On German incremental change, see Mary N. Hampton, 'Institutions and Learning: Explaining Incremental German Foreign Policy Innovation', *European Security* (winter 1997), pp. 543–63.

14. See Hampton, '"The Past, Present, and the Perhaps"', pp. 179–202.

15. Christian Hacke, *Die Aussenpolitik der Bundesrepublik Deutschland: Weltmacht Wider Willen*, reviewed in Hampton, ' "The Past, Present, and the Perhaps" ', esp. pp. 184–6.

16. Volmer, 'Was bleibt vom Pacifismus', pp. 2–4; quotation on p. 4. My translation.

17. Peter Katzenstein (ed.), *Tamed Power: Germany in Europe* (Ithaca, NY: Cornell University Press, 1997).

18. Gerhard Schroeder, quoted in *Die Zeit* (April 2002).

19. Egon Bahr, 'Das Thema: Europa muss erwachsen werden', *Die Welt* online, 6 April 2002; http://www.welt.de/daten/2002/04/06/0406au324335.htx.

20. 'Germany to lead Horn force', BBC News online, 1 May 2002; http://news. bbc.co.uk/hi/english/world/europe/newsid 1961000/1961418.stm.

21. In an interview with *The New York Times* from October of 2000, Rice stated that: 'We don't need to have the 82nd Airborne escorting kids to kindergarten.' Quoted in Michael R. Gordon and Steve Erlanger, 'Bush's Stand on Kosovo Gets Few Cheers in the Field', *International Herald Tribune* (IHT) online, 19 January 2001; www.iht.com. Rice's comments in the interview provoked intense controversy in US–European relations.

22. See discussion in Donald Rothchild, 'The United States and Africa: Power with Limited Influence', in Robert J. Lieber (ed.), *Eagle Rules: Foreign Policy and American Primacy in the Twenty-First Century* (Upper Saddle River: Prentice Hall, 2002), pp. 214–40; esp. discussion on pp. 220–22.

23. Peter J. Schraeder, 'Forget the Rhetoric and Boost the Geopolitics: Emerging Trends in the Bush Administration's Policy Towards Africa, 201', *African Affairs*, Vol. 100, No. 400 (July 2001), pp. 387–404, 390.

24. 'Annan praises Germans as good peacekeepers' (13 July 2001), http:/www. bundesregierung.de/dokumente/Artikel/ix_48610.htm.

25. Kate Connolly, Richard Norton-Taylor, and Ian Black, 'Berlin opens rift over peace force', *Guardian Unlimited* online, 20 December 2001; http://www.guardian.co.uk/ Archive/Article/0,4273,4323468,00.html.

26. On this issue of US unilateralism vs European multilateralism, see Heiko Borchert and Mary N. Hampton, 'The Lessons of Kosovo', *Orbis* (spring 2002).

27. On the distinctions between peacekeeping and peace enforcement missions, see the helpful discussion in the introduction to this volume by David Sorenson and Pia Wood.

28. See charts and discussion regarding German participation in *Redefining German Security: Prospects for Bundeswehr Reform*, esp. pp. 12–15.

29. 'Die ueberforderte Armee', *Der Spiegel*, No. 11 (3 November 2002), p. 173.

30. The numbers are taken from ibid.

31. Among others, see the analysis in Wolfgang-Uwe Friedrich, 'Kosovo and the Evolution of German Foreign Policy in the Balkans', in Wolfgang-Uwe Friedrich (ed.), *The Legacy of Kosovo: German Politics and Policies in the Balkans*. German Issues 22 (Washington, DC: American Institute for Contemporary German Studies, 2000), pp. 1–26.

32. Friedrich, 'Kosovo and the Evolution of German Foreign Policy in the Balkans'.

33. Wolfgang Ischinger, 'Kosovo: Germany Considers the Past and Looks to the Future', in Friedrich (ed.), *The Legacy of Kosovo*, pp. 27–50; quotation on p. 27.

34. On the latter point, see Mary N. Hampton, 'NATO, Germany, and the United States: Creating Positive Identity in Trans-Atlantia', *Security Studies*, Vol. 8, Nos 2/3 (winter 1998/99–spring 1999), pp. 235–69.

35. CBS, 'Macedonia's Peace Process Continues' (27 September 2001), 5 pages; http://www.ok.mk/news/story.asp?id=2533; BBC, 'UN Backs New Macedonia Mission' (27 September 2001), 2 pages, http://www.ok.mk/news/story.asp?id=2535.

36. CBS, 'Macedonia's Peace Process Continues'; BBC, 'UN Backs New Macedonia Mission'; F.A.Z.: 'Mandate Extended For Macedonia Peace Force' (26 March 2002), http://www.ok.mk/news/story.asp?id=3286.

37. 'Bundeswehr bleibt auf dem Balkan', *Spiegel Online*, 22 March 2002.

38. Joschka Fischer, quoted in *Spiegel Online*, 23 March 2002; http://www.spiegel.de/politik/deutschland/0,1518. My translation.

39. Robert Shrimsley, 'Concern over EU force's role in Macedonia', *Financial Times* online, 3 March 2002; http://news.ft.com/ft/gx.cgi/ftc.

40. Judy Dempsey, 'EU and NATO at loggerheads over Macedonian operations', *Financial Times* online (6 March 2002); http://globalarchive.ft.com/globalarchive/article.html?id=020306001798&inquiry=macedonia.

41. *Times On Line*, 'EU And NATO Are Split On Control Of Peace Keepers', 3 April 2002; http://www.ok.mk/news/story.asp?id=3221.

42. See discussions in 'EU Will Coordinate Peacekeeping in Macedonia, Replacing NATO', *Wall Street Journal* (8 February 2002); 'EU And NATO Are Split On Control Of Peace Keepers'.

43. 'Wir Brauchen keine Nato-Mission mehr', *Die Welt* online (20 April 2002); http://www.welt.de//daten/2002/04/20/0420eu327329.htx.

44. See German Defense Ministry, 'Germany's Contribution to the Reconstruction and Development of Afghanistan', from the International Conference on Reconstruction Assistance to Afghanistan, Tokyo (20–22 January 2002).

45. 'Five European soldiers killed in Kabul blast', *Guardian Unlimited* (6 March 2002), http://www.guardian.co.uk/Archive/Article/0,4273,4369084,00.html.

46. The participation of these élite forces, or the Kommano Spezialkraefte (Special Forces Command) actually caused some controversy in Germany and evoked German anger at US leaders. It was the US that first made public the information that the German troops were involved, after the Schroeder government had publicly stated that German troops would not be put into direct combat situations. See 'War dangers shock unprepared Germans', *BBC News* online; see also Hans-Juergen Leersch, 'Berlin ist empoert ueber amerikanische Offenheit', *Die Welt* online.

47. 'Schroeder on Germany's involvement in UN-approved international security assistance force' (12 December 2001), http://www.bundesregierung.de/dokumente/Artikel/ix_66016.htm?

48. 'Schroeder on Germany's involvement in UN-approved international security assistance force' (12 December 2001), http://www.bundesregierung.de/dokumente/Artikel/ix_66016.htm?

49. Interestingly, Washington and London both preferred that Germany take over from the British rather than France, which was the second candidate being considered. See Jakob Menge and Tissy Bruns, 'UN-Mission in Afghanistan unter deutscher Fuehrung?' *Die Welt* online (12 December 2001), http://www.welt.de.daten/2001/12/07.1207de300761.htx.

50. An article in *Der Spiegel* is titled 'Die ueberforderte Armee', or 'The Overtaxed Army', and questions the sustainability of German missions in far-flung places. My translation. *Der Spiegel*, No. 11 (3 November 2002), p. 186.

51. 'The Overtaxed Army', p. 172. My translation.

52. On NATO's DCI, see *NATO Handbook* (Brussels: NATO Office of Information and Press, 2001), pp. 50–53.
53. *Redefining German Security: Prospects for Bundeswehr Reform.* German Issues No. 25 (Washington, DC: American Institute for Contemporary German Studies, 2001), p. 8.
54. For an in-depth analysis of German military reform, see *Redefining German Security.*
55. John Schmid, 'Schroeder Challenger sees tight security ties with US', *The International Herald Tribune* (8 April 2002).
56. Ibid.
57. See Rainer Baumann, 'The Transformation of German Multilateralism: Changes in the Foreign-Policy Discourse Since Unification', paper presented at the International Studies Association Convention, New Orleans, LA, 23–27 March 2002, with permission of author.

THREE

◄○►

Argentina[1]

Cynthia A. Watson

INTRODUCTION

The past few decades have been difficult for the nation of Argentina. A brutal military dictatorship that 'disappeared' at least 9,000 people finally fell from power because of tremendous financial mismanagement and a botched invasion of the Malvinas (the Falkland) Islands. Financial incompetence and pervasive corruption wracked the civilian governments of Raúl Alfonsín and Carlos Saúl Menem. The foreign external debt rose to more than 55 billion dollars in the mid-1980s. The 1990s recovery led to a public sector downsizing previously unknown in a society in which the *Justicialista* movement had played such a central role back to the 1940s. A state with the world's twelfth highest gross national product at the beginning of the century saw its lot sink to the fiftieth ranking a hundred years later. The people of Argentina wondered what hit them as the twentieth century ended.

In 2001, Fernando de la Rua's government suffered complete economic collapse and Argentina had the embarrassment of five presidents in power in less than two weeks because no one wanted to make the changes necessary to begin economic restructuring. The Republic's ability to pay its debts and to restructure its economy is, for many Argentineans, an important symbol of national pride.

This change is perhaps most evident in the Argentine military. The armed forces had been the most prominent institution in society between 1933, when they first seized power from civilian incompetents during the depth of the Great Depression, and the early 1990s, when President Carlos Saúl Menem amnestied them for the *guerra sucia*, or dirty war, between 1976 and 1983. The navy, in particular, had special status for Argentineans as both a national protector and as the developer of nuclear propulsion systems for ships.

The armed forces found the 1990s even tougher. Their living standards dropped precipitously due to slashed budgets resulting from internationally imposed restrictions on government expenditures. Moreover, the human rights brutalities and economic mismanagement of the *guerra sucia* had destroyed their traditional role of intervention when civilians failed. The military's self-confidence was compromised and not all was well.

A major transformation, however, occurred when Argentina's military moved into peace operations. While this was a growth industry in the 1990s because of the end of superpower rivalry and a growing emphasis on multinational enterprises under the auspices of the United Nations, Argentina's participation was still surprisingly strong. This chapter argues that the reasons behind Argentina's peacekeeping efforts are to provide Argentina's military with alternative sources of funding for its existence and to give it an alternative *raison d'être* to assuage much of the humiliation of the past twenty years. This has significantly mitigated, if not completely ended, the national struggle over the role of the military in Argentina.

THE CIVIL–MILITARY EQUATION IN ARGENTINA

Consistent with the region, the armed forces of Argentina have traditionally viewed their role as that of protecting the *patria*, the national essence, culture, soil, history, and belief system. This view is more fundamental and intense than a North American or Western European concept of defense. As this section will attest, the military's role in Argentina historically was an *internal* one, not focusing on the outside nor real threats beyond its border. Argentina's history before the third decade of the twentieth century was exceptional because the military had *not* been the determining factor in politics, as militaries so often were elsewhere (Peru or Paraguay, with multiple coups per decade, were the classic examples of the intervention the military found necessary to 'save the nation' from the flawed civilians).[2] Instead, the Argentine political system functioned relatively well as a 'democratic' entity based on a small segment of the society: the landed, traditional élite.[3] However, between 1930 and 1989, no elected government in Argentina completed its elected term in office. Instead, *golpes del estado* by the military curtailed elected governments whenever the threats to the established stability became too overwhelming.[4]

As the Cold War unfolded, Argentina's military – like others of the region – took on a decidedly more active role in trying to protect the *patria*. As with most Latin American countries, the vast majority of the conflicts that the armed forces have fought have been domestic counter-insurgencies in the 1960s and 1970s. The military gave itself a larger portion of the budget, at the cost of Argentina's economic growth. Because the political system failed to respond to demands for greater apportionment of political power, insurgencies and domestic discontent were widespread. Thus, the armed forces almost invariably (Peru in 1968 was a notable exception) took the role of defending the existing socio-economic balance through whatever steps were necessary.

This approach became known as the 'national security doctrine' and had a particular edge that allowed Latin American militaries, including Argentina's, to commit serious human rights abuses believing that they were defending society against the worst kinds of threats.[5] The United States encouraged this pattern because it feared, particularly after the 1959 Cuban Revolution, that Marxist-Leninism was snaking its way into the western hemisphere. The United States was willing to sacrifice democracy and basic human rights to ensure that the region was free of communism. Latin American militaries, with their concerns about defending the *patria* – as they defined it – were more than willing to adhere to this view and to carry out their missions.

Therefore, Argentina's armed forces developed, first, a strong and widely held opinion that they alone understood the needs and priorities of the Republic and, second, that they were responsible for reconstructing society. When the military seized power in March 1976 from Juan Domingo Perón's widow, it immediately created a blueprint to redesign society. Unlike prior occasions, the military took power in 1976 intending to keep it, not for a brief transition back to civilian stewardship, but as part of a permanent remaking of society.[6] Civilians, in the military's view, were not to be entrusted with Argentina's development, as the military believed that it alone understood societal needs and development goals, and had the brute force to ensure their accomplishment.

The military interlude between 1976 and 1983, when Raúl Alfonsín was elected president, proved a watershed both for the nation and for the armed forces. While the initial years of their governance proved more stable and led to increased foreign direct investment for development, it was at tremendously high costs. The military waged a campaign against dissidents in Argentina that created a new term still used to chill Latin American societies: *desaparecidos*, or the 'disappeared'. People whose political beliefs differed from the national reorganization or *were thought to differ* were seized from their homes, classrooms, workplaces, across society in the dead of the night – or in broad daylight. Being wealthy was no protection, as the prominent Argentine newspaper editor Jacobo Timerman discovered. The military even victimized foreigners. A total of between 9,000 and 30,000 persons were 'disappeared', according to the 1984 national reconciliation commission. Subsequent admissions from members of the military, such as Lieutenant Alfredo Astiz, indicate that many of them were simply thrown into the Rio de la Plata or off the coast into the South Atlantic. The infamous Navy Mechanics School, near Buenos Aires, was the site for horrific acts against many before they were killed.[7]

One of the issues with which Argentine society has had to come to grips over the past decade is the tolerance a large segment of society had for this activity over a number of years. A major justification was that the military seemed able to manage the economy better than elected civilians, but even that myth was destroyed by the early 1980s. Argentina was in the same straits by 1982, when the Mexican government admitted to the International Monetary Fund that its burgeoning debt prevented it from meeting financial obligations. Part of the reason was simple corruption; the viaduct that ends 60 feet above the street in central Buenos Aires is a tribute to the pocketing of funds that did not complete large-scale infrastructure projects planned to make the nation proud. Other indications of corruption were rampant, including tax evasion, customs fraud and politicians enriching themselves at public expense.[8]

Equally important, however, was the change in the international economic scene. By the early 1980s, the 'Reagan' recession plagued international economics. At the same time, OPEC (Organization of Petroleum Exporting Countries) still wielded a strong stick and petroleum prices were only just beginning to fall because of overproduction by Iran and Iraq in the midst of their bloody war. Argentina, while a net importer of less than 13 percent of its petroleum, had tried to reduce reliance on petroleum by developing a nuclear power grid. Nuclear power was expensive, however, and Argentina encountered combined technical problems and corruption associated with the power plants that delayed the projects, subjecting the country to high OPEC prices for petroleum imports. Buenos Aires had to take out more loans.

The international banking community was complicit in this activity. Instead of holding Argentina to a high standard for the planning on projects or for having the collateral to repay debts, bankers in the late 1970s and early 1980s were only too happy to recycle petrol dollars for a promised high return. This put Argentina (along with Venezuela, Brazil, Mexico, and a number of other states in the Third World) into an increasingly disadvantageous position. The problem then simply compounded.

The people of Argentina were fed up by the time the armed forces initiated the South Atlantic conflict in early April 1982 by landing troops on islands long disputed with Britain. Often forgotten as people replay the events leading to the Argentine attacks on South Georgia and the Falklands were the bread riots in the streets of Buenos Aires the week of the invasion.

The military campaign was a dismal failure. While Argentine media continued to praise the valiant contributions of the soldiers and sailors fighting to protect the *patria*, the British, with a 6,000-mile logistics trail but support from the United States,[9] tossed the Argentines back to the mainland. Argentines who had been afraid to question the armed forces' rule now took to the streets in droves and the junta was forced to acknowledge that a civilian government was needed. Argentina finally held elections in October 1983, and the feared victory by the Peronists, the only thing that might have allowed the military a glimmer of hope of retaining power, did not materialize.[10]

During the Alfonsín government (1983–89), the military launched several attempts at *golpes* to stop the civilians from prosecuting officers who had conducted themselves in accordance with what they believed their national responsibility: to protect the *patria*. Human rights trials, a national commission to discover what had really happened, imprisonment of junta members, and a significant reduction in funding were major threats to the military's role in Argentine society, a role embedded as 'above the law' during several generations.

Some funding cuts were beyond Alfonsín's control, mandated by the stiff IMF requirements to tighten the economy in exchange for loans to get the external debt crisis under control. But this did not placate the military. The soldiers may have left office in disgrace (unlike the Chilean armed forces later in the decade, a reason Chile is still finding civil–military tensions so high), but they were not comfortable with an incompetent, weak civilian regime.

Additionally, the military resented that the civilians judged its ability to carry out the defense of the *patria*. Alfonsín survived in office but, in view of his inability to run the battered economy, he was unable to finish his term and Peronist Carlos Saúl Menem succeeded him six months early, in 1989.

CARLOS SAÚL MENEM AND THE NEW WORLD

Initially, Menem also faced a number of military *golpes*, but he partially remedied the problem when he declared an amnesty for all service members involved in the *guerra sucia*. This partially mollified the armed forces, although the tough issues of whether the military was acting on behalf of society remains a sore point in Argentina today. By granting the amnesty, Menem made further prosecutions of uniformed officers impossible and set society on the path of reconciliation.

Menem assumed the presidency in 1989, a year of major changes around the world. He took control of the *Casa Rosada* a month after the Tiananmen Square incident in China, when the world saw that the Communist Party of China was unwilling to brook political debate which might lead to its loss of power. This was also not quite six months before the Berlin Wall came down and superpower competition collapsed. The international situation facing Menem forced him into a more internationalist stance, including looking at ways by which he could use international events to help domestic problems. Circumstances prevented Menem from pursuing his Peronist policies, including a stridently anti-US position and manipulating of superpower rivalry for Argentina's national interests. He faced a completely different environment in two major ways that affected the military.

First, the ascendant economic model after 1989 was the *laissez-faire*, market economy championed by Washington and, increasingly, the International Monetary Fund. Argentina had no option except to abandon its 50-year history of strong unions, corporatist organization for society, and protectionist policies. The United States overnight became the major source of funding for anyone needing assistance. Washington made it absolutely clear that funding would be limited and available only on its terms. The days of playing off the East against the West were gone.

Second, the United States began to dictate the terms of the international arena in a way that no one had in the twentieth century, if ever. The George H. W. Bush Administration talked of the New World Order, a term that would have made Perón and fellow 'Third World advocates' (Nasser, Sukarno, and Nehru, for example) distinctly uncomfortable. This smacked of hegemony, but no one could challenge Washington's view of the world. This was not a new order at all, to Argentina, but a calcification of its less advantageous position. For the humbled Argentine military, this was a further indication that the world was a disappointing place. Once proud Argentina looked more and more like a weakling.

The first Bush Administration view of the New World Order was different: instead of a world where the United States acted in every capacity, Bush's vision included a role for a moribund institution that Argentina actually supported, the United Nations. As Argentina understood, the United Nations had no troops to carry out the actions the Bush Administration sought to guarantee stability and *status quo* around the world.

CONDITIONS GREETING MENEM

Here the two realities that Menem saw came together to form the basis of a new Argentine military, a military with a decidedly strong commitment to peace operations as the guarantee of its survival as an institution. The military could take a major role in peace operations, which would provide funding directly back to Argentina, but also indicate Argentina's reformed views of its role in the global community, a role that made it cooperative rather than competitive. By assuming such a posture, Menem calculated that he would have a better chance to increase assistance to his country and eventually take a position as a major US ally. With that position, Argentina would be able to reclaim its historical role as a leader in the region.

As had been true when Alfonsín assumed the presidency in 1983, Menem faced significant economic and budgetary constraints limiting his ability to satisfy the military. The soldiers thought Argentinean society subjected them to more criticism and harsher standards than it had their civilian counterparts after they surrendered power to civilians in 1983. They began believing that military budget cuts, the continuing probing about torture and human rights abuses, and the military's generally low stature in society were demeaning and unjustified.

Further, the economy took the first two years of Menem's presidency to bottom out and begin to improve. Inflation, which had haunted Argentina during the 1980s, continued as a major problem and caused the country to adopt somewhat unusual economic remedies to get things under control. For instance, Economic Minister Domingo Cavallo took the remarkable step of tagging Argentina's peso to the US dollar, a scheme known as convertibility, which meant that each peso printed in Buenos Aires had to be backed by dollars in the central bank. The program prevented Buenos Aires from simply creating pesos to satisfy Argentina's commercial community. Critics did not believe the populist Menem would carry through the program, but under Cavallo's heavy-handed rule, the program held, convincing the international community that Argentina was finally engaging in serious free market reform.[11]

Market reform takes many shapes, but a primary and immediate requirement is generally to slash public expenditures of all types, including that on the armed forces. The budget for the Argentine military dropped dramatically and the government had to consider alternative sources of funding and missions. There were benefits to this since the military expenditures from the late 1970s and early 1980s would not be replicated (nor would the fraud and graft which ensued) and the armed forces, with less money available, would have a more balanced position in society to that of earlier times. However, the reality that something had to pay the bills was urgently attracting people's attention.

THE PEACE OPERATIONS EMPHASIS

Global changes in 1989 included a greater global attention to peace operations. Beginning with the United Nations peacekeeping force deployed at the end of the Iran–Iraq War in 1988, the world seemed to notice that the UN had no troops of its own but was calling upon the forces of member states to carry out the supranational organization's business. Many of the states were sending small numbers that the UN joined together into a large fighting force. The increasing number of deployments made difficult the method of relying on smaller island nations of the Pacific, such as Fiji, or African countries, such as Ghana. These states did not have large enough forces, the transportation to get there, or the budgets to carry out logistical work required; indeed, many states participated in peace operations because they serve as a funding mechanism for their militaries.

The major issue, however, was that the Cold War was over and Third World militaries were no longer needed to protect their countries from communism at home or abroad. The fairly large forces relative to national population in some countries, such as those of sub-Saharan Africa or Central America, became a concern for fear they would be underemployed, hence dissatisfied. An additional motivation for many governments to send their forces to act as peacekeepers was to get them out of the country so that they would not be tempted to involve themselves in domestic politics. This was the beginning of the 'era of democratic reawakening' and keeping the civilians in charge would require finding something to do with militaries besides telling them to return to the barracks.

All of these incentives were at work for Menem as he sought to deal with the Argentine military. He could not pay them an amount that the armed forces found satisfactory. The economy drove many Argentine officers and enlisted men to take second and third jobs well into the 1990s. The Argentine military was also beginning to ask what a country of just under 30 million people with no serious external threats needed with armed forces of roughly 100,000.

Argentina and Menem still sought global presence, however. Menem, in particular, more energetically curried favor with the United States than had any of his predecessors. While Peronists had always been antagonistic towards US dominance, Menem deliberately cultivated better relations first with George H. W. Bush, and then with Bill Clinton. Peronist members of the Buenos Aires Congress howled at the prospect of Argentina putting its interests in line with those of Washington. The economic steps taken by Cavallo were criticized as in Washington's best interest, not Buenos Aires', and this view was reinforced when Menem's economic reforms began including privatization of state-owned utilities, a backbone of the Republic since the mid-1940s. These privatizations, combined with reduction in the state sector, increased unemployment through the 1990s, at times reaching almost 20 percent of the population. Unemployment led to greater economic stresses, including those of the families of the Argentine armed forces. The military could not be asked to take a decrease in salary and standard of living without some compensation; it had been asked to stomach too much over the prior decade. When the economic deprivation reached well into each family because of the generalized nature of the economic change, Argentines recognized that their new commitment to democracy was threatened.

Menem made several choices that were extraordinary for Argentina. First, he served as an intermediary during the Persian Gulf War of 1990–91.[12] He also sent a token force of Argentine troops to participate in the Gulf coalition. Menem also tried playing an increasingly central role in Latin American regional discussions as the 1990s progressed, to include taking fairly critical positions against Castro's authoritarianism in Cuba. In October 1993, he was the only Latin American leader to advocate sending his own troops with the US forces to restore democracy to Haiti, although his congress eventually prohibited any Argentine deployment. The congressional reaction reflected a more traditional Latin American reluctance to intervene in the affairs of a sovereign state, particularly when the intervention was in concert with the United States, the country most prone to violating Latin American sovereignty in the past. Even though the Organization of American States, in 1992, invoked a new stance on sovereignty if its violation could lead to the reinstallation of a democratically elected government, the Argentine Congress took a fairly traditional view that such intervention was not justifiable in Haiti.

Menem understood that he needed support from Washington to accomplish a number of goals. First, he could not manage economic reform unless it appeared that Argentina would benefit in some tangible way – and Menem hoped that he would lead the first state admitted to NAFTA (North American Free Trade Agreement) or at least an expanded NAFTA. While this was misreading the politics of the United States, it was a clear-cut aim for Menem. Second, he needed to show that Argentina's change in world posture was paying off in some way that could be seen to keep it competitive with arch-rival Chile. As the Chileans continued getting international praise for their 1980s economic reforms and 1990s return to democratic politics, Argentina needed something that appeared to keep the country from falling behind. At a time when Argentina's economic woes were not solved, this was crucial to Menem encouraging people to tolerate their temporary pain for longer-term gain. Third, Menem needed to show that he had some part to play and that Argentine forces could play a role in the international community, justifying this transformation in the nation's orientation. He believed that a prominent Argentine role in peace operations was a tremendous step in raising the country's international prestige, while also keeping the armed forces busy.

Curiously, peace operations also fit Argentina for a reason peculiar to multi-ethnic immigrant nations. Argentina is a community of immigrants from all over the world. While one in every three people in Buenos Aires and one in four in the country is of Italian heritage, more recent immigrants have been predominantly from the parts of the world where peace operations are more often conducted these days: Southeastern Europe and the Middle East. These new arrivals raise attention in their new homeland to the traumas of the places they left behind and bring those places more fully into Argentina's national debate. Because so much of the time over the past few years has focused on domestic economic reform, the ties to traditional homelands has not been as heated an issue for the Republic as it might have been, but the various groups with relatives in some of the areas requesting international peace missions, such as Southeastern Europe, remain important.

One other change that Menem initiated which fit with the peace orientation was the 1994 decision to turn the military into a volunteer force. The president ended conscription in early 1994 because it was expensive and because he believed that a smaller military was justified. Ending the draft altered the social responsibility to serve but meant that those entering the Argentine armed forces did so voluntarily and, eventually, they gained an understanding that their role would involve peace operations around the world.

The presence of Argentine forces in various 'hot spots' around the world provided the Menem government with the presence it so desperately needed to justify its change in foreign policy, as well as economic compensation which partially funded the military. Additionally, Argentina's role as a peacekeeper was an important method of erasing its international perception as a militant state resulting from the 1982 confrontation with Britain.

Most significant was the need to provide the economic justification to maintain the armed forces at a relatively high level. By improving its reputation, Menem was banking that he would be able to leverage that change in view into economic benefits such as greater chance of entry into NAFTA, as well as greater foreign investment from the United States and Europe.

Menem also sought to make Argentine an important ally of the United States as a method of justifying ties with Washington at the same time he was giving the armed forces a new, non-traditional mission. In October 1997, President Bill Clinton declared that Argentina was a 'major non-NATO ally' of the United States, giving it special status within the hemisphere as the only state with such a title. While this may not have been a surprise to Menem,[13] it was a noteworthy title, only one of seven such states, for a country which had taken on a new relationship with its self-described traditional rival. With the Clinton Administration's emphasis on peace operations, Menem was also clearly going to raise Argentina's visibility in the peace field.

ARGENTINA: PEACE OPERATORS

As Herb Huser notes, Argentina deployed peace forces abroad in the late 1950s for UN observer missions.[14] For most of the past five and half decades of the United Nations, Argentina was only sporadically interested and quite nominally committed. Instead, in 2002, peace operations participation has taken on a life of its own.[15] The Republic boasted the seventh largest contingent of peacekeepers in 2000, with 743 men wearing blue helmets.[16] The Republic remains proud that the initial UN-flagged naval unit for peacekeeping was created by Argentines.[17]

Argentine commitment grew dramatically with the 865 soldier *Batallon Ejercito Argentino* (BEA, Argentine Army Battalion) sent to western Slavonia, Croatia in mid-1992, along with additional UNPROFOR (United Nations Protection Force) personnel.[18] This battalion, rotating forces through the peace zone regularly, operated in Croatia for three years.

More gratifying was the 1997 elevation of Brigadier-General Evergisto de Vergara to the position of head of the UN peace forces in Cyprus where he would be the first Argentine to command a United Nations 'blue helmet' mission. De Vergara, a prominent soldier who had just completed studies as an International Fellow at the National War College in Washington, DC, represented Argentina's prominence as a participant in these activities.

In the 1990s, Argentina also sent forces to the MOMEP (Military Observer Mission Ecuador Peru) to pacify the border where Ecuador and Peru fought a brief war in 1995. Argentine forces also served in Haiti for a brief period, in Kuwait (including military engineers), and in East Slovenia where Argentine forces provided civil police.

The missions account for roughly a thousand dollars per participant monthly. While not a substantial amount of money compared with what forces are paid in the United States or European militaries, it was a considerable portion of Argentina's defense requirements, particularly under the all-volunteer force that went into effect in 1993. The primary gain, however, remains the message that Argentina is a willing and interested participant in the evolving international coalition system. Argentina's commitment of 636 peacekeepers places it in twenty-first place in a list of 87 countries providing peacekeepers to UN missions as of May 2002.

The largest contingent (412) of Argentina's troops is located in Cyprus, with an Argentine general serving as the overall UN commander of forces between 1998 and 2000. Argentine forces also have command over the Cyprus operations' helicopter force. Other contributions for Argentina, as of June 2000, included:

UNAMET (UN Assistance Mission in East Timor) 15
UNMIK (UN Mission in Kosovo) 38
UNMIBH (UN Mission in Bosnia and Herzegovina) 88
UNTSO (UN Truce Supervision Organization, Middle East) 4
MINURSO (UN Mission for the Referendum in Western Sahara) 1
UNMOP (UN Mission of Observers in Prevlaka (Croatia)) 1
MONUA (UN Mission in Angola) 1
MINUGUA (UN Mission in Guatemala) 8
MIPONUH (UN Civilian Police Mission in Haiti) 142

Another important aspect for the Republic is the two training centers, located near Buenos Aires, open to UN member states' forces. These are the CAECOPAZ (Argentine Joint Training Center for Blue Helmets), directed by the Argentine Army at Cinco de Mayo near Buenos Aires, which opened in 1995, and the CENCAMEX (Training Center for Members of Peace Missions Abroad), directed by the Argentine National Gendarmerie (Civil and Border Police).

CAECOPAZ is seen as helping to further the Republic's goals in the international system as well as helping to earn respect that will bring more financial assistance to an increasingly cooperative Argentina. CAECOPAZ trains military peacekeepers from around the world, hosting seven US delegations alone between November 1995 and the following October.[19]

Additionally, Argentina originated the idea of White Helmets in 1993. These are specially trained volunteer corps intended to provide humanitarian assistance to peoples suffering extreme emergencies. Voluntary contributions from states around the world pay for the forces. Their role is to leverage the international community to provide basic assistance for reconstruction and rehabilitation as well as to alleviate the worst of the suffering.[20] This was an initiative more in line with the traditional non-aligned position of the Peronists than much of Menem's work in a decade as president. The White Helmets are intended to have a non-political but 'just' approach to basic needs of people around the world.

PEACE OPERATIONS IN THE NEW TIME OF CRISIS

Argentina's crisis at the beginning of the new century is economic, social, and political as the old system clearly has stopped functioning. While presidents after Menem might have wanted to return the nation its pride and might have turned to peace operations as a method of returning Argentina to a prominent role in the international system, most of the time for the nation is spent on debating a course for national recovery. Peace operations simply cannot play as prominent a position. In the era of the International Monetary Fund and the Bush Administration's steadfastly refusing to support a bailout for Buenos Aires, expenditures in the Republic are zero-sum. What would go into peace operations for a military that cannot be completely funded by external sources is money that can go into keeping Argentines off the streets and from looting stores and business establishments, as occurred in December 2001 and January 2002 as the politicians sorted through presidents. It would appear that peace operations will retain a low level of interest for the Republic as long as the severe economic turmoil persists.

At the same time, Argentina in the initial period after the 11 September attacks on the United States pledged to join UN peacekeepers in Afghanistan. Forces initially announced included a mobile hospital unit that had operated in Kosovo and a light mechanized infantry battalion.[21] While President de la Rua announced his intentions to support President Bush and the United Nations in the global war against terrorism, President Eduardo Duhalde has had far more trouble keeping his head above water because of the economic turmoil which brought him to power. In fact, Argentina's profound sense of frustration that the United States blocked

International Monetary Fund emergency assistance to get the country through the economic crisis it has faced for the past decade makes support for the war on terrorism and international peacekeeping forces far less likely today than it would have been in late 2001.

CONCLUSIONS

Argentina is likely to continue as a credible participant in coalition peace operations in the western hemisphere and around the world. The economic benefits that President Carlos Saúl Menem envisioned have not been realized, however, with the prognosis for the Republic's economic health not entirely positive and with substantial unemployment and corruption issues still plaguing the country. In fact, the economic collapse characterizing 2001–2002 continues to plague this proud, once wealthy nation.

However, the move towards Argentina as a peacekeeper has paid some of the dividends anticipated. First, it has generated revenue for the state, at a time when the armed forces were squeezed domestically and all sources of revenue were appreciated. Second, it has restored Argentina's credibility as a nation to be called upon to cooperate with neighbors around the world. The two training centers have also brought focus to Buenos Aires' willingness to share what it has learned. Finally, the Argentine peace experience has helped to defuse some of the distrust of civilians. As David Pion-Berlin and Craig Arceneaux pointed out recently, 'In the past, armies involved in internal projects often lost sight of the boundary between their responsibilities as soldiers and the political authority of civilian leaders. In exchange for the valuable services they rendered – services that civilians were unwilling or unable to provide – they would demand positions or policy input.'[22] Clearly under Menem and now de la Rua, the Argentine armed forces believe they have regained their reputation, their economic viability within the budget process of the Republic, and their role in a national mission.[23] That mission is external to the Republic but remains one of defending the *patria* in the sense of projecting more positive virtues of Argentina abroad. This is a noteworthy and welcome transformation.

Whether this signals the end of civil–military strife in Argentina is a longer-term question. The lack of economic stability may eventually raise questions in both the public's and military's minds in the future, but at present this represents a radical transition from the past.

NOTES

1. This chapter represents the personal opinions of the author, not those of the National War College or the US government.
2. In particular on this point, see Alain Rouquié, *The Military and the State in Latin America* (Berkeley, CA: University of California Press, 1987), chapter 2, or Brian Loveman, *For the Patria: Politics and the Armed Forces in Latin America* (Wilmington, DE: Scholarly Resources, 1999).
3. Once electoral reforms at the beginning of the twentieth century broadened the electoral base, tensions arose about who had the best interests of the nation at heart. The Unión Cívica Radical (UCR) party's victory in 1916 heightened concerns about Argentina's future, but it was Hipólito Yrigoyen's second election, and the complete economic collapse due to the Depression, that finally persuaded the military to seize power in 1930.
4. In the 1940s, *golpes* were occasionally conducted against other military governments, to include the one when Juan Domingo Perón first seized power in 1944.
    Military affiliations divided into pro- and anti-Peronist factions in the aftermath of Perón's ouster in 1955. The *Justicialista* movement, as Peronism was known in Spanish, was a labor-based, corporatist organization. Its sheer dominance polarized Argentine society, including the armed forces. Rather than military intervention based on economic mismanagement, Peronism itself became a reason to prevent civilians from seizing control. Since Peronism was a nationalist, anti-communist movement, this was somewhat ironic. The US attempt to portray Perón as a leftist, possibly communist, sympathizer in the late 1940s was demonstrably false. From 1944 until his exile in 1955, and during his brief return in 1973 until his death on 1 July 1974, Perón and *justicialismo* became equated with chaos, strong union control of the country, protectionism, and all the policies the international community began roundly condemning in the 1960s. Those outside *justicialismo* did all they could to prevent it from returning to power in 1973, and the military was as much a party to this as anyone else.
5. See Jack Child, *Geopolitics and Conflict in South America: Quarrels Among Neighbors* (New York: Praeger, 1985).
6. The September 1976 'National Reorganization Plan' for Argentina made this point clearly.
7. There are several books on the topic. One of the most readable is John Simpson and Jana Bennet, *The Disappeared* (New York: Penguin Books, 1985).
8. See 'Death and Corruption', *The Economist*, Vol. 347 (30 May 1998), p. 37; 'Argentines May Act on Fatigue over Reform, Disgust Over Graft', *Christian Science Monitor* (22 October 1997), p. 7.
9. This was a further problem for the Argentine military. With its impeccable anti-communist credentials, the junta in Buenos Aires had started training US-sponsored insurgents in Nicaragua against the Sandinista government since Washington could not do so. Such activity, along with the commitments laid out in the 1947 Rio Pact which *pre-dates* NATO, led the junta to miscalculate that Washington would support Argentina in this venture rather than its traditional ally, London. Once this perfidy was realized in Argentina, the anti-communist junta began entertaining grain sales to the Soviet Union, to the frustration of the Reagan Administration. For national debate, however, the junta's credibility was shot and turning to the Soviets only appeared comical.

10. Polls several months before the election indicated that the Peronists were inevitable winners. The individual put forth as presidential candidate, however, proved a completely lackluster personality, particularly against Alfonsín. The latter also won at least partially because of his personal story of having weathered the physical abuses and not fled the country when he had been harassed as a Senator questioning the junta's commitment of human rights crimes.

11. The implications of this were tremendous for Argentina. Part of the reason that no government had finished its term for so long was the repeated bouts of hyperinflation that had wracked the economy so often. The international community had a particularly jaded view that no government in the Casa Rosada was willing to threaten its powerful union base, especially not the Peronists, to satisfy external economic orthodoxy. Cavallo and Menem, from the beginning, were not considered any more likely than others but proved exceptional.

12. Menem is a first-generation Argentine of Syrian extraction. Throughout his tenure in office, he tried on several occasions to play peacemaker in various Middle Eastern conflicts. With Argentina's large Jewish population and two major terrorist bombings against Argentine-Jewish organizations in the 1990s, this made for a prominent place in the Argentine national dialogue.

13. Much has been made of President Clinton initiating this but stories of Menem requesting this status had been circulating through Washington for over a year by the 1997 announcement.

14. Herbert C. Huser, 'Democratic Argentina's "Global Reach"': The Argentine Military in Peacekeeping Operations', *Naval War College Review*, summer 1998 (Internet edition), p. 2.

15. Briefing by visiting Argentine peacekeepers, 10 August 2000, National Defense University, Washington, DC.

16. Argentina's Permanent Mission to the United Nations website, www.un.it/argentina

17. Ibid.

18. Huser, 'Democratic Argentina's "Global Reach"', p. 3.

19. Ibid., p. 7.

20. Argentina's Permanent Mission to the United Nations website, www.un.it/argentina

21. 'Argentina to Send Contingent to Join UN Peacekeeping Forces in Afghanistan', *Foreign Broadcast Information Service*, LAP20011122000042, 22 November 2001 (Internet edition), p. 1.

22. David Pion-Berlin and Craig Arceneaux, 'Decision-Makers or Decision-Takers? Military Missions and Civilian Control in Democratic South America', *Armed Forces & Society*, Vol. 26, No. 3 (spring 2000), pp. 413–36, 414.

23. Comment supported by discussion with three Argentine officers, 10 August 2000, National Defense University, Washington, DC.

FOUR

———◄○►———

France

Pia Christina Wood

INTRODUCTION

The end of the Cold War had a dramatic impact on the United Nations and its peacekeeping operations. The Security Council, no longer immobilized by the veto power of the five permanent members, approved UN observer and peacekeeping missions to conflict-ridden states in growing numbers. Between 1988 and 1991, ten UN observer missions and peacekeeping operations (PKOs) were created, a number which almost equals the 13 observer missions and PKOs mounted between 1948 and 1988. In addition, the nature of peacekeeping operations changed in several important ways. First, the permanent members of the UN Security Council began to send troops to participate in UN PKOs. Second, the Security Council began to approve PKOs (named 'second-generation' operations) under Chapter VII as their mandates expanded to include peacemaking and peace enforcement. Third, the right to intervene for humanitarian purposes was accepted as a new justification for UN peacekeeping operations based on two resolutions passed in the General Assembly.[1] Finally, in the wake of the disastrous UN peacekeeping experience in the former Yugoslavia, some countries, including France, have shifted their participation from UN PKOs to multinational peacekeeping operations with a UN Security Council mandate.

As one of the five permanent members, France welcomed the revitalization of the Security Council and has become a highly active and engaged participant in UN peacekeeping operations.[2] This chapter will analyze the reasons for this support and participation. In addition, the role and motivations of domestic players in the decision-making process, including the president, prime minister, the military, the media, and public opinion, will be examined in the context of several peacekeeping operations

(Cambodia, Rwanda, Kosovo, and Afghanistan). Because France has participated in too many UN peacekeeping operations to be examined here, four examples were chosen for their illustrative purposes: the first two occurred during the Mitterrand presidency, one (Cambodia) before cohabitation[3] with little disagreement and one (Rwanda) during cohabitation with substantial internal disputes. The second two occurred during the Chirac presidency, both during cohabitation with Socialist Prime Minister Lionel Jospin. France's participation in UN peacekeeping in Bosnia (United Nations Protection Force – UNPROFOR) will be briefly examined in terms of its impact on the conceptualization of subsequent French peacekeeping.[4]

BACKGROUND

France fought hard at the end of World War II to gain one of the permanent seats on the UN Security Council, but relations between the organization and the French government deteriorated. Throughout the 1950s, the UN General Assembly drew the ire of successive French governments by repeatedly serving as a forum to criticize France's colonial policies. France argued that the UN had no authority to interfere in the internal (i.e. colonial) affairs of any country and denounced the shift in decision-making power from the Security Council to the General Assembly. When Charles de Gaulle returned to French politics as president in 1958, France–UN relations did not immediately improve. Determined to reassert France's independence, restore its 'grandeur', and find a solution to the Algerian imbroglio without outside interference, de Gaulle had little use for the United Nations. He denounced the General Assembly on numerous occasions, reputedly called the United Nations 'le machin',[5] and, in 1961, announced that France would neither finance nor participate in the UN peacekeeping force to the Congo.[6]

The 1962 Evian Accords and Algerian independence removed a major obstacle to better relations and, by 1967, Armand Bérard, French Ambassador to the UN, could write that the 'difficult years' between France and the UN were over.[7] In fact, France's popularity rose in the United Nations in response to de Gaulle's rejection of the bipolar system dominated by the two superpowers and his championing of the Third World. In turn, the French government returned to full participation in the UN, believing that the organization could now help further French interests. France did not, however, take part in any UN peacekeeping operations largely due to the unwritten rule that permanent members of the Security Council were barred from them.

The year 1978 marked a decisive turning point in France–UN relations. In response to Israel's invasion of Southern Lebanon, France sent paratroopers to participate, for the first time, in a UN peacekeeping operation – the United Nations Interim Force in Lebanon (UNIFIL). This decision by President Valéry Giscard d'Estaing reflected a serious reevaluation of the role of the United Nations in French foreign policy. The UN as an institution was viewed as an increasingly important arena for French foreign policy. In turn, France hoped that its participation in UNIFIL would help the Lebanese people augment its influence in the Middle East peace process, and provide a means to assert and legitimize France's presence in world affairs.[8] However, given the difficulties confronting UNIFIL from its ambiguous mandate to the numerous threats against its peacekeepers, France did not participate in another UN PKO until the end of the Cold War.[9] At this time the perception of the UN as a powerless, static institution changed and international confidence in the use of UN peacekeeping to resolve long-standing conflicts rose. The French government embraced the growing role of UN peacekeeping for a variety of reasons and, by September 1993, France could declare that it was the largest troop contributor, with over 9,000 men to UN-controlled and -mandated peacekeeping operations.[10]

MOTIVATIONS

France's active participation in UN peacekeeping operations since the end of the Cold War reflects its view that the United Nations is an important asset to French foreign policy. As a 'middle power' with a strong desire to play an independent and leading role on the international stage, France considers international organizations such as the UN and the European Union as important tools to support its aims and protect its national interests.[11] In the post-Cold War world, dominated by the United States, France views the UN above all as the multilateral forum in which it can play a substantive role based on its permanent membership on the Security Council. The importance of the UN has been clearly expressed by numerous French officials, including President François Mitterrand, who declared in 1990, 'our policy is that of the United Nations'.[12] Alain Juppé, Minister of Foreign Affairs in 1994–95, stated that 'we are profoundly convinced that the UN, by its universal character, must remain the keystone of the international system'[13] and 'we have made our engagement within the United Nations a fundamental axis of our foreign policy'.[14] French support for the UN, however, is not given priority over a national, independent foreign policy. Instead, the benefits of its permanent membership on the UN Security Council are weighed against any costs this might have for French foreign policy. However, as John Trent points out, 'All in all, the United Nations is relatively inexpensive for France, provides high status, and rarely threatens its vital interests. So it pays to balance UN cooperation with national goals.'[15]

French support for the United Nations is accompanied by the firm belief that the Security Council must remain the preeminent decision-making body of the organization. The authority of the Security Council translates into prestige and influence for France as one of its five permanent members. Moreover, France's position and status is further enhanced by its inclusion in the informal P3 group (permanent three Western nations on the Security Council), where initial discussions and preliminary resolutions are often reached.[16] As Réné-Jean Dupuy points out, 'France has always considered its quality as permanent member of the Security Council as essential and has watched out to protect the prerogatives of the Council'.[17] In addition, France champions the Security Council because it is both an organization of the *status quo* and a multilateral forum that may serve to rein in the unilateral tendencies of the United States.

In addition to supporting the primacy of the Security Council, France has strongly defended its right to a permanent seat on the Council, particularly in light of post-Cold War debates on UN reform and Security Council enlargement. Successive French governments have argued that France's nuclear arsenal, its active participation in UN PKOs, its monetary contribution to the UN budget, and its status as one of only a few countries with a 'world vocation' combine to justify fully France's permanent seat on the UN Security Council.[18] France views its participation in UN peacekeeping operations, in particular, both as a justification for its permanent seat and as almost an obligation in its quest to assert its influence on the world stage. In fact, France contends that the UN and the Security Council have the primary responsibility for both conflict resolution and the maintenance of world peace. Further, a UN Security Council mandate is indispensable in order to legitimize intervening in another country, including with peacekeeping operations.[19] As the Raimond Report explains, 'This condition is a guarantee for France that no intervention may be undertaken without its approval, due to its veto over Security Council decisions.'[20] For example, when discussing the situation in Afghanistan in November 2001, Jacques Chirac argued that a political solution was urgently needed and it should 'necessarily go through the United Nations'.[21] In July 2002, both Chirac and German Chancellor Gerhard Schroeder stated that any military intervention against Iraq must be founded on a UN Security Council mandate.[22]

While protection of its 'rank' is one important, underlying motivation, other motivations for France's participation in UN peacekeeping include protection of national interests, continued influence in countries formerly part of its empire, regional instability, and political and humanitarian reasons. The 1994 French White Paper divided national interest into three categories: vital interests, strategic interests, and power interests. The first concerns the protection of France itself, the second is aimed at regions geographically close and/or economically important to France and Europe, and the third focuses on France's 'international responsibilities' stemming from 'her obligations as a permanent member of the Security Council, her history, and her particular vocation'.[23] With a few notable exceptions, such as in the former Yugoslavia, France's decisions to participate in UN PKOs have been largely based on the third category of interests. Examples include French participation in UN PKOs to Cambodia, Somalia, Salvador, Haiti, and Angola. France's decision to launch 'Operation Turquoise' to Rwanda, a multinational PKO under UN mandate, reflected a combination of reasons including concern over regional instability, domestic and international pressure, and humanitarian considerations. In the late 1980s and early 1990s, the Mitterrand government was at the forefront of several initiatives designed to broaden the justifications for intervention to include humanitarian assistance. Some success was achieved with the passage of two General Assembly Resolutions (1988, 1990) initiated by France and, in 1992, humanitarian concerns were instrumental in the decision to send a PKO to Somalia. The UN Security Council Resolution 794 (3 December 1992) stated 'that action under Chapter VII of the Charter of the United Nations should be taken in order to establish a secure environment for humanitarian relief operations in Somalia ...'. France's agreement to send forces to Afghanistan can be viewed as a response to a combination of interests, one of which was humanitarian. In November 2001, Jacques Chirac announced that some 300 French forces were leaving for Afghanistan 'to participate in an international action of aid and assistance to the populations', and that French planes would create a humanitarian air bridge to bring help to Afghans in distress.[24]

DOMESTIC PLAYERS

President vs prime minister

The decision to participate in peacekeeping operations cannot be explained without reference to the relevant domestic actors and the interplay between them.[25] Although the weight and position of some actors may change depending on the time frame and the specifics of each PKO, some general comments are in order. The 1958 French constitution gives a tremendous amount of power to the president in foreign policy. The president is head of state as well as the guarantor of national independence, of the integrity of the territory and of respect for treaties (Article 5). He is the commander of the armed forces, presides over national defense higher councils and committees (Article 15), negotiates and ratifies foreign treaties (Article 52), and is solely responsible for firing strategic nuclear weapons.[26] In the Fifth Republic, all presidents have considered themselves to be the decision-maker in the areas of foreign and defense policy. For example, although he consults with his ministers, the president authorizes UN peacekeeping participation (or any other types of intervention) by French forces. Mitterrand listened to his prime ministers, his foreign and defense ministers, and his military leaders, but foreign intervention was his decision, and one that he sometimes made rapidly.[27] Hubert Védrine, former French Foreign Minister, explained: 'My conviction is that, in the first 48 hours, the president had made his strategic choices, even if he divulged them piece by piece. I did say the president.'[28] Thus, when the president's party holds a majority in the Parliament, his control over foreign policy is virtually absolute. In other words, the president has a special role or a *domaine réservé* in foreign and defense policy, granted to him by the constitution and past experiences, practices, and decisions.[29] It is important to note that the principle of a presidential *domaine réservé* in foreign policy is not present in the French constitution and President Mitterrand specifically rejected the concept in 1992.[30] In practice, however, all French presidents have believed that they should have the preeminent role in foreign and defense policy decision-making.

A role for the prime minister and the Parliament in foreign and defense policy is also present in the constitution. Article 20 states that the government shall direct the policy of the nation and have at its disposal the armed forces and Article 21 gives the prime minister responsibility for national defense. The Parliament authorizes any declaration of war (Article 35) but this power has no bearing on peacekeeping operations. Until 1986, there was little disagreement among the various branches of the government that the president and not the prime minister controlled foreign and defense policy despite the above-mentioned articles. However, with the arrival of cohabitation in 1986, the textual ambiguity in the constitution came to the fore.[31] Former Minister of Foreign Affairs Védrine argued that during cohabitation, foreign policy is not a *domaine réservé* of the president but is a *domaine partagé* (shared role). Both the president and the prime minister have to agree on the objectives as well as the implementation of any foreign policy action.[32]

During the first period of cohabitation, various disagreements over foreign policy specifics between the president and prime minister occurred but an underlying, general bi-partisan consensus in foreign policy and defense policy over the big issues remained. Realizing that open conflict in public would damage France's credibility in foreign policy, both men emphasized that France had only one foreign policy. This tacit agreement that French foreign policy, at least publicly, should be presented with a united front was generally accepted, with a few exceptions, by the president and prime minister(s) in the subsequent cohabitation experiences. In April 1987, Chirac reiterated that 'France has a single position, a single policy, and speaks with a single voice.'[33] Nevertheless, Jacques Chirac wanted to play a role in foreign policy and he insisted on attending summit meetings and occasionally attempted to conduct forays into foreign policy. According to Jolyon Howorth, 'on the basics – major European policies, security policy, relations with the USA and the USSR and even international economic and trade policy – the Prime Minister was obliged to accept presidential primacy. Chirac challenged Mitterrand – but lost. His defeat created a precedent which deterred subsequent prime ministers from repeating the experience.'[34] As France did not participate in UN peacekeeping operations in 1986–88, this issue did not trouble the first cohabitation experience.

The second period of cohabitation went smoothly, as Edouard Balladur made no effort to take a leading role in foreign policy but cooperated with the Elysée on all major foreign policy decisions. Right from the beginning, Balladur promised cooperation and coordination, made it clear that he would not compete with the president at international summits, and stated he 'would see to it that we [Balladur and Mitterrand] find common positions'.[35] Discussions and disagreements did occur over the use of troops for peacekeeping operations in the former Yugoslavia and in Rwanda, and Mitterrand's general authority prevailed. 'The president was always the actual and final decision-maker in Rwanda as for all crises.'[36] According to foreign policy advisor Hubert Védrine, Balladur was actually more cautious than Mitterrand when the use of French troops was being considered, Mitterrand and Foreign Minister Alain Juppé generally were in agreement, and French foreign policy was well managed and coherent during the two years of cohabitation.[37]

There were few disagreements over French participation in peace-keeping operations during the third period of cohabitation.[38] In 1999, Chirac and Jospin, in 'harmonious complementarity', agreed that France should participate in both NATO air strikes against the Serbs in Kosovo and the multinational peacekeeping force that followed (KFOR). There was similar agreement over French participation in US-led military operations against Al Qaeda after the 11 September terrorist attacks on the United States and in the multinational peacekeeping force (ISAF) to Kabul authorized by the UN Security Council in December 2001. Interestingly, in October 2001, *Le Monde* reported on a quarrel between Jospin and Chirac concerning the use of French forces (Jospin was highly irritated that Chirac had promised additional French military support to the United States without adequate consultation), but concluded that the president was in charge of foreign policy: 'Matignon is furious. In silence. Jacques Chirac is head of the armed forces, it's the Constitution that says it, and the Prime Minister can do nothing.'[39]

Parliament, public opinion, media

The French Parliament is noticeably absent both from foreign policy decision-making, in general, and from specific governmental discussions leading to the use of French forces in PKOs.[40] Participation in UN peacekeeping operations, even those falling under Chapter VII of the UN Charter, are implemented without any declaration of war, which only the Parliament can authorize under the constitution (Article 35). Several members of Parliament have floated proposals to amend the constitution to give it greater control over foreign interventions but none of them garnered much support and they have not been adopted.[41] According to Marie-Claude Smouts, 'Apart from a few rare exceptions, Parliament has given in as far as defense and foreign policy matters are concerned. At most, it plays the role of a sounding board but exerts no real pressure.'[42]

During the Afghan crisis, a number of deputies, largely communists and Greens, demanded a vote on French military intervention in Afghanistan. This proposal was rejected by Jospin and Defense Minister Alain Richard, who stated, '[I]n our constitutional system, there is no vote by the deputies on the engagement of operations.'[43]

Public opinion generally supports French participation in peacekeeping operations and does not demand 'zero casualties'. According to a 2001 public opinion poll conducted by the Ministry of Defense, the French public approved the use of the French military to deliver humanitarian aid (92 percent), to destroy a terrorist site (87 percent), to intervene in the UN framework to enforce international law (83 percent), and to contribute to bringing peace to a region of the world (75 percent). The same poll also asked what circumstances warranted risking the lives of French soldiers. Fifty-eight percent approved risking French lives in a military action within a NATO or European coalition.[44] As former Minister of Defense Pierre Joxe explains, '[I]n France, one can attest that public opinion tolerates and accepts the use of armed forces in causes that are just and can dignify sacrifices of human life.'[45] This is not to argue, however, that public opinion is uninterested in the safety of French peacekeepers. The Armed Forces Information and Public Relations Service (SIRPA), Sofres, IFOP (l'Institut Français d'Opinion Publique), and the Institute BVA all conduct regular public opinion polls to gage support for a variety of foreign policy initiatives including foreign interventions and peacekeeping. On several occasions from 1991 to 1995, the public was asked if they approved or disapproved of the use of French forces in three circumstances: 'within the framework of the UN for the respect of international law', 'to bring assistance to populations in distress', and 'to contribute to the re-establishment of peace in a region of the world'. Public approval was consistently over 50 percent and generally stood at 70–80 percent.[46] In April 1999, in response to the question 'would you be somewhat favorable or somewhat less favorable toward a ground intervention by NATO in Kosovo if the air strikes are not sufficient to end the massacres?' 63 percent replied 'more favorable'.[47] In September 2001, 66 percent of the public favored French participation in a military alliance to respond to the terrorist attacks against the United States.[48] While polls are not always an accurate reflection of the public's views and support has varied for specific PKOs, the opinion poll data suggest that the French public supports the general principle of participation by French forces in military interventions and UN PKOs.

The importance of public opinion to Mitterrand and Chirac in the peacekeeping decision-making process is a second but related question. It is important to note that many French politicians and decision-makers often consider the media to represent public opinion, particularly the national press and television.[49] Moreover, the connections between the government and the media are very close, which allows the former to get its message out to the public.[50] While there is agreement that the media and public opinion can exert some influence depending on the circumstances, there is disagreement over the decisiveness of their role. There are those who argue that the media and strong public opinion can force the president to act and they point to Rwanda as a relevant case. On 10 May 1994 Mitterrand announced that French troops could not intervene everywhere and yet two weeks later, he approved an intervention (Operation Turquoise) by French forces in Rwanda. The outcry from the media, charging the French government with 'responsibility' and 'culpability' in the massacres, was deafening. Mitterrand remarked, 'When I read certain commentaries, I think I'm dreaming. We must, nevertheless, maintain reason which is very difficult in the face of such a spectacle.'[51] Prime Minister Balladur explained the government's volte-face: 'The entire world and all of France were overwhelmed by the images that we saw, and it was apparent that the French government could not remain indifferent or immobile.'[52] In contrast, however, is the case of the former Yugoslavia, where Mitterrand refused to intervene or 'add war to war' despite tremendous criticism from the press and political leaders (right and left) and public opinion support for military intervention. In the final analysis, the president (and prime minister) does pay attention to public opinion and the press on foreign policy issues. At the same time, the means at his disposal to frame the debate, exert influence, and gain support for his decisions are impressive.

POLITICS OF PEACEKEEPING: EXAMPLES

Cambodia

Beginning with the Vietnamese invasion of Cambodia in 1978 and throughout most of the 1980s, there were few opportunities to solve the conflict between the People's Republic of Kampuchea (PRK) government, supported by the Soviet Union and Vietnam, and the rival factions (Khmer Rouge, Prince Sihanouk's FUNCINPEC (National United Front for an Independent, Neutral, Peaceful and Cooperative Cambodia), former Prime Minister's KPNLF (Khmer People's National Liberation Front)), supported by China, the US, and ASEAN.[53] By 1989, however, a variety of internal and external developments, including Vietnam's decision to withdraw from Cambodia, made peace negotiations possible. France seized the initiative and offered to host an international conference with Indonesia in Paris in July 1989. The French government considered the conference as a means to play an active, diplomatic role on the international stage and an opportunity to reestablish a French presence in Indochina. The conference, comprising 18 countries including the five permanent members of the UN Security Council (P5), failed initially as the factions could not agree over a host of issues, including power sharing. However, the end of the Cold War had made cooperation between the US, China, and Russia possible and revitalized the UN Security Council as forum for peace negotiations. The P5 took the initiative to re-start the negotiations among themselves in early 1990 and reached a framework agreement that included a major role for the United Nations by August. Under the co-presidency of France and Indonesia, talks followed between the Cambodian factions and the P5, eventually resulting in the Paris Peace Accords on 23 October 1991.

The French government played a significant role in the difficult and drawn-out negotiations, and agreed to send French forces to participate in both UNAMIC (United Nations Advance Mission in Cambodia) and in UNTAC (United Nations Transitional Authority in Cambodia). According to Mitterrand, the Paris Peace Accords were 'a great success for French diplomacy' because 'it was thanks to France that this result was achieved' and 'France is more than ever active on the world scene'.[54] Throughout the negotiation process and peacekeeping operation itself, President Mitterrand's control over the direction of France's foreign policy was complete and Foreign Minister Roland Dumas was his point-man for Cambodia. Michel Rocard, Edith Cresson, and Pierre Bérégovy, serving consecutively as prime minister from 1988 to 1993, all accepted the president's leadership and command over foreign policy. In addition, a reading of the national press indicates little disagreement or criticism of France's Cambodia policy. In the end, the French government provided one of the largest contingents to UNTAC (1,500 men out of a total of more than 22,000), which contrasted sharply with France's lack of participation in UN peacekeeping operations during the 1980s. The explanation for this policy shift is multi-faceted.

As discussed earlier, France's perception of the value of the United Nations increased significantly in the early 1990s with the end of the Cold War. It appeared to many in France and other countries that the UN has regained its international responsibilities and would begin to play an important role in conflict resolution. In turn, the French government considered its permanent membership on UN Security Council as an important asset and one that it would justify and protect by participating actively in UN peacekeeping operations. As Cambodia was one of the first crises of the 'new world order', France was determined to make its mark by sending a large number of forces and supporting the new role for peacekeeping. UNTAC's responsibilities were dramatically different from earlier PKOs. Defined as a 'second-generation' operation, it was given numerous tasks including maintaining law and order, repatriating refugees, promoting human rights, and, most important, overseeing the elections for the new government. In fact, UNTAC was the first example of what UN Secretary-General Boutros Boutros-Ghali defined as 'peacebuilding' in his 1992 *Agenda for Peace*.

In addition to protecting its 'rank', the French government had other reasons to participate in UNTAC. Clearly, it hoped the PKO would help to end permanently the conflict that had devastated the country. With peace came the opportunity for France to reestablish its presence in a country and region of the world formerly part of the French empire. Dumas explained, '[w]e hope that Cambodia will regain its place on the Indo-Chinese peninsula, that Indochina will regain its place in South East Asia, and consequently, France will regain its place on the Indo-Chinese peninsula and in South-East Asia'.[55] A reestablished presence encompassed both diplomatic and economic interests, and in November 1991, Roland Dumas visited Cambodia, Vietnam, and Laos accompanied by 20 CEOs of the biggest French companies, including Air France, BNP (Banque National de Paris), Thomson, Elf, and Peugeot. *Agence France Presse* commented that the French government hoped to gain economic advantage from its active role in the Paris Peace Accords and consolidate a greater foothold in the three countries before Japan or the United States.[56]

Rwanda

Unlike in Cambodia, the internal decision-making process leading to France's 1994 peacekeeping operation (Operation Turquoise) to Rwanda was fraught with disagreement. It should also be noted that the decision to intervene occurred in the context of France's political/military engagement in the Bosnia quagmire and the up-coming presidential elections. The events leading up to the massacres of thousands of Tutsis and Hutu moderates by Hutu militias in Rwanda in 1994 have been analyzed in great detail and need not be retold here.[57]

In the early 1990s, there were close political and military ties between the French government and the Hutu-dominated Rwandan government led by President Juvenal Habyarimana.[58] Throughout the early 1990s, the French government was actively engaged both militarily and diplomatically to find a solution to the escalating ethnic conflict. In response to the Tutsi Rwandan Patriotic Front's (RPF) invasion of Rwanda from Uganda in 1990, the French government sent in troops to protect French expatriates. On the diplomatic front, France encouraged negotiations between the Rwandan government and the RPR (Rassemblement pour la République) and supported the Arusha peace process. The Arusha Accords, signed in August 1993, provided for a power-sharing, transitional government followed by democratic elections, the integration of the Rwandan Armed Forces (FAR) and the RPF, the return of refugees, and the deployment of a neutral international force by September. The UN Security Council voted in favor of Resolution 872 on 8 October to establish the United Nations Assistance Mission in Rwanda (UNAMIR) and UNAMIR troops began to arrive at the end of October. On 6 April, the presidents of Rwanda and Burundi were killed when their plane was shot down over Kigali, and the massacres in Rwanda began almost immediately. After first passing a resolution to withdraw UNAMIR troops, the UN Security Council voted to establish UNAMIR II on 17 May, when the extent of the tragedy unfolding in Rwanda could no longer be avoided. The difficulty, however, lay in organizing the force quickly and UN Secretary-General Boutros-Ghali estimated a delay of three months before full deployment.

France's position regarding intervention shifted quickly from that of May, when President Mitterrand stated that the responsibility for intervening rested with the United Nations and it was not France's role to be a substitute for the UN. By June, the French government had changed its position, stepped forward, and offered an interim solution, a multinational peacekeeping force under French national command. As mentioned previously, the outcry from the media and public opinion played a role in this policy shift. France asked for a UN mandate under Chapter VI and, despite some objections, the UN Security Council voted in favor of Resolution 929 on 22 June to endorse a French intervention (Operation Turquoise) with a two-month time limit.

France's motivations for launching Operation Turquoise are not only multi-faceted but have led to tremendous debate and disagreement. The French government stressed that the operation was for humanitarian reasons and indeed Resolution 929 endorsed this. Foreign Minister Juppé first announced the decision to intervene as a means 'to protect groups in danger of extermination'.[59] In addition, one of the five conditions for deployment posed by Prime Minister Balladur was that 'all operations would be limited to humanitarian actions'.[60] Considerations of 'rank', an active world role, and defense of French interests in a region of the world long considered to be under French influence were also part of the equation. In Balladur's words, 'France sees herself as a world power, it is her ambition, it is her honor, and I wish to preserve this ambition. . . . She has a prominent role to play in Africa, specially Francophone Africa.'[61] Lieutenant Colonel Hogard, former commander of 'Groupement Sud' of Operation Turquoise, expressed similar views: 'I would add that for

France, today a middle power from a demographic and economic point of view, . . . the only way to remain in the "great power" club is to preserve the influence conferred on her by history in certain regions [Africa] of the world.'[62]

Others have argued that geopolitical concerns, specifically the desire to counter Anglo-American influence in Africa, lay behind France's policy in Rwanda.[63] The Anglophone RPF was supported by the United States and Uganda and was viewed as a threat to the pro-French Hutu government and French influence in what it viewed as its 'backyard'. In this scenario, Nelson Mandela's call for action on 13 June pushed the French to intervene to prevent any Anglo-Saxon interference. The launching of Operation Turquoise and subsequent creation of the 'Safe Humanitarian Zone' (ZHS) in southwest Rwanda was designed to protect fleeing refugees and members of the pro-French Hutu government and FAR, including perpetrators of the genocide. Moreover, the French made it clear that the military would use force against the RPF if it attacked the ZHS.[64]

In the storm of accusations just before, during and after Operation Turquoise, government officials were forced to defend their policy decisions and actions. Both President Mitterrand and Prime Minister Balladur asserted that the intervention had been undertaken for humanitarian reasons. In July Balladur stressed that Operation Turquoise had been a 'moral duty', France's honor was at stake, 'no economic or strategic interest could have justified such an intervention', and nobody accused of participating in the massacres was in France.[65] Mitterrand, Juppé, and Védrine also defended French policies in Rwanda and stressed that the operation had saved thousands of lives.

Although the Elysée spokesman, Jan Musitelli, announced in mid-June that there was a perfect understanding between the president and the government over Rwanda, there is ample evidence of tremendous internal disagreement over the decision to intervene. Mitterrand and Juppé supported intervention while Balladur, Admiral Lanxade, and Defense Minister François Léotard were firmly against the idea. But once Mitterrand had decided in favor of intervention, the only room left for debate was over the conditions. Here there was agreement that the operation would be humanitarian, limited to weeks in duration, and mandated by the United Nations. Presidential election politics also cannot be ignored as at least two of the four players had presidential ambitions. Prunier charges that Balladur and Léotard considered an intervention in Rwanda to be fraught with danger. 'If it failed, the Prime Minister was bound to be blamed; if it worked, the initiators – Mitterrand and Chirac's man Juppé – would get the credit. In this political minefield, the Defense

Ministry felt it should act with great prudence.'[66] In the final analysis, the French decision to launch Operation Turquoise cannot be explained without taking into account the whole range of motivations.

IMPACT OF UNPROFOR

France's participation in UNPROFOR (1992–95), first in Croatia and then in Bosnia and Herzegovina, represented a watershed for French peace-keeping. In 1991, the Mitterrand government was determined to take a prominent role in efforts to find a solution to the escalating conflict. In September 1991, France took the lead in bringing the crisis to the attention of the United Nations and supporting the deployment of a UN peacekeeping force to the former Yugoslavia in 1992. The French decision to enlist the United Nations in the early stages of the conflict can be explained by several factors: first, France's privileged position as a permanent member of the UN Security Council allowed it to play a leading role in all issues taken up at the United Nations. Second, the French government believed that the neutral UN 'blue helmets' might be more acceptable to the Serbs, and UN authority in general would be more compelling than that of the EC. Moreover, agreement could not be reached among the members of the WEU (Western European Union) to send a peacekeeping force. Finally, participation in UN peacekeeping operations supported France's goals of presence and 'rank'.[67]

The real difficulties for UNPROFOR arose when the UN Security Council decided to create a second element of UNPROFOR for Bosnia in 1992, and it soon became clear that the peacekeeping force was unable to end the violence. The world watched as the Serbs bombed and laid siege to Sarajevo, carried out 'ethnic cleansing' campaigns, and continued to attack designated 'safe areas' such as Srebrenica, Gorazde, Bihac, and Tuzla. As reports of rape camps and mass executions of Muslims by the Serbs appeared in the French media, the spotlight increasingly focused on the impotence of UNPROFOR and a growing crescendo of criticism was leveled against the Mitterrand government. Mitterrand, however, repeat-edly refused to consider the military option (direct confrontation with the Serb army).

When Chirac was elected president in 1995, French policy towards Bosnia and UNPROFOR did not immediately change. But when the Serbs decided to take UN 'blue helmets' hostage (more than 100 were French troops) in May, Chirac hardened his position. France, in conjunction with the British and the Dutch, created the Rapid Reaction Force to support UNPROFOR with force if necessary. Denouncing the 'congenital impotence of the UN', Chirac decided to 'renationalize French foreign policy', reclaim command and control of its forces and set aside the United Nations.[68] The marginalization of the UN was complete when the United States took the lead in launching NATO air strikes (Operation Deliberate Force) against the Serbs in August. France participated in the operation, the Serbs capitulated, and the Dayton Peace Accords were signed in November 1995. In December 1995, UNPROFOR's mandate ended and it was replaced by IFOR (Implementation Force), which was replaced in turn a year later by SFOR (Stabilization Force). Although both forces were authorized by the UN Security Council, NATO was in charge.

UNPROFOR led the French government and military to reassess France's role in UN peacekeeping and French military doctrine. At the top of the list was the determination to avoid another disastrous peacekeeping operation. The military, in particular, was highly critical of UNPROFOR and warned against the problems associated with ill-defined peacekeeping missions under UN control.[69] The 1994 White Paper on Defense laid out guidelines to address some of the problems of French participation in UN peacekeeping operations. They included a clear chain of command, a willingness to withdraw troops, explicit national and multinational support, a clear political goal of the operation, and a correspondence between the operation and French strategic issues.[70] In 1995, Admiral Lanxade's 'directive' defined three major types of intervention: peace maintaining (Chapter VI), peace imposing (Chapter VII), and peace restoration (Chapter VII). For the first time, French doctrine recognized that 'conflicts operate on a spectrum and that operations to "restore peace" fall within the ambiguous middle of the spectrum'.[71] Therefore, UN troops must be prepared for and trained to use force both for 'restoring peace' operations and for 'maintaining peace' operations that escalate. General Jean-Philippe Douin's 1997 'directive' entitled 'Concept of the Use of Force' emphasized that future French military engagements would often be multinational and coordinated through the United Nations, the OSCE, the EU, and NATO. However, in general, the operational chain of command would remain French although it could be delegated for a clearly defined, specific mission.[72] France also recognized from its UNPROFOR experience that peacekeeping operations under UN command, requiring the use of force, were less likely to be successful. As a result, France has moved to supporting peacekeeping operations under national command, an *ad hoc* coalition, or a regional organization. However, France continues to argue that peacekeeping operations require a UN mandate.

Kosovo

When violence broke out in Kosovo between the Serbs and Kosovo Albanians, France's response was informed by its experiences in Bosnia (UNPROFOR), Albania (Multinational Protection Force) and Macedonia (United Nations Preventative Deployment Force). The specter of another Bosnia was every Western leader's nightmare. Right from the beginning, the French government was determined to play an active diplomatic, and if necessary military, role in seeking a solution to the conflict. As Jospin explained, 'France is ready to take part in any response necessary to avoid a repetition in Kosovo in a different context, of the tragedy that we experienced in the former Yugoslavia.'[73] Protecting France's 'rank' and position as an influential actor, particularly in Europe, was every bit as much an ambition for Chirac as it had been for Mitterrand. Given France's position as a permanent member of the Security Council, it is not surprising that French diplomacy centered, at least initially, on this forum. Discussions over the possible use of force surfaced immediately and Chirac made it clear that France would both support and participate in military action. He agreed with President Clinton that NATO planning for possible military action should begin without delay. However, Chirac argued that force would have to be authorized by the UN Security Council.

On 23 September, France voted in favor of Security Council Resolution 1199 which demanded a ceasefire, the end of Serb attacks against civilians, and a safe return of refugees. The resolution did not specifically mention the use of force but it did discuss taking additional measures to maintain the peace. (Chirac later argued that this resolution did authorize the use of force.) In October, Serb leader Slobodan Milosevic agreed to withdraw his forces and allow a group of OSCE (Organization for Security and Cooperation in Europe) international inspectors forming the Kosovo Verification Mission (KVM) to monitor compliance with UN SC Resolution 1199. When Serb forces did not withdraw, France pressed for a peace conference, which it hosted in February 1999 in Rambouillet (outside of Paris). Despite threats from numerous leaders that consequences would follow if an agreement were not reached, the Serbs remained intransigent. On 24 March, NATO launched its first air strikes. French forces participated in the operation despite the lack of an explicit mandate from the UN Security Council, prevented by Russian reticence. Chirac settled the internal debate over whether France should participate in NATO air strikes without a UN mandate. Given his determination to promote France as a player with 'great power' stature, non-participation was simply not an option. Chirac explained: 'France was at the head of this fight. It was her duty. It is her honor.'[74] At the same time, he was careful to point out that France remained an independent decision-maker despite Franco-American cooperation, '[t]o say that France was content to follow the Americans is simply an error'.[75] He went on to explain that France had the ability to veto any air strike targets, which it had exercised on several occasions.

French participation in KFOR (Kosovo Force), the multinational peacekeeping force under NATO command deployed in June to provide security (and, quickly, protection of minorities), was also a given. A presence and a role required participation. France had been particularly concerned not to deploy KFOR without a UN Security Council Resolution, an objective it achieved with Resolution 1244 on 10 June 1999. Not only was KFOR authorized to use force under Chapter VII, but Kosovo was divided into five sections, each under the command of a major NATO country (France, the UK, the US, Italy and Germany). The possibility of a UN-controlled KFOR was a non-starter. France and other participating countries had taken the lessons from UNPROFOR to heart. France, however, did support the creation of the United Nations Interim Administration Mission in Kosovo (UNMIK) as part of Resolution 1244 which in essence provided an international administration to run Kosovo.

An analysis of the domestic politics surrounding the Kosovo crisis leads to several conclusions. Cohabitation between Chirac and Jospin created few difficulties for the smooth functioning of French foreign policy as both men were in agreement over the course of action for Kosovo. In the months preceding the air strikes, Chirac, Jospin, and French Foreign Minister Hubert Védrine publicly supported the use of force on numerous occasions. They also reiterated that they were in complete agreement and that France spoke with one voice. On 7 April, for the first time, television cameras were allowed to film a meeting called to discuss Kosovo between Chirac, Jospin, Védrine, Alain Richard (Minister of Defense), and other top officials. The purpose was to 'show the country, in these difficult times, that the two highest authorities of the State were completely cooperating to manage the crisis'.[76] The national press did report some vocal opposition to the use of force against Serbia from within Jospin's political coalition, including from the communist ministers, Green leader Dominique Voynet, and Minister of Interior Jean-Pierre Chevènement. This criticism, however, dissipated as images of Kosovo Albanian refugees appeared on television and public opinion supported both the president and prime minister.

Given the number of public addresses on Kosovo given by the president and prime minister between March and June 1999, it appears clear that they considered support from the public to be, if not required, at least important. Just before the air strikes began, Chirac addressed the public on the radio and television. Stressing his complete agreement with the government, the military, and the NATO allies over the use of force, Chirac blamed the Serbian authorities for 'the destruction of village, the assassinations, the massacres' of Kosovo Albanians. Peace in Europe and respect for human rights were at stake and the only option left was force.[77] By the end of May, Chirac had appeared six times on the radio and television to explain France's policies in Kosovo. The public responded positively. According to a poll conducted by ISOF in April 1999, the French massively approved of both the president's (79 percent) and the prime minister's (73 percent) actions regarding Kosovo.[78]

Afghanistan

The bi-partisan foreign policy, evident with Kosovo, continued with Afghanistan despite the looming presidential elections in which both men were candidates. In the immediate aftermath of the terrorist attacks on the United States on 11 September 2001, both Chirac and Jospin expressed complete solidarity with the United States and promised French support for retaliatory action. At the same time, both men stressed their agreement and close cooperation over how France would respond. According to Jospin, 'You can well imagine that the government and the president together will act, in circumstances of this type.'[79] France also voted in favor of both UN Security Council Resolution 1368 which condemned the attacks and expressed a readiness 'to take all necessary steps' in response and NATO's decision to invoke, for the first time, Article 5 which equated the terrorist attack on the US with an attack on the whole alliance.[80]

As the United States weighed its retaliatory options, Chirac met with President Bush in Washington on 18 September and reiterated France's support in the fight against terrorism. But he added that France's participation in any military intervention against Al Qaeda and the Taliban in Afghanistan depended on prior consultation over methods and objectives. Nevertheless, it appeared clear that Chirac was intent on playing an active role, which, as in the Gulf War and Kosovo, necessitated military participation. To facilitate France's ambition of having a voice in the political future of Afghanistan and the region, its military participation was considered essential. Moreover, as the terrorists' target was first and foremost the United States but also included the West, solidarity among the Western democracies was critical. According to Chirac, 'France can not stand apart from a combat against a scourge which challenges all the democracies.'[81] A few days later, he stated, 'Everyone understands that a riposte is inevitable ... it is obvious that neither England nor France could be absent if the riposte is both suitable and effective.'[82] Chirac's bilateral diplomacy with the United States was coupled with a call for a role for the United Nations, which he argued was the best place to coordinate international support for policies to fight terrorism. As the United States appeared to be on the verge of embarking on unilateral action, the association of the United Nations to the effort would keep multilateral diplomacy and France, as a permanent member, in the picture.

In the weeks that followed the US retaliatory attack against the Taliban and Al Qaeda, Chirac pursued an ambitious international diplomatic schedule designed to give France a leading role in the political decision-making process. Meetings followed with Tony Blair, Prime Minister of the UK, European Union (EU) leaders, Gerhard Schroeder, Chancellor of Germany, President Bush for a second time in November, Israeli Minister of Foreign Affairs Shimon Peres, Pakistani President Pervez Musharraf, UN Secretary-General Kofi Annan, Chinese Vice-President Hu Jintao, and Arab leaders including Hosni Mubarak, President of Egypt. In particular, Chirac emphasized that military action must be accompanied by political and diplomatic efforts to address the Afghan crisis. This necessitated UN involvement and he supported Lakhdar Brahimi, the UN special representative to Afghanistan, in his efforts to craft a political solution. Humanitarian aid to the Afghan population was also at the forefront of French actions, and in early November, Chirac proposed an international conference of major donor countries, countries bordering Afghanistan, and UN and other non-governmental agencies to address the issue.

While Chirac was willing to give political and military support to the US retaliation against the Taliban and Al Qaeda, the French 'difference' was also evident. He pressed for UN involvement in a political solution for Afghanistan, argued that fundamental and fanatical terrorist groups should not be automatically equated with Muslims and the Arab world, and obliquely warned the US that its response should be proportional, have clear targets and should not be extended to other countries such as Iraq. In November, during his visit to Washington, Chirac argued to George W. Bush that the fight against terrorism required an immediate resuscitation of the peace process and a solution to the Israeli–Palestinian conflict. Bush publicly rejected any linkage, stating that Al Qaeda would be defeated 'peace or no peace in the Middle East',[83] but went on to state that he was 'trying to bring peace to the Middle East'. In sum, France defined its relationship with the United States as 'a supporter but not a follower'.[84]

On 5 December Afghan leaders of the major factions signed the Bonn Accords, establishing an interim Afghan government until elections could be held and calling for the deployment of an international security force to the country. Although Védrine explained that the choice of Germany to hold the talks was 'purely technical', others commented that the 'constraints of cohabitation' had prevented France from hosting them.[85] It was quickly agreed that the international security force would not be UN controlled (no blue helmets) but would be a multinational force under UN mandate. Within the context of the negative experiences of past UN peacekeeping operations (Bosnia, Somalia), UN officials, in particular, were not anxious for the UN to assume responsibility for the operation to Afghanistan.[86] On 12 December, France announced that it would participate in the force as long as it received a UN mandate. Given Chirac's political activism, his desire to have France play an influential role in the UN, in the EU, and in the region, and his determination to enhance France's 'rank' and 'grandeur' in the international arena, non-participation was not a viable option. After several weeks of discussions over the details of command and control, the UN Security Council passed Resolution 1386 on 20 December 2001 authorizing the International Security Assistance Force (ISAF) under Chapter VII. The resolution authorized ISAF to assist the interim Afghan authority in maintaining security, but only in Kabul and its surrounding areas. The first French forces (approximately 550) arrived on 2 January 2002.

Domestic politics regarding the Afghan crisis was similar to that over Kosovo in 1999, although the upcoming presidential elections created some additional tensions. As with Kosovo, Chirac and Jospin agreed over the basic direction of French foreign policy. Extensive consultation, meetings, and daily communications between Matignon and the Elysée were the norm. According to Chirac, '[c]oncerning the plan of foreign interests, France always speaks with one voice and it is not today, in such a difficult situation, that she [France] will change this behaviour'.[87] Two disagreements were reported in the press. Both times, complaints were leveled by Matignon over the lack of communication, but according to Jospin, 'There is the form and there is the content. On the content, there is no question.'[88]

Criticism from the Parliament, particularly the communists and the Greens, was also heard. The Greens argued that bombing Afghanistan was an act of war against the Afghan people, while the communists warned against the possibility of becoming embroiled in a conflict. It is important to note that Prime Minister Jospin's Socialist Party did not by itself hold a majority of seats in the National Assembly. Instead, the 'plural majority' was a coalition of the parties on the left (Socialist Party, Green Party,

Communist Party, MDC (Mouvement des Citoyens), and PRG (Parti Radical de Gauche)), a situation that complicated but did not fundamentally change the position of Jospin. Ironically, by November 2001, some deputies had shifted to criticizing the government for its modest engagement in the military campaign, thus relegating France to second place behind Germany and the UK. These criticisms, no doubt intensified by the upcoming presidential elections, had little effect on the basic direction of French foreign policy. Moreover, public opinion supported the Chirac/Jospin approach to the conflict. As during the Kosovo crisis, the president and prime minister frequently appeared on the television/ radio to inform the public and gain their support. In October, according to an IFOP public opinion poll, more than 69 percent of the French approved of the American military riposte in Afghanistan and 55 percent were in favor of increasing France's military engagement. Chirac's approval rating jumped dramatically as well, and he was given higher marks (65 percent) than Jospin (22 percent) in terms of managing the crisis.[89]

FINAL REMARKS

In the post-Cold War world, support for the United Nations forum and participation in UN peacekeeping remain important aspects of French foreign policy. The Ministry of Defense's 2001 Annual Report stated, 'the military deployments ... illustrate the constants of our defense policy, particularly the contribution to international stability through the participation in peacekeeping operations under international mandate'.[90] The motivations of 'rank' and 'world presence' discussed above remain valid. At the same time, there has been a distinct decline in enthusiasm for UN-controlled operations seen in the early 1990s. Instead, French participation in UN-mandated multinational peacekeeping forces will likely continue for difficult missions. The numbers in December 2001 support this approach. Some 14,000 French troops were deployed in multinational peacekeeping operations (Bosnia, Kosovo, Macedonia, Operation Hercules) but fewer than 500 military observers, civilian police, and troops were assigned to UN-controlled peacekeeping operations.

In terms of domestic politics, the president's dominance over foreign and defense policy, and particularly the decision to participate in UN peacekeeping operations, was uncontested except during periods of cohabitation. Even during the two periods of cohabitation in the 1990s, the president and prime minister agreed over French participation in peacekeeping operations, with rare exceptions, and were supported by the media and public opinion. France did generally 'speak with one voice' although disagreements between the Elysée and Matignon existed and the decision-making process was more complicated and more time-consuming. The elections of 2002, which returned Chirac to the Elysée and gave his party a majority in the National Assembly, ended the third period of cohabitation and any ambiguity over foreign and defense policy.

Chirac has promised to prioritize the modernization of France's defense capabilities and would like to counterbalance NATO with a European Rapid Reaction Force of 60,000 troops, which could deploy in 60 days and be available for humanitarian and peacekeeping missions. At present, however, this force would still be dependent on NATO for transport and other military support functions. In addition, a major increase in defense spending to improve France's ability to conduct peacekeeping operations among other military objectives has to compete with other domestic priorities and will be politically difficult.

NOTES

1. The two General Assembly resolutions were Resolution 43–131, 8 December 1988 and Resolution 45–100, 14 December 1990.
2. For the purposes of this chapter, UN peacekeeping operations include UN operations and multinational operations with a UN mandate as approved by the Security Council.
3. Cohabitation occurred when the prime minister and the majority of the National Assembly represented a different political party than that of the president.
4. For an outstanding study of this topic, see T. Tardy, *La France et la gestion des conflits yougoslaves (1991–1995): Enjeux et leçons d'une opération de maintien de la paix de l'ONU* (Brussels: Établissements Émile Bruylant, 1999).
5. Jean Lacouture, *De Gaulle, le souverain* (Paris: Seuil, 1986), p. 429. See also Alain Plantey, 'Le général de Gaulle et l'ONU', in André Lewin (ed.), *La France et L'ONU depuis 1945* (Paris: Arlea-Corlet, Collection Panoramiques, 1995).
6. Charles de Gaulle, *Discours et messages*, Vol. 3 (Paris: Plon, 1970), p. 296.
7. Armand Bérard, *Un Ambassadeur se souvient: L'ONU Oui ou Non, 1959–1970* (Paris: Plon, 1979), pp. 317–18.
8. See remarks by Valéry Giscard d'Estaing, *Le Monde* (23 March 1978).
9. Pelcovits writes that there was widespread agreement that 'the UNIFIL command was put into an impossible operational position because of the ambiguity of the mandate, the lack of specificity in the definitions of objectives, and the territorial constraints'. Nathan Pelcovits, *Peacekeeping on Arab–Israeli Fronts: Lessons from the Sinai and Lebanon* (Boulder, CO: Westview Press, 1984), p. 20.
10. Marie-Claude Smouts, 'Political Aspects of Peace-keeping Operations', in Brigitte Stern (ed.), *United Nations Peace-Keeping Operations: A Guide to French Policies* (Tokyo: United Nations University Press, 1998), p. 19.
11. See for example: Ministère de la Défense, *Livre blanc sur la défense 1994*, La documentation française (March 1994), p. 43.

12. *Le Monde* (25 September 1990).
13. Alain Juppé, 'La diplomatie française à l'ONU', *Le Trimestre du monde* (1994), p. 10.
14. *Le Monde* (6 January 1995).
15. John E. Trent, 'Foreign Policy and the United Nations: National Interest in the Era of Global Politics', in Chadwick Alger, Gene Lyons, and John Trent (eds), *The United Nations System: The Policies of Member States* (Tokyo: United Nations University Press, 1995), p. 468.
16. Smouts, 'Political Aspects of Peace-keeping Operations', p. 27.
17. Réné-Jean Dupuy, 'La présence de la France à l'ONU', in Lewin (ed.), *La France et L'ONU depuis 1945*, p. 57.
18. Gabriel Keller, Deputy Director of the United Nations and International Organizations at the Ministry of Foreign Affairs, wrote: 'Our place on the Council is certainly justified by our contribution to the general budget of the organization and to peacekeeping operations.' Gabriel Keller, 'La France et le conseil de sécurité', *Le Trimestre du monde*, Vol. 4 (1992), p. 51.
19. François Léotard, 'Les Casques bleus français: cinquante ans au service de la paix', in Lewin (ed.), *La France et L'ONU depuis 1945*, p. 207.
20. J.-B. Raimond, *La politique d'intervention dans les conflits*. Assemblée Nationale, Commission des affairs étrangères: Les documents d'information, 150 (Paris, 1995), p. 58. (J.-B. Raimond was a député in the National Assembly and a Minister of Foreign Affairs.)
21. *Le Figaro* (17 November 2001).
22. *Agence France Presse* (30 July 2002). Chirac stated: 'I do not want to imagine an attack against Iraq, which, in the event, could not be justified unless a decision existed by the UN Security Council. This is the position of Germany and France.'
23. Ministère de la Défense, *Livre blanc sur la défense (1994)*, pp. 50–51.
24. *Le Figaro* (17 November 2001). In October 2001, two French ships were participating in Operation Enduring Freedom in Afghanistan and French airspace and ports were open to American ships and planes. In late October, the French government announced that French reconnaissance planes had joined the operation and in November, Chirac announced that more than 2,000 French troops and reconnaissance planes were engaged in Afghanistan and additional combat planes were being sent. *Le Monde* (17 November 2001).
25. See several excellent works: M.-C. Kessler, *La Politique étrangère de la France: Acteurs et processus* (Paris: Presses de la FNSP, 1999); S. Cohen, *La monarchie nucléaire: Les coulisses de la politique étrangère sous la Ve République* (Paris: Hachette, 1986); S. Cohen (ed.), *L'opinion, l'humanitaire et la guerre: Une perspective comparative* (Paris: Fondation pour les études de défense, 1996).
26. For a detailed analysis see Cohen, *La monarchie nucléaire*.
27. Frédérique Dufour and Jean-Louis Dufour, 'François Mitterrand et l'emploi des forces armées', in S. Cohen, *Mitterrand et la sortie de la guerre froide* (Paris: Presses universitaires de France, 1998), p. 404.
28. Hubert Védrine, *Les Mondes de François Mitterand. À l'Elysée, 1981–1995* (Paris: Fayard, 1996), p. 526.
29. Jolyon Howorth, 'The President's Special Role in Foreign and Defence Policy', in Jack Hayward (ed.), *De Gaulle to Mitterrand* (New York: New York University Press, 1993), Chapter 6; Dmitri Georges Lavroff, 'La pratique de la conduite des Affaires étrangères sous la Cinquième République', in Dmitri Georges Lavroff (ed.), *La*

conduite de la politique sous la Cinquième République (Bordeaux: Presses Universitaires de Bordeaux, 1995), pp. 79–105.

30. According to Mitterrand, 'There is not and there should not be a *domaine réservé*, an expression employed under circumstances related to the Algerian war and which did not have a constitutional reality.' Kessler, *La Politique étrangère de la France*, p. 25.

31. For the first time in the Fifth Republic, the president's (Mitterrand) Socialist Party lost control of the Parliament. The leader of the opposition party (RPR), Jacques Chirac, then became prime minister from 1986 to 1988. A second period of cohabitation occurred from 1993 to 1995, with Mitterrand as president and Edouard Balladur (RPR-UDF) as prime minister. A third period of cohabitation began in 1995 until 2002, with Jacques Chirac as president and Lionel Jospin (PS) as prime minister.

32. H. Védrine, *Les cartes de la France à l'heure de la mondialisation: dialogue avec Dominique Moïsi* (Paris: Fayard, 2000), p. 66.

33. *Le Monde* (2 April 1987).

34. Jolyon Howorth, 'Foreign and Security Policy in the Post-Cold War World', in Alain Guyomarch, et al. (eds), *Developments in French Politics 2* (Basingstoke: Palgrave, 2001), pp. 158–9.

35. Pierre Favier and Michel Martin-Roland, *La Décennie Mitterrand: Les déchirements (1991–1995)*, 4 (Paris: Éditions du Seuil, 1999), p. 395.

36. D. Ambrosetti, *La France au Rwanda: Un discours de légitimation morale* (Paris: Éditions Karthala, 2000), p. 42.

37. Védrine, *Les cartes de la France*, pp. 648–51.

38. The same could not be said, however, for other domestic political issues. See article, 'Cohabitation: Five Years of Combat without Mercy', *Le Monde* (8 May 2002) and O. Schrameck, 'Matignon Rive Gauche, 1997–2001' (Paris: Éditions du Seuil, 2001).

39. *Le Monde* (10 October 2001).

40. See Paul Quiles, 'Le rôle du Parlement en matière d'interventions extérieures des forces armées', *La Revue Internationale et Strategique*, Vol. 29 (spring 1998), pp. 15–25.

41. For more detail on the proposals see Yves Daudet, 'Legal Aspects', in Stern (ed.), *United Nations Peace-Keeping Operations*, pp. 57–61.

42. Smouts, 'Political Aspects of Peace-keeping Operations', p. 33.

43. *Le Figaro* (9 October 2001).

44. Ministère de la Défense, 'L'Opinion des français sur la défense nationale', in *Rapport d'activité 2001* (Paris: Ministère de la Défense, 2001).

45. Cohen, *Mitterrand et la sortie de la guerre froide*, p. 427.

46. Smouts, 'Political Aspects of Peace-keeping Operations', pp. 34–5.

47. Sondage IFOP, *L'Express* (22 April 1999).

48. Sondage IFOP, *Dimanche Ouest France* (23 September 2001).

49. Natalie La Balme, 'L'influence de l'opinion publique dans la gestion des crises', in Cohen, *Mitterrand et la sortie de la guerre froide*, p. 414.

50. Smouts, 'Political Aspects of Peace-keeping Operations', pp. 35–6 and Anne Stevens, *The Government and Politics of France* (New York: St Martin's Press, 1996), p. 82.

51. Favier and Roland-Martin, *La Décennie Mitterrand*, p. 479.

52. *Le Monde* (29 June 1994).

53. FUNCINPEC stands for United National Front for an Independent, Neutral, Peaceful and Cooperative Cambodia. KPNLF stands for Khmer People's National Liberation Front.

54. *Le Monde* (24 October 1991).
55. *Agence France Presse* (22 October 1991).
56. Ibid. (19 November 1991).
57. See for example: Favier and Roland-Martin, *La Décennie Mitterrand*; Gérard Prunier, *The Rwanda Crisis: History of a Genocide* (New York: Columbia University Press, 1995); H. Adelman and A. Suhrke (eds), *The Path of Genocide: The Rwanda Crisis from Uganda to Zaire* (New Brunswick, NJ: Transaction Publishers, 1999).
58. Prunier explains that Rwanda was considered a 'pays du champs', which meant it received more French aid and loans, enjoyed a special cultural and political relationship with France, and was considered to be a 'junior member in the francophone family'. G. Prunier, 'Operation Turquoise: A Humanitarian Escape from a Political Dead End', in Adelman, *Path of Genocide*, pp. 281–2.
59. *Agence France Presse* (15 June 1994).
60. Ibid. (21 June 1994). See also J. Lanxade, 'L'opération Turquoise', *Défense nationale* (February 1995).
61. *Le Monde* (29 June 1994).
62. Lieutenant Colonel Hogard, 'L'intervention française au Rwanda', in L. Balmond (ed.), *Les interventions militaires françaises en Afrique* (Paris: Éditions A. Pedone, 1998), p. 105.
63. See, for example, F.-X. Vershave, *Complicité de genocide? La politique de la France au Rwanda* (Paris: Éditions la Découverte, 1994) and Prunier, *The Rwandan Crisis*.
64. Ibid.
65. *Le Monde* (13 July 1994).
66. Prunier, 'Operation Turquoise', p. 286.
67. See my article: Pia Christina Wood, 'France and the Post Cold War Order: The Case of Yugoslavia', *European Security*, Vol. 3, No. 1 (spring 1994), pp. 136–7.
68. Tardy, *La France et la gestion des conflits yougoslaves (1991–1995)*, pp. 280–3.
69. Ibid., pp. 338–9.
70. *Livre blanc sur la défense*, pp. 75–6.
71. Sten Rynning, *Changing Military Doctrine: Presidents and Military Power in Fifth Republic France, 1958–2000* (Westport, CT: Praeger Publishing Company, 2001), Chapter 5.
72. *Le Monde* (5 February 1998).
73. *Agence France Presse* (9 June 1998).
74. *Le Monde* (5 June 1999).
75. Ibid. (12 June 1999).
76. Ibid. (9 April 1999).
77. Ibid. (26 March 1999).
78. *Agence France Presse* (15 April 1999).
79. *Le Monde* (14 September 2001).
80. Discussion followed over whether another specific UN SC Resolution was needed to authorize the use of force by the US. On 26 September, the UN SC decided that Resolution 1368 was sufficient and the US required no further UN permission to act.
81. *Agence France Presse* (19 September 2001).
82. Ibid. (20 September 2001).
83. *The Times*, London (8 November 2001).
84. *Le Figaro* (7 November 2001). (Loosely translated from the French: 'Solidaire mais pas suiviste'.)

85. François Heisbourg, director of the Foundation for Strategic Research, explained that the site of the peace talks stemmed from Schroeder's greater political freedom of maneuver while 'The constraints of cohabitation and the nature of the pluralist majority [in France] weighed heavily.' *Agence France Presse* (22 November 2001). See also *Financial Times,* London (24 December 2001).
86. *Libération* (11 December 2001).
87. *Le Figaro* (12 October 2001).
88. Ibid.
89. Ibid. (15 October 2001).
90. Ministry of Defense, *Rapport d'activité* (2001), Chapter 1, p. 1.

◄o►

The United Kingdom

Tom Woodhouse and Alexander Ramsbotham

INTRODUCTION

The development of British peacekeeping policy (doctrine) and practice can best be explained in the context of forty years of experience in 'low-intensity operations', as Britain gradually pulled out from its colonies, often in the face of violent unrest and conflict. In the attempt to withdraw in some kind of orderly and controlled fashion, Britain became involved in a succession of counter-insurgency operations in places like Cyprus, Kenya, Palestine, Malaysia and Aden. The approach of British peacekeeping was defined in *Keeping the Peace*, published in 1963, which drew on experiences in the campaigns in Cyprus, Malaya and Kenya. During the 1970s and 1980s, experiences in the conflict in Northern Ireland shaped the British approach, as it was in the 1990s by experiences in the wars in the former Yugoslavia. The essence of British doctrine, going back to *Keeping the Peace* in the early 1960s, was that the use of force was only a means to an end. Military force in peacekeeping was necessary to create the conditions from which economic, diplomatic and political initiatives could achieve an overall solution to the conflict.

There was, however, a subtle difference in British thinking compared with the concept of self-defence characteristic of classic UN peacekeeping. British doctrine allowed for the use of force more than reactively for self-defence. However, the use of force had to be positively justified in that each act must be constructive and not punitive. It was vital that the use of force was credible and impartial in order to fulfil another criterion of the British approach, the winning of 'hearts and minds' among the local population, and isolating insurgents and extremists. British doctrine also placed great emphasis on decentralisation and the delegation of command to the lowest level. In this chapter we trace the development of the doctrine and practice of British peacekeeping after the Cold War. The key characteristics of this development are (i) the definition of a 'robust' doctrine and practice of peacekeeping which was deemed necessary after the experiences of the UK military in civil wars in the 1990s, especially in Bosnia, where post-deployment assessments suggested that the rules of engagement and principles which characterised traditional UN peacekeeping were danger-ously ineffective in these environments; (ii) the development of projects which aim to support the emergence of more robust peacekeeping capacities in Africa, which has witnessed some of the worst civil wars during the post-Cold War period; and (iii) the emergence and influence of a concept of humanitarian intervention which justified the use of peacekeeping forces to protect human rights and also to protect civilian populations from militias, warlords and other 'predators' such as criminal mafias. This form of peacekeeping has been deployed now in a number of conflicts where justification for deployment has come, initially at least, not from a UN mandate but from some kind of reference to international human rights and humanitarian norms (Sierra Leone and Kosovo). More recently Britain has deployed peacekeepers to take action against international terrorism and (controversially) to confront rogue states which threaten international peace and security by harbouring terrorists (Afghanistan) and developing weapons of mass destruction (Iraq, April 2003). We review controversies about the motives for these more recent deployments of UK peacekeepers in Sierra Leone and in Kosovo, and suggest in conclusion that while robust or muscular peacekeeping as developed in UK doctrine (referred to as peace support operations) has had some success militarily, the challenge is to develop in policy and in practice the mechanisms for harnessing military peacekeeping power to the longer-term and more arduous tasks of conflict resolution and democratic post-conflict peace building. In particular we conclude that the use of military forces as peacekeepers in the 'war on terror', in which UK forces are now involved in both Afghanistan and in southern Iraq, will require a renewed commitment to the multilateral coordination of policies centred on long-term conflict prevention and post-conflict peace building.

THE DEVELOPMENT OF CONTEMPORARY BRITISH PEACEKEEPING DOCTRINE

Despite a wealth of experience based on managing the process of decolonisation since *c.* 1950, British military thinking did not treat peacekeeping very seriously until the production of the first *Army Field*

Manual on Peace Keeping Operations in 1988. The subject was not taught at the Royal Military Academy until 1994.

In the UK the first attempt to 'modernise' peacekeeping came with the publication of the *British Army Field Manual on Wider Peacekeeping*.[1] *Wider Peacekeeping* was constructed not just from theory but from post-operational reports and observations particularly from UNPROFOR in Bosnia and from contrasting experiences in Somalia, where a distinction was observed between the armies of Europe and the Commonwealth on the one hand, and units of the United States on the other. In general the 'lessons learned' here were that: 'Avoidance of escalation, impartiality, negotiation, patience, trust, confidence, the developing of relationships, mediation and restraint do not constitute a disparate collection of useful characteristics and principles. They each serve to develop cooperation by protecting and supporting consent. The requirement for consent is the parent of the principles and techniques ...'[2]

From the late 1990s Joint Warfare Publication 3–50 (JWP) replaced Army Field Manual Vol. 5 (*Wider Peacekeeping*) as the British doctrine for peacekeeping and peace enforcement operations. Here, the term peace support operations (PSOs) was used to cover a wide range of potential operations from conflict prevention to peacemaking, and to provide a doctrine which was relevant to the post-Cold War geo-strategic environment. It was intended to define a *modus operandi* for commanders and staff of all services in the conduct of PSOs. The peacekeeping policy of the UK set out in JWP is placed within the context of responding to what have been termed complex political emergencies (CPEs) which are seen to pose the main threat to the security of states and of peoples since the Cold War. Subsequently, and since 11 September 2001, it was these CPEs that were seen as the breeding grounds for terrorism. CPEs were defined as having some or all of the following characteristics:[3]

- numerous parties to the conflict;
- undisciplined factions and militia which may not be responsive to their own authorities;
- collapse of the civil infrastructure;
- absence of law and order;
- ineffective or non-existent ceasefire;
- risk of local armed opposition to UN forces;
- deliberate abuse of human rights and use of violence against civilians (including genocide);

- high levels of human deprivation and suffering;
- large numbers of refugees and displaced persons;
- an undefined area of operations; and
- the growth of crime and the involvement of external organised crime syndicates.

In JWP, peace enforcement is significantly redefined to have a place within a broader framework of intervention options that nevertheless sees consent and peace building (not victory) as end goals. In *Wider Peacekeeping*, the primary emphasis was placed on consent, with peace enforcement characterised as breaking the consent principle and risking escalation to war and the consequent loss of the impartiality principle. In JWP, the so-called Mogadishu line is crossed not when consent is breached, but when impartiality is breached. Here the vital division is between peace enforcement and war, with peacekeeping and peace enforcement operating on the correct side of the impartiality line, and with the objective of sustaining or restoring consent in the interests of the long-term demands of peace building. However, what defines the essence of peace support here is the need to preserve not so much consent as impartiality.

It is evident from this conceptualisation that peace enforcement has to contain within it two dimensions of activity, one of which brings it close in fact to a state of war (i.e. it must be prepared for combat and have an enforcement capability), while at the same time, in order not to breach the impartiality principle, it must be capable, in a genuine sense, of building consent so as to limit the necessity for enforcement of compliance. The danger is that if this is not done, the prospect of being drawn into prolonged military enforcement actions will be more likely, and increase the danger, consequently, of crossing the Mogadishu line; that is, of taking sides and being drawn into the conflict directly. This danger is honestly recognised in the JWP doctrine. Thus, while there may be consent at the strategic level where there have been agreements between political élites, at the tactical level there may be local groups who violently disagree and who may be actively destabilising the PSO. In these cases, in the latest British doctrine it would be prudent to deploy a robust peace enforcement force from the outset. Should there be persistent non-compliance, then the political decision may be taken to move to full enforcement against the offending party: i.e. to designate an enemy and move to war.

In order to reduce the chances of this undesirable escalation, JWP identifies the dimension of operations, which are referred to as consent-promoting techniques. This dimension is related to Kofi Annan's idea of building and strengthening positive inducements in PSOs. Operationally, there are two categories of techniques that are relevant to PSO doctrine. The first category is composed of techniques to promote cooperation and consent. The second refers to control techniques, where 'in particular circumstances the selective use of C2W may be appropriate'.[4] C2W is Command and Control Warfare incorporating military activity which includes psychological operations (PSYOPS), electronic warfare (EW), and operational security (OPSEC). Since it is aimed at influencing communications, information and perception, rather than physical destruction, command and control warfare may have a key part in PSOs. It may even extend to combat techniques appropriate to war. The likelihood of using combat techniques will be reduced significantly if consent and cooperation techniques are commensurably developed.

The following consent-promoting techniques are defined in PSO doctrine:

- community information;
- media operations;
- civil affairs; and
- negotiation and mediation.

Negotiation and mediation is described as a skill required at all stages of a PSO and relevant at every level of the operation. All service personnel may be involved, from senior commanders meeting with faction leaders to soldiers at isolated observation points who may become involved in trying to control an incident or even arbitrate a dispute. At the wider level, and in a critical sense linking PSO objectives to the goals of conflict resolution, the doctrine includes the objective of making parties to the conflict stakeholders in the peace process by providing opportunities to cooperate and by incentives, rewards and penalties.

PEACEKEEPING AND HUMANITARIAN INTERVENTION

The fashioning of this more robust model of peacekeeping and its linkage to the goals of conflict resolution and peace building took place in the context of a new emergent foreign and security policy, developed by the Labour Party under the leadership of Prime Minister Tony Blair since

1997. This policy provided the basis for UK intervention in conflicts in Europe (Kosovo) and in Africa (Sierra Leone). This section reviews evolving thinking in British approaches to peacekeeping since New Labour's arrival in power, beginning with the Strategic Defence Review (SDR), launched in 1998 by the then Secretary of State for Defence, George Robertson, which looked at British defence needs for the forthcoming millennium. In 1997, Robertson had warned that new challenges were likely to stem from weapons proliferation, the drugs trade, terrorism, ethnic and population pressures and the break-up of states.[5]

The UK Ministry of Defence's (MOD) 2002 *New Chapter* to the SDR stressed the continued significance of PSO in the post–11 September strategic environment, now also seen as an integral part of the war on terror as a means to prevent instability and so reduce the likelihood of state support or protection for terrorists. Thus, it predicts an even greater demand for expeditionary operations such as those in the Balkans, Sierra Leone, East Timor and in and around Afghanistan than that identified and planned for in the original SDR.[6]

Under the influence of humanitarian and lobby groups such as Oxfam, the SDR helped to define a role for British forces in responding to humanitarian crises (complex emergencies). But, while it is accepted that the UK should retain sufficient military capability to uphold international obligations, the reality is that participation in particular operations remains a matter of hard choice, constrained by the basic responsibilities to which the UK is committed. These include the continuing commitment to security in Northern Ireland, the internal and external security of 13 dependent territories, a commitment to European security and, as mentioned above, more recently participation in the war on terror.

The commitment of UK military peacekeeping forces outside of Europe is clearly a possibility because of the UK's position as a permanent member of the UN Security Council, but in reality UK involvement in major operations outside Europe has remained limited, at least until recently.[7] The MOD's 2002 *New Chapter* warned that: 'While the core regions identified in the SDR of Europe, the Gulf and the Mediterranean are likely to remain the primary focus of our interests, it is increasingly clear that a coherent and effective campaign against international terrorism – and indeed other contingencies – may require engagement further afield more often than perhaps we had previously assumed.'[8]

However, while recent developments may indeed have shown an increased willingness to deploy British troops beyond continental limits, such as in Sierra Leone, Afghanistan and now the Democratic Republic of the Congo (DRC), these contributions have either been small and restricted to a non-combat role – such as the approximately 100 troops sent to support the French-led, 5,000-strong Interim Emergency Multinational Force deployed in summer 2003 to Bunia, a town in the DRC that is within the Ituri region of Orientale Province – or, alternatively, these contributions have relied on very particular national interests being at stake, such as the historical, colonial legacy in Sierra Leone and allied support for the US-led war on terror in Kabul and Basra, inflated due to London's 'special relationship' with Washington.

Moreover, the UK has continued to shy away from contributing troops to UN operations. Even within Europe, British troops are serving with NATO operations in both Bosnia and Kosovo. British troops have, by and large, remained outside the command and control structure of the UN mission in Sierra Leone, while the UK's non-combat contribution to the French-led force in DRC are also operating *alongside* – as opposed to as part of – the UN Organization Mission in the Democratic Republic of the Congo (MONUC) to restore stability in Bunia. The International Security Assistance Force (ISAF) in Kabul and British involvement in Iraq both operated as part of non-UN coalitions (in the case of Iraq, without even explicit authorisation from the Security Council). It remains the case, therefore, that much of the focus of British peacekeeping activity outside Europe is likely to remain through infrastructural and other non-combat support for the peacekeeping capabilities of other nations, especially in Africa.

The influence of British peacekeeping policy in Africa has involved less direct involvement in missions, emphasising instead sector reform, capacity building and training. Since the adoption by the OAU of the Conflict Prevention Mechanism in 1993 the UK commitment has been to enhance the capacity of African governments and organisations. For instance, as part of its obligations under the 2002 G8 Action Plan for Africa, the British government has pledged to 'Support the development of a long-term plan to build conflict management capacity in Africa, and specifically, support for an effective African peacekeeping force by 2010'.[9]

The UK African Peacekeeping Initiative was launched in September 1994 in order to help build indigenous capabilities to respond to regional crises. In January 1995, senior military officers from 17 African countries met in Zimbabwe to participate in a seminar jointly organised between Zimbabwe and the UK, to examine peacekeeping theory and practice. Berman and Sams describe how UK capacity-building initiatives incorporate three branches of government: the Foreign and Commonwealth Office (FCO); the MOD; and the Department for International Development

(DFID). All three departments have been seeking to coordinate their activities more consistently.[10]

More recently, the UK African Peacekeeping Training Support Programme, launched in 1996 with a yearly budget of approximately $4 million, is directed primarily at officer level through 'training the trainer' programmes. The British programme has been aimed at developing African national military staff colleges as centres of excellence for regional training, using British Military Advisory and Training Teams (BMATTs). For instance, the UK supported UN peacekeeping training in Zimbabwe and the Zimbabwe Staff College became the first regional centre of excellence for training for UN peacekeeping (BMATT Southern Africa). A similar centre of excellence has since been established in Ghana (BMATT West Africa).

The overall strategy for peacekeeping in Africa was clarified in the Anglo–Nigerian paper on *Conflict Prevention and Peacekeeping in Africa* (April 1995) and the Anglo-French Peacekeeping Initiative. Subsequent statements have reinforced British policy towards Africa. For instance, under the aforementioned G8 Action Plan for Africa, the UK has committed itself to assist 'African countries and regional and sub-regional organizations . . . to engage more effectively to prevent and resolve violent conflict on the continent, and undertake peace support operations in accordance with the United Nations Charter – including by: Continuing to work with African partners . . . for the development of African capability to undertake peace support operations, including at the regional level'.[11]

Peacekeeping strategy towards Africa is therefore composed of three essential elements: (i) strengthening the structures through which peacekeeping operations are conducted (especially the African Union and subregional groups); (ii) joint assessment of logistic and equipment requirements to assist African troop contributors to be well equipped and swiftly deployed when needed; and (iii) training troops from different countries to work alongside each other.[12] It should be noted that British policy in relation to Africa (where complex emergencies are most likely to demand some form of peacekeeping intervention) is consistent with European Union policy. The conclusions of the Council of the European Union on 'Preventive diplomacy, conflict resolution and peacekeeping' of December 1995 stipulated that EU involvement in Africa would be based on (i) increasing indigenous capability and (ii) improving interlocking and coordinating mechanisms between the EU and African countries.

In the later 1990s, while the US and France were accused of disengagement from Africa, Berman and Sams point out that the UK is widely perceived as having increased African aid and military assistance: a rise from 9 per cent of the Foreign and Commonwealth Office's (FCO) total budget in 1995–96 to 11 per cent in 1998–99; and a similar rise in the Department for International Development's (DFID) bilateral aid to Africa from $480 million in 1996–97, when New Labour came to power in the UK, to an estimated $780 million in 2001–2002. While the budget of the MOD's African Peacekeeping Training Support Programme has not grown noticeably, expansion of DFID's Security Sector Reform Programme and additional funding granted on an *ad hoc* basis should significantly enhance UK spending on capacity building.[13]

The sophistication of UK PSO doctrine has given it considerable currency abroad. Malan describes how NATO doctrine has been heavily informed by British Army doctrinal thinkers drawing on UK experience in counter-insurgency (COIN) operations. These ideas have allowed NATO to produce some clear doctrinal policy on peace enforcement as the significant alternative to peacekeeping in semi- or non-consensual operational environments, but where there is also a convincing rationale for multinational intervention. More broadly, Malan suggests that such UK-influenced NATO doctrinal advances are relevant to the development of an agreed, pan-African doctrine, particularly as it relates to peace enforcement which he describes as 'clearly a *sine qua non* for meaningful "peacekeeping" capacity-building' in Africa, although he acknowledges the limits to the applicability (or desirability) of NATO's high-technology approach to intervention in the African context.[14]

At the time of writing, the UK MOD had not yet published its latest PSO doctrine. However, hints at evolving British thinking have been disseminated in other official fora, indicating a continued interest in the development of British PSO capacity at a governmental level. For instance, the MOD established its Joint Doctrine and Concepts Centre (JDCC) in the late 1990s, whose rationale expresses the desire to become an internationally respected centre for promoting the development of joint doctrine, concepts and PSO in order to advance joint, national and multinational operational effectiveness through:[15]

- formulating, developing and reviewing joint doctrine at the military-strategic, operational and joint-tactical level;
- coordinating tactical-level doctrine between the armed services and providing British input to allied and multinational doctrine; and
- leading Britain's contribution in promoting PSO doctrine in association with other government departments, NGOs and the broader international community.

More specific reference to UK doctrinal developments appeared in the MOD's 1999 Defence White Paper, which re-emphasised how contemporary UK PSO doctrine has continued to develop the approach outlined in Kofi Annan's 1997 paper, centering both on 'inducing consent' and on 'coercive inducement'. The White Paper further stressed the links between UK and international doctrinal evolution, asserting that the MOD's military approach to PSO was being developed in close cooperation with NATO. It stated how doctrinal thinking was tackling the complete range of military peace support activities, from conflict prevention and other developmental and diplomatic initiatives, to conflict management and support, to broader post-conflict peace building. It stressed the overarching objective of achieving consensus among the widest possible range of nations and international agencies, as well as trying to promote methods to improve civil and military cooperation and coordination in PSO towards integrating all their activities and achieving unity of purpose and effort, such as through coordination of the MOD's Defence Diplomacy activities with the FCO's ASSIST programme and DFID's Security Sector Reform strategies as part of the conflict prevention element of PSOs.

The White Paper highlighted the MOD's efforts to develop doctrine acknowledging that military forces involved in PSO would have to deploy to semi-consensual operational environments. These would require peacekeepers to have the capacity to coerce compliance while continuing the need for combat-capable forces either to contain violence or to establish consent. It describes how British military forces, working in conjunction with DFID and the FCO in Bosnia and Kosovo, successfully developed procedures to ensure the coordination of their activities that had then improved cooperation between government and non-governmental bodies. Finally, the White Paper highlighted ongoing progress in the development of PSO doctrine to incorporate recurrent lessons learned from the field, a feature of the dynamic nature of PSO doctrine in general.[16]

More recently, the MOD's 2002 *New Chapter* updated British defence posture to accommodate the new, post-11 September strategic environment. As the British Secretary of State for Defence, Geoff Hoon, stated in his introduction, the supplement was not designed to examine all aspects of defence, as a more comprehensive review would come in the form of a Defence White Paper to be published in 2003. Rather, it would examine those defence issues specifically affected by the events of 11 September and the role of the British military as part of the international war on terror.

The *New Chapter* emphasises the long-term nature of counter-terrorism, incorporating efforts to address its root causes. Conflict prevention has a major and significant role in helping less capable states to construct an environment in which terrorism is less likely to emerge. Specifically, it highlights the importance of PSO as an aid to preventing instability or assisting stabilisation. In post-conflict, peace-building phases, security sector reform initiatives can help to transfer UK military skills and expertise – such as in PSO doctrine and techniques. In such operational environments, the use of coercive or enforcement measures should be aimed at supporting peace-building programmes, in this context particularly as a means to undermine conditions conducive to developing terrorism. To this end, the *New Chapter* promises increased government resourcing for conflict prevention, management and resolution, again highlighting the importance of intra-government coordination through the establishment of cross-departmental budgets. In doctrinal terms, therefore, the primary function of the *New Chapter* has been to reinforce the relevance of existing PSO doctrine to the post-11 September context of the war on terror.[17]

UK PSO DOCTRINE IN PRACTICE: SIERRA LEONE AND KOSOVO

UK involvement following the near collapse of the UN Assistance Mission in Sierra Leone (UNAMSIL) presented an early example of UK PSO doctrine in practice. UNAMSIL was deployed to help implement the 1999 Lomé Peace Agreement between Sierra Leonean warring parties. The UN force was mandated to assist in the demobilisation of armed groups, to monitor adherence to an agreed ceasefire and eventually to provide electoral support towards establishing a lasting peace. However, there was a strong likelihood of violent non-compliance by some of the parties, notably the Revolutionary United Front (RUF), not least due to acknowledged flaws in Lomé. Indeed, the RUF duly violated the ceasefire, continued to abuse human rights and opposed demobilisation. Ultimately, widespread fighting resumed, with which UNAMSIL proved unable to cope, resulting in the seizure of 500 of its peacekeepers.

According to Wilkinson, some of UNAMSIL's fundamental shortcomings included:[18]

- a consensual peacekeeping and not peace enforcement mandate;
- poorly equipped and trained troops;
- the lack of a 'lead nation' to coordinate command and control structures; and

- inadequate support from the Department of Peace Keeping Operations (DPKO) at UN Headquarters in New York.

Doctrinal confusion was a major contributing factor in UNAMSIL's problems. The operational environment clearly demanded an enforcement capability but, despite UNAMSIL's Chapter VII mandate, agreement over such a robust approach within the UN system has proved much harder to achieve and many of the original troop-contributing countries (TCCs) to UNAMSIL did not, in fact, subscribe to PSO doctrine. An effective enforcement capacity requires a common 'doctrine, standard operating procedures, joint and combined operational planning and common training standards and experience' among TCCs, which was not the case in Sierra Leone. At the time of the kidnappings, UNAMSIL was a disparate collection of contingents from over 30 countries, with no consistent operational infrastructure. Moreover, they arrived piecemeal and many had neither been trained nor equipped to cope with the rigours of enforcement. The British army had also learned that enforcement requires an accomplished military formation based on the lead-nation concept. Indeed, not only did the independent *Report of the Panel on United Nations Peace Operations* published in 2000 (the Brahimi Report) acknowledge the UN's incapability of taking on robust peacekeeping, but also the UN itself has subsequently eschewed assuming enforcement responsibilities, such as in postwar Afghanistan. Finally, UNAMSIL's operational support was supplied by planning capacity within DPKO in New York whose already insufficient capability had been further eroded by the withdrawal of 'gratis' officers for political reasons by the General Assembly in 1999. While, as a result of recommendations in the Brahimi Report, around 200 additional personnel have since been assigned to DPKO, the UN has largely continued to delegate enforcement responsibilities to other bodies.[19]

UK PSO doctrine highlights three fundamental features of what was required to support peace in Sierra Leone effectively;

1. the threat to peace was multi-dimensional, demanding a multi-functional political approach, including national and regional diplomatic activities, military initiatives, humanitarian assistance and economic and development programmes;
2. the volatility of operational environment meant that it was injudicious to take parties' commitments at face value; and

3. as these same parties only appeared to respect the use of force, so only an enforcement-capable force could establish the necessary stability to facilitate peace building.

The UK's commitment of a balanced and capable combat force to assist UNAMSIL enabled the conduct of operations across the entire PSO spectrum.[20]

UK intervention at such a critical juncture in Sierra Leone ultimately saved both the mission and the peace process. Bernath and Nyce describe how UNAMSIL was initially doomed until after the hostage crisis, which in fact spurred the UK and the international community not to allow another peacekeeping failure – a decision from which followed all of the subsequent success factors.[21] Indeed, British interest in Sierra Leone and its position as a permanent member of the Security Council was likely to have been a major catalyst in the Council's agreement to expand UNAMSIL's strength to 17,500. The depth of the UK's contribution to UNAMSIL was summed up by Defence Minister Geoff Hoon, who declared that the UK was 'to all intents and purposes running the day-to-day operation of UN forces'.[22] Although the UN and the wider international community were grateful for the UK input, there was some discontent that the UK had not been prepared to place the majority of its troops within UNAMSIL's command and control structure. The British troops' rescue of UNAMSIL and their combined success in getting the peace process back on track, ultimately enabling 'free and fair' elections to return President Kabbah to power the following year, suggests the effectiveness of UK PSO doctrine in practice.

Kosovo provided another early test of UK PSO strategy. UK peace-keeping forces entered Kosovo under NATO command and led by British general Sir Mike Jackson on 12 June 1999. The peacekeeping mission (United Nations Mission in Kosovo – UNMIK) was established under UN Security Council Resolution 1244 of 10 June 1999. In Kosovo the international community has developed a pillar system for post-conflict reconstruction where different actors undertook responsibility for different dimensions of the peace process: the UN for transitional government and administration; the European Union and the World Bank for economic reconstruction; and the OSCE for human rights monitoring, democratisation and the development of civil society. The NATO-led and UN-authorised multinational peacekeeping force KFOR provides security. The peace-building model used here includes the linkage between social, economic, and political development and the capacity to enforce compliance with the terms of the UN mandate governing Kosovo. This capacity to enforce is guaranteed by the operation of KFOR using rules of engagement which are defined in a 'muscular' form of peacekeeping (i.e., peace support operations). Under these rules of engagement KFOR has the capacity and authority to engage criminal mafias, warlords and 'spoilers' of the peace process. While there was much concern in Kosovo about the generation of chaos, instability and a return to guerrilla-based terrorism, this has not happened because of the robust peace-building package applied to the conflict.

CONTROVERSIES: MOTIVES FOR INTERVENTION

While the British peacekeeping presence in Sierra Leone and Kosovo may be evaluated as a success, the mass media have portrayed peacekeeping as either humiliatingly ineffective, narrowly nationalistic, or representing a new paradigm for effective twenty-first-century conflict prevention and peace building.

Recent debates in the British press have seen an increasing emergence of both opponents and champions of intervention from across the political spectrum. Detractors from the political right tend to condemn interventionists as idealistic, while those on the left portray British peacekeeping as neo-colonialist. Many rightist and leftist champions, on the other hand, see intervention as a necessary evil to support a moral imperative. Nor are critiques confined to the domain of the *ad bellum* rationale, the practical application of PSO technique '*in bello*' in the post-combat phase capable of creating equally lively debate. This perhaps misplaced application of the term *bello* to peacekeeping deployments – which, after all, the military refer to as operations *short of war* – itself alludes to controversy in media commentary on contemporary interventions. In operations like those in Kosovo, Afghanistan and Iraq, the peacekeeping dimension followed what was essentially a war-fighting approach: the objective being military victory over the respective enemies of the Milosevic regime, the Taliban/Al Qaeda and Saddam Hussein as a means of creating the necessary conditions to allow for a peacekeeping deployment. However, beyond critiques of the morality of these interventions – which have themselves been affected by doubts over their legitimacy in terms of international law and UN Security Council authorisation – there appears to be an analytical separation of the war-fighting phase from the post-combat peacekeeping phase.

Writing in the London *Times* during the build-up to the recent war in Iraq, Jenkins asserted that the champions of intervention ... have taken up Kipling's white man's burden and his demand that 'a courthouse stands where the raw blood flowed'. They are abetted by a potent coalition of soldiers, aid donors, charity bosses, lawyers and United Nations plutocrats ... UN Secretary-General Kofi Annan, the Innocent III of our age, blesses every soldier of philanthropic fortune. He declares that, under globalisation, human rights are more important than state sovereignty.[23]

Jenkins' analysis covers many of the actors involved in intervention and brackets them inclusively as essentially injurious. His last phrase reveals the realist rationale behind his anti-intervention attitude, when he questions that in these circumstances individual human rights should take precedence over the rights of states to sovereignty and non-interference in their internal affairs.

Regarding media coverage of military performance, on the other hand, British troops receive a broadly positive response from their national press. Contrasting media attitudes to the aerial bombardment tactics employed in Kosovo, which drew profuse criticism, and the capture of Basra in southern Iraq, which received much wider approval, suggest that, where ground troops are concerned at least, this is true even in the war-fighting phase. Beyond the combat role and into peacekeeping proper (although, of course, allowing for the use of enforcement measures, in line with contemporary UK PSO doctrine), the performance of British military personnel again is widely admired.

Henley, writing in the London *Guardian* in the aftermath of the Iraq War, chronicled the effectiveness of UK peacekeeping in Kosovo, Sierra Leone and then Afghanistan. His basic message from all three case studies was that British military peacekeepers have performed admirably, the big problem emerging in resourcing and other support for broader peace-building initiatives. In Kosovo, for example, Henley surmises that intervention had largely established security, but there was little progress beyond this. Similarly, intervention had changed some things for the better in Kabul, such as life in general for women, but there was little security or other progress towards peace beyond the capital. Finally, in Sierra Leone, Henley describes how 'They love the Brits to bits here', since 'we played a big part in bringing the place back from the dead'. Again, however, the establishment of a more enduring peace remained elusive, not least from broader instability throughout the sub-region. He sums up his impressions by declaring that Tony Blair 'can rest assured of one thing: British troops ... are doing a remarkable job. In Kosovo, Afghanistan and Sierra Leone you will not hear a word said against them.' However, the problem remains in consolidating peace in the long term.[24]

Finally, in May 2000, the London *Guardian* featured a debate after the seizure of 500 UN peacekeepers in Sierra Leone, asking whether UN involvement in such conflicts was a basic moral responsibility of the international community, or in reality merely risked exacerbating the conflicts the peacekeepers had been sent to resolve. The Sierra Leone instance is different from Kosovo, Afghanistan and Iraq in that Security Council authorisation for – and so the moral basis of – the intervention was less equivocal. Thus, much of the media interest circumvented the *ad bellum* issue and concentrated on the *in bello*. A significant aspect of the debate was its timing, as media interest in such grand questions does not tend to follow the announcement of good news (there was much less press speculation after the official announcement of peace by President Kabbah the following year). A fundamental issue within the debate was whether the performance of the peacekeepers themselves was relevant to peace-keeping's effectiveness as a tool to manage conflicts like the one in Sierra Leone.[25] The subsequent British rescue of the UN mission and the outcome of Henley's research above would suggest a resounding but very limited yes.

CONCLUSION: PEACEKEEPING, ACCOUNTABILITY, AND THE 'NEW MILITARY HUMANITARIANISM'

British peacekeeping intervention in Sierra Leone and to a more marked extent the crisis in Kosovo were events seen by many academic and political commentators to have heralded a 'landmark in international relations' characterised by an idealistic new world determined to end ethnic cleansing and other transgressions of human rights. When US air forces and European allies joined in the attack on Serbia in March 1999, British Prime Minister Blair declared that this was a new kind of war: 'We are fighting for a world in which dictators are no longer able to visit horrible punishments on their own people in order to stay in power ... [and entering] a new millennium where dictators know they cannot get away with ethnic cleansing or repress their people with impunity.' In Germany Foreign Minister Joschka Fisher also bought into what Ulrich Beck called 'NATO's new military humanism' in which the defence of human rights was a form of mission where 'enlightened states' were able to use force in situations in which they believed it to be just.[26] For sceptics such as Chomsky, NATO and British peacekeepers serving as the effective force within it both concealed and legitimised US imperial ambitions. In Chomsky's view the Kosovo intervention was not an example of a new model of robust peacekeeping targeted on the defence of human rights and seeking to engage in democratic post-conflict peace building, but an attempt to establish US credibility as the dominant superpower.

We conclude here with a different analysis, which nevertheless urges caution about peacekeeping as the front-line instrument of the new interventionism. Debates about the Kosovo and Sierra Leone interventions in which UK peacekeeping forces played central roles must be understood in a wider context of changing norms of international relations. There has been a significant qualitative change in the response of the international community to civil wars since the end of the Cold War. Crucially, in a line of policy development which stretches from the Agenda for Peace, formulated at the beginning of the 1990s, to the Brahimi Report at the end of that decade, the main objective in the international management of civil wars was one of multilateral 'third partyism' aimed at operating impartially between warring parties, rather than a bilateral approach which seeks to support one side or the other. In this model a variety of actors from UN agencies to NGOs and peacekeeping forces are all recognised as conducting humanitarian operations where the use of force is an option, but not a determinant of the intervention.

Hugo Slim has suggested that this new form of interventionism has raised four main operational challenges for international society: the art of 'mid-war' operations; the need to protect civilian populations from violence; the management of military and humanitarian components in peacekeeping operations; and the focus on peace programming as a means of ending the war.[27] UK peacekeeping doctrine as presented in its PSO format has attempted to engage with these issues and challenges. Significant difficulties have emerged in applying the doctrine in practice but the ultimate test is that of legitimacy and democratic accountability, by which we mean the accountability of the whole intervention mechanism to the humanitarian 'target' of the intervention, the civilians in the conflict zone who are the subjects of the conflict being managed. While it is not the main subject of this chapter, it is clear that the crisis currently under way in postwar Iraq and the wider 'war on terror' pursued by the Bush Administration (with UK military forces now deployed in a peacekeeping mode in southern Iraq) raises a number of worrying questions about intervention, post-conflict peace building and the role of peacekeeping forces in such interventions. If intervention is defined primarily as a military-directed activity, and if the more sophisticated elements of conflict prevention and peace building contained both in UK PSO doctrine and in a decade of UN practice of multilateral peacekeeping and peace building are disregarded, then the Chomsky thesis will begin to look increasingly convincing.

NOTES

1. C. Dobbie, 'A concept for post-Cold War peacekeeping', *Survival*, Vol. 36, No. 3 (1994), pp. 121–48.
2. Ibid., p. 126.
3. Ministry of Defence (MOD), *Peace Support Operations* (Joint Warfare Publication 3–50, 1997), section 2–2.
4. Ibid., section 7–9.
5. G. Robertson, Strategic Defence Review, Speech to Royal United Services Institute, London (18 September 1997).
6. MOD White Paper, *The Strategic Defence Review: A New Chapter* (2002), section 2, para. 16.
7. M. Chalmers, 'The Strategic Defence Review: British Policy Options', *RUSI Journal* (1998), pp. 36–8.
8. MOD White Paper.
9. DFID and FCO, *G8 Africa Action Plan: Towards the 2003 Summit* (November 2002), http://www.dfid.gov.uk/News/News/files/bg_brief_g8africaactionplan.pdf
10. E. Berman and K. Sams, *Peacekeeping in Africa: Capabilities and Culpabilities*, Geneva: UN Institute for Disarmament Research; Pretoria: Institute for Security Studies, 2000), pp. 317–21.
11. DFID and FCO, *G8 Africa Action Plan*.
12. L. Chalker (Baroness), 'Britain and Africa: Working Together to Prevent and Resolve Conflicts', Address by Minister for Overseas Development to OAU, Addis Ababa (November 1996).
13. Berman and Sams, *Peacekeeping in Africa*, pp. 328–9.
14. M. Malan, 'Towards an Integrated Doctrine for Peace Support Operations in Africa', in *Challenges for the New Millennium*, Institute for Security Studies Monograph 46 (February 2000).
15. MOD Website, Joint Doctrine and Concepts Centre, Overview, http://www.mod.uk/jdcc/oview.htm
16. MOD, White Paper (1999), Chapter 6, paras 119–24.
17. MOD, White Paper.
18. Col. (Ret.) P. Wilkinson (OBE), 'Peace Support Under Fire: Lessons from Sierra Leone', *ISIS Briefing on Humanitarian Intervention*, No. 2 (June 2000).
19. Ibid.
20. Ibid.
21. C. Bernath and S. Nyce, Report on the United Nations Mission in Sierra Leone (UNAMSIL) – A Peacekeeping Success: Lessons Learned, Relief Web (October 2002).
22. M. Malan, P. Rakate and A. McIntyre, 'Peacekeeping in Sierra Leone: UNAMSIL Hits the Home Straight', *Institute for Security Studies Monograph*, No. 68 (January 2002).

23. S. Jenkins, 'The New Order that Splits the World', *The Times* (31 January 2003).

24. J. Henley, 'Did We Make it Better?' *The Guardian* (29 May 2003).

25. Prof. C. Clapham and A. Ramsbotham, 'Should the UN Get Out of Sierra Leone?', *The Guardian* (22 May 2000).

26. N. Chomsky, *The New Military Humanism: Lessons from Kosovo* (London: Pluto Press 1999); quotes in this paragraph from pp. 3–4.

27. H. Slim, *International Humanitarianism's Engagement with Civil War in the 1990s: A Glance at Evolving Practice and Theory* (CENDEP, Oxford Brookes University, 1997).

———◄o►———

The United States[1]

David S. Sorenson

INTRODUCTION

Since the end of the Cold War, the United States has dispatched peacekeepers to a variety of conflict-ridden areas. This participation, though, heavily favors UN-mandated peacekeeping operations (PKOs) over UN-operated missions, reflecting a strong American desire to avoid UN command and the UN bureaucracy that operates its PKOs. It also reveals that the US sends its peacekeepers to regions it considers strategically or politically important, and then gains a UN sanction over the consequent peacekeeping operation.

In May 2002, for example, the US ranked eighteenth on the list of countries contributing peacekeepers to UN-operated PKOs, with only 704 military and civilian police in place.[2] Bangladesh, by comparison, had over 5,000 peacekeepers in the field while Pakistan had over 4,000. However, the US participated more fully in UN-sanctioned operations, including deploying some 3,000 troops in the NATO Bosnia Stabilization Force (SFOR) and 4,800 in the NATO Kosovo Force (KFOR), along with another 1,309 in Macedonia offering indirect support to KFOR.[3] The commitment reflected an American strategic interest in the Balkans more than it does American support for UN peacekeeping as a principle, however.

The large US PKO commitments to the Balkans developed under the Clinton Administration, but the second Bush Administration has scaled them back. The 'war on terrorism', coupled with a different philosophy about the US global role by the Bush foreign policy team, may explain part of the reduction in US peacekeepers. However, a broader picture of US peacekeeping policy suggests that the Clinton Administration greatly expanded the US role in UN peacekeeping, but that role reached its peak and headed downward while Clinton was still president. Peacekeeping, in other words, is a policy instrument used sparingly and only for brief periods by the US, and only in areas that the US considers strategically important.

US peacekeeping commitment to UN-operated and -sanctioned peace-keeping missions and the announcement of peacekeeping cutbacks by the second Bush Administration may say something about the broader strategic aspirations underlying American foreign policy.[4] Does this apparent lack of interest signal a reduced American global engagement? Or do American national policy-makers view other instruments of power and influence as more significant than peacekeeping? Alternatively, do US domestic political actors play a role in limiting US peacekeeping policy and, if so, how?

Another element in US peacekeeping policy is the insistence that such missions be multilateral. Recent American presidents have demanded multilateral participation with US forces as a way to spread the peacekeeping risks and costs, and to attempt to build domestic political support for such missions. This follows from the belief that otherwise skeptical US political constituencies will be more willing to accept US peacekeeping if the burden is widely shared with other countries.

This emphasis on multilateral US peacekeeping highlights the impor-tance of domestic politics and its influence on US involvement in peacekeeping, and particularly UN peacekeeping. What political constitu-encies support, and which oppose, peacekeeping, and why? What role, in particular, does the US professional military play in peacekeeping politics? Does the military eschew such operations as drains on resources needed for more traditional military missions? Alternatively, does the military support peacekeeping because it gains the military assets and a seat at the foreign policy-making table? Is the State Department more eager than Defense to commit troops to peacekeeping missions? Where does Congress sit on peacekeeping missions? Do congressional positions reflect bipartisanship on foreign policy, or has party politics shaped peacekeeping policy in Congress? Is peacekeeping stimulated at the behest of US constituencies in response to atrocities or other wrongdoings that gain public attention (the so-called 'CNN effect')? Does the public pay attention to reports of atrocities, invasions of sovereign territory, and ethnic conflict in ways that force political leaders to dispatch US peacekeepers to troubled areas of the world?

US PEACEKEEPING POLICY EVOLVES

The US played a significant role in shaping the text that ultimately became the UN Charter, particularly in drafting the language involving peacekeeping. Rather than supporting an organic peace force under UN control, the US instead pushed for a provision where each UN member would make available forces to the UN when requested, with a significant role for air forces.[5]

Most UN Cold War era peacekeeping was done either by neutral nations or by three nations together representing the 'West' (often Canada), the 'East' (usually Poland), and a neutral nation (generally India). Therefore, the United States did not have a clear doctrine on UN peacekeeping when the Cold War ended. The George H. W. Bush Administration attempted to remedy this shortfall in formulating National Security Decision Directive (NSDD) 74, calling for US participation in UN peacekeeping operations only if the mission required its 'unique' military capabilities.[6] NSDD-74 represented the first US peacekeeping doctrine since the Truman Administration, but it would fall to the Clinton Administration to expand dramatically the US role in UN peacekeeping.

The new Clinton Administration envisioned a much broader and more active global role for the US than did its predecessor, and swiftly began to review US peacekeeping policy. In drafting one of its first documents on US peacekeeping, Presidential Decision Directive (PDD-13), the Clinton Administration formed an interagency team to explore US participation in UN peace operations. The team initially developed ideas for a 'rapid reaction force' but the concept attracted opposition from the Defense Department because of concerns that such a force would deplete troops from regular units. The document did identify guidelines for the use of American peacekeepers, including threats to an established democracy or gross violation of human rights.[7] However, by the summer of 1993 the Administration failed to reach internal consensus (on the draft PDD-13, largely due to the unraveling of the Somalia peace operation – see below). Sixteen dead American soldiers became symbolic of the cost of UN missions.[8] That symbol was unfortunate; as Hirsh noted, the mission failure that cost them their lives was an American, not a UN, failure.[9] However, an influential body of Republicans in Congress chastised the UN while the Clinton Administration viewed it with studied indifference.[10]

At the urging of then Secretary of Defense Les Aspin, the Administration refocused on limiting US peacekeeping and issued a new document, PDD-25, in March 1994. In PDD-25 the Administration responded to competing pressures to both limit and encourage US peacekeeping operations by clarifying doctrine for such roles. PDD-25 acknowledged that peacekeeping can advance US national security objectives, if done selectively. It also called for reducing the costs of peacekeeping operations and a clear definition of the circumstances under which a foreign commander might assume operational control of US forces in a peace operation.[11]

While the 1993 débâcle in Somalia reinforced US reluctance to participate in future UN peacekeeping missions, it was only part of the problem. Americans perceived the UN as a highly bureaucratized structure that was incompatible with a military organization. US leaders complained that the UN agencies that dealt with peacekeeping operations did not have any military experience.[12]

The US also tried to influence the UN Department of Peacekeeping Operations (DPKO) to enhance the organization's expertise on the military dimensions of peacekeeping, attempting to get Ambassador Jacques Klein a position as deputy undersecretary for peacekeeping. France, however, blocked the effort, complaining that the US had too much involvement in UN peacekeeping management.[13] France frequently expresses concerns about US power, but it may not be alone in its views. At the UN millennium celebration in September 2000, Algeria's former foreign minister Lakhdar Brahimi, who headed the expert panel that studied UN peacekeeping, sharply criticized the major powers on the Security Council for interference in UN peacekeeping functions.[14] While he did not specifically mention the US by name, the inference was there, particularly given the smaller role played by the other four Security Council permanent members on peacekeeping responsibility.

US PARTICIPATION IN SELECTED PEACEKEEPING OPERATIONS

The US did increase its peacekeeping participation after the end of the Cold War, but it did so selectively. In almost every case, the US justified its peacekeeping roles by referring to its *national* interest rather than to the *collective* interest, as the missions described below indicate. Somalia, as noted below, would be the exception to the rule and, because of this, laid the groundwork for a retreat from purely humanitarian peacekeeping missions.

Bosnia and Herzegovina

In the wake of the Yugoslav break-up, ethnic rivalries turned violent in several former Yugoslav regions, including Bosnia and Herzegovina. Serb attacks on civilians drove initial US involvement there, along with the concern about the conflict spilling over to the larger Balkan region.[15] In 1995, the UN mandated the United Nations Mission in Bosnia and

Herzegovina (UNMIBH) after the parties to the conflict reached a settlement in Dayton, Ohio in November 1995 and the US entered as part of the Combined Joint Task Force (CJTF). UNMIBH undertook a wide range of activities, including the restoration of civil law, prosecution of alleged war crimes, and the maintenance of the multilateral Stabilization Force (SFOR), created by the UN in 1996. Under the Clinton Administration, the US contributed over 4,000 troops to UNMIBH, but the Bush II Administration reduced the commitment by 1,000 troops in March 2001 in one of its first foreign policy actions. A year and a half later, the Bush Administration threatened to veto a six-month extension of the UN mission itself because the Security Council refused to grant immunity from the new International Criminal Court (ICC) to the remaining American forces serving in Bosnia.[16] The US later relented, and agreed to maintain its troops in Bosnia, while expressing strong reservations about the ICC, but the action indicated a US willingness to veto UN support of an entire UN peacekeeping mission in order to protect its own interests.

Haiti

The deteriorating political situation in Haiti that began to flood the US with illegal refugees set the stage for the United Nations Mission in Haiti (UNMIH), chartered in 1993. At its peak it had over 6,000 troops from Algeria, Bangladesh, Canada, Djibouti, France, Mali, the Netherlands, Pakistan, the Russian Federation, Togo, Trinidad and Tobago, and the United States.

The purpose of UNMIH was to implement the Governor's Island agreement of 1993 where the Haitian military rulers of the island agreed to step down and allow free elections. UNMIH also attempted to professionalize the Haitian military to free it from civil policing so that a non-political police force might be established. Haiti held elections in June 1995, and the UNMIH completed its mission in June 1996. Haiti's president requested an extension of that mission until July 1997 in an effort to complete the training of civilian police.

US participation in UNMIH was slow, conditioned by the débâcle in Somalia in October 1993 (see below), and an initial rebuff of US and Canadian peacekeepers at Port-au-Prince in the same month. However, the Clinton Administration came under pressure from civil rights groups who objected to the fact that Haitians fleeing to the US were either repatriated or housed at the US base at Guantanamo, Cuba, while Cuban refugees were admitted to the US under the 1966 Cuban Adjustment Act. The Congressional Black Caucus demanded that the Clinton Administration not only solve the unequal treatment of Haitian refugees, but also address the root cause for refugees, the Haitian political system.[17]

Somalia

Ethnic conflict has torn Somalia almost from the time of its independence in 1960, but televised views of the famine stemming from Somalian violence stirred the US into action in August 1992. As in the case of Haiti, the Congressional Black Caucus demanded that the US lend assistance to the struggling country. The policy started in a limited way, with US forces airlifting food to displaced refugees. However, as armed militia fighters interfered with food delivery, the US stepped up its participation, landing troops in December 1992. That commitment quickly grew to over 28,000 US troops.

Questions arose about the scope and duration of the peacekeeping mission in Somalia, but they were initially in the minority. During the Bush presidency, most Republicans and Democrats in Congress backed the mission, as did President-elect Clinton.[18] The military initially under-estimated the situation in Somalia: 'The Pentagon official described the two clan leaders as "intimidated" by the imminent arrival of US troops and noted that the United States is generally well respected in Somalia.'[19] That turned out not to be the case, as UN peacekeepers increasingly got caught in the cross-fire of rival militias and armed gangs, culminating in the loss of 18 American troops caught in an ambush by Adid's forces in October 1993.[20] The televised results of that tragedy ended the mission for the US, and the US left the peacekeeping mission shortly afterward.[21] Later, President Clinton refused to intervene in another violent ethnic conflict in Rwanda, partly because of the brutal lessons learned in Somalia (though he would later apologize for having not used US peacekeepers to help prevent the horrific slaughter in that central African country).

Current US peacekeeping operations

The intensity of the debate in the United States over United Nations peacekeeping commitments gives the impression that thousands of uniformed American men and women patrol tense areas around the globe. However, in May of 2002 the US had only 704 personnel in such roles.[22] That is around one percent of the 45,159 troops supporting UN peacekeeping operations as of May 2002. While no single nation commits more than 2,000 troops to peacekeeping, still the US is dwarfed by such nations as Poland with 1,054, Bangladesh with 867, and Ghana with 774. The US is currently involved in dozens of peacekeeping operations, but only a few troops in UN-supported operations. They include 15 troops in the MINURSO force in Western Sahara, 26 civilian police in Haiti supporting MIPONUH, 168 in Bosnia and Herzegovina with UNMIBH, and 11 on the Kuwaiti-Iraqi border in association with UNIKOM (UN Iraq–Kuwait Observation Mission). It is also noteworthy that the US began its most significant engagements with UN peacekeeping missions in the early 1990s under former President George H. W. Bush, and has not joined any UN peacekeeping missions in several years. Under the George W. Bush Administration, the rhetoric from senior national security policy advisors emphasizes a retrenchment even from that limited commitment. Moreover, the Bush II Administration warned the UN Security Council in June 2002 that the US would refuse participation in future UN peacekeeping missions unless the SC granted immunity to US soldiers from prosecution by the International Criminal Court (ICC). The Bush II Administration initially indicated that it was not bound by the Clinton Administration's agreement on the treaty creating the ICC, then redoubled its efforts against the ICC even though traditional allies France and the UK objected to the US tactics.[23] Several days later the Bush Administration quietly withdrew its threat, but then shifted its tactics, attempting to extract promises from over 180 countries never to deliver an American to the ICC.[24] The efforts only reinforced the possibility that the US might refuse participation in both current and future peacekeeping operations as long as the ICC existed.

THE STRATEGIC CONTEXT FOR US PEACEKEEPING DECISIONS

The end of the Cold War stimulated a debate within US scholarly and policy-making circles over the purpose and extent of American involvement in the world. Some reasoned that with the collapse of the USSR, the US no longer needed to pursue global interests. Others argued that America faced a post-Cold War world where chaos and uncertainty replaced the somewhat orderly competition of the Cold War.[25] Those in the latter group argued that only American involvement met both strategic and moral criteria to respond to the uncertain world that followed the Cold War. Opponents also feared that American unipolarity efforts would only trigger a 'bandwagon' effect where other powers would coalesce against the US in order to deny it the potential to threaten their interests.[26]

Lake argues that those who predicted the rise of other powers attempting to offset American predominance by balancing against it were wrong. This has happened in part, Lake claims, because the US has successfully linked its power to multilateral coalitions.[27] Wohlforth agrees that other potential hegemons have not risen since the collapse of the Soviet Union, and that unipolarity is both stable and durable. Such a condition might give the US the expected license to intervene widely throughout the world. However, as Wohlforth puts it, 'Constrained by a domestic welfare role and consumer culture, ... Washington tends to shrink from accepting the financial, military, and especially the domestic political burdens of sole pole status.'[28] Kupchan agrees, stating that 'the American electorate will tire of a foreign policy that saddles the United States with such a disproportionate share of the burden of managing the international system'.[29]

The debate over global versus limited engagement may also be influenced by the reactions to Kosovo, where a US-led air campaign toppled Serbian leader Slobodan Milosevic after Serb forces engaged in a campaign of atrocities against the Kosovar Albanians. If Kosovo was at least partially a case of global expansion for the US, some argue that it may be the beginning of new limits. As Marcus claims, 'Applying the concept of humanitarian intervention in Kosovo highlighted the problems that this approach poses for Washington's bilateral relations with both Moscow and Beijing.'[30] Furthermore, as again Marcus notes, American allies may be less willing to join the US in global expansion, and evidence of fissures between the US and its allies grows, as attested by differences on sanctions against Iraq and Cuba.[31]

If Wohlforth and Kupchan are correct, then American decisions on supporting UN peacekeeping missions are not solely reflective of the international security environment, but also echo domestic national security constraints posted by domestic political preferences. Thus, this chapter uses two differing yet complementary approaches in an effort to explain American perspectives on peacekeeping.

THE STRATEGIC ARGUMENTS OVER US PEACEKEEPING

Strategic-level decisions on peacekeeping reflect perspectives on the nature of US strategic interests in the unipolar era. At the scholarly level, debate over the range of those interests and the instruments to address them divides into distinct camps. Those who argue that the US has global interests represent the 'global engagement' camp, while those who claim that US interests are more limited fall into the 'limited engagement' school.

The global engagement argument

The global engagement argument for peacekeeping rests on both moral and national interest foundations. Its proponents argue that the US is the only nation capable of unilateral peacekeeping operations that can terminate conflict or 'ethnic cleansing' in troubled parts of the world. That capacity alone, they argue, undergirds the moral need to commit such forces. Michael O'Hanlon claims that a moral foundation is traditional for the US: 'moral foreign policy has been a part of our country. Ronald Reagan stood for it, Roosevelt and Truman stood for it. This has been a very important thing.'[32]

The global engagement position is more than a moral argument, though. The proponents of global engagement also claim that US national interests are served when peacekeeping succeeds. Edward Luck, for example, advances nine reasons for active involvement of the United States in peacekeeping efforts:

1. US leadership (others will fill the void if the US withdraws);

2. curbing weapons proliferation;

3. containment of local conflicts;

4. deterrence of local aggressors;

5. reinforcement of international norms;

6. expanding the number of democratic governments;

7. multilateral cooperation between the US and potential adversaries;

8. trade and jobs (from the stability following successful peacekeeping operations); and

9. controlling the long-term costs of conflict.[33]

The limited engagement argument

The 'limited engagement' proponents take a different tack on US participation in peacekeeping. They claim that the unipolar status of the US is not justification enough to engage in peacekeeping, particularly outside of traditional US areas of interest. Christopher Layne offers counter-arguments on both moral and national security grounds. Moral wrongdoing, he notes, is rarely clear enough to identify the guilty parties, and then to take sides against them. Who, for example, was guilty in Bosnia – the Croats, the Muslims, or the Serbs?[34] Additionally, Layne argues that the rationale for US participation in international peacekeeping at the national-interest level includes efforts to deter future aggressors by responding decisively to present aggression. However, Layne suggests that US actions against Iraq failed to deter Slobodan Milosevic, that Saddam Hussein was undeterred by US actions in Panama, and that Manuel Noriega was not deterred by US action against North Korea.[35]

The 'limited engagement' argument also rests on the premise that the US has limited interests outside the western hemisphere, and especially in the developing world where peacekeeping missions are most likely. There are few threats from escalating conflicts in places like sub-Saharan Africa. Moreover, the American economy is less dependent on trade than many other industrial economies, and only one-third of US exports and imports are to the Third World.[36]

When US participation grew under the Clinton Administration, it had many of the earmarks of global engagement, expanding from the first Bush Administration. However, the second Bush Administration has a much more limited view of peacekeeping. Part of that view stems from the 'war on terrorism' that draws military resources away from peacekeeping, but the key players in that administration also appear to value peacekeeping as a principle less than did the Clinton Administration, as their readiness to veto all UN missions over the ICC issue noted above.

The multilateral dimension of peacekeeping

In virtually every post-Cold War peacekeeping effort, the US has refused to go it alone. Even in the smaller, less risky missions like in Haiti, the US insisted that other nations join the effort. Moreover, the US appears to prefer implementation under the aegis of a multilateral organization. In some instances the US has agreed to join a UN peacekeeping effort; however, in others the lead multilateral organization is NATO, or, in the case of Haiti, the Organization of American States.

The multilateral context also applies to the UN itself. Here the US has been inconsistent, sometimes insisting on UN support for peacekeeping operations it has an interest in (such as in Haiti), yet at other times eschewing such a role for the world body (as in Kosovo, where the US peacekeepers are under NATO authority despite a UN presence there). Then-UN Ambassador Albright declared her support for 'assertive multilateralism' after an attack on Pakistani peacekeepers in Somalia, but the Clinton Administration quickly retreated from the stance after US peacekeepers died there soon after.[37]

The strategic context framework gives a partial understanding of US peacekeeping decisions, but for a more comprehensive examination, the next part of this chapter focuses on the domestic politics of peace-keeping.

THE DOMESTIC POLITICS OF PEACEKEEPING

To accept the 'strategic objectives' reasoning for peacekeeping decisions, one must accept the argument that military commitments stem from the calculus of national interests, and a fit between such interests and the means employed to secure them. However, other forces have an impact on peacekeeping choices, including the interests of domestic actors. Such interests may include greater access to resources, a chance to display particular capabilities (thus leading perhaps to greater shares of resources), or avoiding employments that might lead to negative consequences, such as losing. Commonly, such objectives fall under the rubric of 'bureaucratic politics' since they emphasize organizational rather than national inter-ests.[38] The purpose of including the bureaucratic politics model in this chapter is not to provide a test of the validity of the model, but only to use it as an organizing concept.

Bureaucratic politics emphasizes organizational keenness for maintaining the *status quo* in the face of pressures for change. As Rosen notes, organizations are not only difficult to change; their design facilitates resistance to change.[39] Militaries, almost by their very nature, often resist change that runs at variance with their established traditions and routines. So, for that matter, do foreign policy bureaucracies, again for the same reason. Both are highly functional, and both recruit their professional members (as opposed to their political leaders) from a small cross-section of society. Membership in both includes the rites of passage into the deep traditions of the organization, and sometimes those passages include inculcation into the dangers of outside interference. It is not surprising that the professional military may resist peacekeeping while the professional State Department may embrace it.

ACTORS IN THE DECISION-MAKING PROCESS

The policy-makers who advise the president clearly shape the motives underlying peacekeeping commitments. The president thus seeks con-sensus on military operations such as peacekeeping in order to build a policy that essential agencies can minimally support. However, those agencies, the State Department and the Department of Defense may disagree on fundamental objectives and operational rules for peace-keeping.[40] Observers note that the State Department is sometimes more supportive of the general use of military force abroad than is the Defense Department.[41] Within the Defense Department, the Secretary of Defense may be more eager to commit force than are uniformed military leaders. Moreover, the uniformed military is likely to resist what it considers 'unorthodox' military operations, such as those required for peacekeeping, preferring instead to emphasize more traditional missions like those requiring the heavy weapons infrastructure that the military had invested billions of dollars in over the years.[42]

Divisions across bureaucracies raise barriers to effective policy-making, and for several decades now, Washington has pursued and continues to pursue the notion of an 'interagency process' to bridge such divisions. Given the inevitable divisions inherent in the peacekeeping process and the complex combination of political and military objectives, the Clinton Administration developed PDD-56 in 1997. Officially called 'Managing Complex Contingency Operations', PDD-56 emphasizes interagency coordination across the peacekeeping process. However, as Langford notes, 'lack of inter-agency cohesion regarding the principles of PDD-56 impedes its progress'.[43] Unsurprisingly, a doctrine alone is insufficient to breach organizational divides on peacekeeping, so it is necessary to examine the perspectives of both lead agencies in US peacekeeping operations, the military and the State Department.

The military

The US military has tended to oppose peacekeeping missions, although there are exceptions. Military leaders understand that both political leaders and the public will hold them accountable for peacekeeping missions that ultimately fail for political reasons. As Hendrickson has observed, the military received blame for problems or mission failures in Grenada, Desert One (the 1980 Iranian hostage rescue), Beirut 1982, and Vietnam, even though the failure of these operations reflected poor political judgement about undertaking them at all.[44] The consequences for the military from these failures ranged from large budget reductions after the Vietnam War and demands for outside reform of the services after Beirut and Desert One. While some of those measures may have ultimately helped the military improve its operations, no organization likes outside criticism and pressures from outside for reform.

Many peacekeeping missions also violate the American military preference for clear-cut objectives. The ideal is World War II, where 'unconditional surrender' gave considerable latitude to the military for force application and a clearly defined end–state. The dissatisfaction with objectives in Korea and Vietnam (both 'limited wars' with unclear military objectives) only nourished military unhappiness with the even more vague objectives of peacekeeping. Peacekeeping also falls outside the normal set of military combat capabilities, and for the US military in particular, these capabilities are technologically intensive. The military, for much of its twentieth–century history, emphasized large ships, planes, and armor, to the detriment of the kinds of light forces most appropriate for peace–keeping roles.[45]

The military also expresses concern about the stresses that peacekeeping missions place on the readiness of the overall force. Army Chief of Staff Eric Shinseki tied low readiness ratings of two Army divisions to the fact that almost half of their strength was tied up in Balkans peacekeeping missions.[46] The pace of deployments has increased sixteen–fold since the Cold War, which puts a particular strain on the airlift and sealift capacity that moves the troops and their supplies overseas.[47] Peace operations also disrupt training for regular war–fighting missions.[48]

Therefore, the US military did not support a peacekeeping role in Afghanistan after the 2001–02 campaign against the Taliban and Al Qaeda forces there. Instead, the UK took the lead on peacekeeping, while the US concentrated on ridding the country of opponent forces. The Defense Department also pushed for ending some long–standing peacekeeping operations, including the MFO in the Sinai, noted above, although the White House resisted the plan, claiming that it sent the wrong signals about US interests in the Middle East.

Part of the readiness problem is obvious – the military, and the Army in particular, has shrunk considerably since the late 1980s. The Army, which supplies most peacekeeping personnel, is smaller by some 630,000 soldiers from 1989, yet Army deployments have increased since the end of the Cold War. According to General William Crouch, Army Vice Chief of Staff, army deployments averaged one deployment every four years during the Cold War, but they have averaged 14 deployments every four years since 1989, with some 31,000 soldiers deployed away from their home units in 1998.[49]

Related to this concern is a less commonly voiced concern in the military that peacekeeping lies beyond the traditional missions that military forces perform. As Green states, 'When US combat forces are sent to faraway places to monitor cease–fire agreements, patrol buffer zones, or deliver humanitarian assistance, they are performing duties wholly unrelated to, and at various times in clear opposition to, their mission to prepare to fight and win wars.'[50] These differences became apparent in the Somalia operation, when US senior military officials found themselves in a clash with UN Secretary-General Boutros Boutros-Ghali over the scope of the mission. The military wanted only a 'clear and precise' aid distribution program, after which US forces would leave Somalia. Boutros-Ghali, on the other hand, wanted US forces to remain in Somalia to undertake the more difficult and time-consuming task of disarming the roving armed gangs who were terrorizing the country.[51]

Not all military officers express opposition to peacekeeping. The Marine Corps, for example, initially welcomed peacekeeping operations in Somalia, noting that such an effort might help the Marines avoid budgetary reductions.[52] General Colin Powell, Chairman of the Joint Chiefs of Staff in the first Bush Administration, claimed that Somalia was a 'paid political advertisement for the base force', the bottom-line military size advocated by that administration to protect from possible congressional cutbacks.[53] MacKinnon also noted that some mid-level military officers saw peacekeeping as a way to stem the post-Cold War decline in defense budgets.[54] Another unnamed officer claimed that troops 'thrive on foreign assignments because they add a sense of adventure to the job'.[55]

However, a sub-organization of the US military has taken a different view of peacekeeping, the regional commanders-in-chief, or CINCs. The regional CINCs, representing Europe and Africa (EUCOM – US European Command), Latin America south of Mexico and the Caribbean (SOUTHCOM), the Middle East and Southwest Asia (CENTCOM), and the Pacific and most of Asia (PACOM), gained influence relative to the Joint Staff through the Goldwater–Nichols Defense Reform Act of 1986. The growing influence of the CINCs, at least in Europe, appeared in Bosnia under CINCEUR (Commander-in-Chief Europe) General Wesley Clark (now retired), who ordered his peacekeepers to engage in operations beyond the scope of those approved by the Defense Department. They included anti-corruption activities and disrupting the operations of Croatian radicals by using both Special Forces and an interagency anti-corruption team. The Secretary of Defense ultimately opposed some of General Clark's operation since it gave more of an activist role to the military in peacekeeping than the Secretary of Defense or the Joint Staff desired.[56]

In the face of concerns about peacekeeping, the military attempted to minimize the damage to its own reputation and to its forces. It can also try to curtail the most undesirable outcomes by affecting such things as the scope of the operations and the rules of engagement under which it may operate. Avant reports on the considerable efforts by the US Central

Command (CENTCOM) to modify UN rules of engagement in Somalia to allow for force protection, and to limit the scope of the operation.[57]

The US military can also try to increase the capacity of other militaries to engage in peacekeeping operations in order to reduce its own involvement. In working towards this objective, the US has actively trained militaries of other nations, and in June 2000 this effort was put under one program, the Enhanced International Peacekeeping Capabilities (EIPC).[58] According to the initializing message, EIPC sets aside funding for training foreign peacekeepers with an explicit purpose: 'EIPC will help reduce the likelihood and expense of future US involvement in peacekeeping . . .'[59] The US has encouraged sub-Saharan African nations to organize peacekeeping efforts through such regional organizations as the Economic Community of West African States (ECOWAS). Several member nations of ECOWAS contributed a significant peacekeeping force in Liberia, including the use of Ghanaian and Nigerian naval forces to land troops to enforce UN-imposed economic sanctions against Liberia.[60] In August 2000, the US announced that it would train Nigerian peacekeeping troops for use in Sierra Leone. The move, coming after congressional and foreign criticism of US inactivity in Sierra Leone's brutal civil war, calls for several hundred Special Forces troops to go to Nigeria and both train and equip Nigerian troops to actively pursue and defeat guerrilla forces.[61] More recently, US Special Forces personnel arrived in Ghana and Senegal to train troops from those countries as a part of Operation Focus Relief.[62]

While it is useful to generalize about the military, it is also necessary to note unique perspectives that differ across military leaders. This is clear in considering the military reaction to peacekeeping missions in the US. Two successive Chairs of the Joint Chiefs of Staff had considerably different positions on the issue. General Colin Powell, the Chair under President George H. W. Bush, lobbied privately (and sometimes publicly) against peacekeeping missions for US forces. His successor, General John Shalikashvili, who served under President Bill Clinton, took a much more nuanced approach to peacekeeping. As Goldstein observed about General Shalikashvili's posture on US peacekeeping, 'Shalikashvili did not take the position that peacekeeping was either wholly worthy or wholly worthless, but examined each case on its own merits, bringing his professional military expertise to bear on each.'[63]

The US military has also shifted some peacekeeping responsibility to units outside of the regular military structure. One such group is the special forces of the various services, who have engaged in a number of operations, including mine clearance, cease-fire monitoring between Ecuador and Peru, support for civil–military relations in East Timor, and other responsibilities.[64] National Guard forces are also increasingly used for major peacekeeping responsibilities, including command of the US sector of the NATO-led Bosnia peacekeeping mission, the first time a guard unit had commanded active Army troops in such an area.[65] In 2002, the National Guard took over much of the SFOR mission, using troops from Kansas, Michigan, Minnesota, Indiana, and New York.[66] The National Guard argues that its members may bring more appropriate skills to peacekeeping than does the regular military. Water engineers, medical professionals, teachers, and computer programmers, jobs held by National Guard members in civilian life, may be more appropriate for rebuilding war-torn areas like Bosnia and Kosovo than infantry or armor.[67] Since guard units have closer links to their communities in the US than do regular military units, support for peace operations may increase as citizens back home learn directly about the work of peacekeeping.[68] Using guard forces also reduces the pressure on regular forces, where personnel leaving in response to the pressures of long deployments overseas leaves increasingly thin active ranks.

In addition to guard and reserve forces, the US contracts with private firms to provide police officers for peacekeeping missions. According to reports, the George W. Bush Administration favors increasing the number of civilian police officers so that it can scale back on the number of military personnel performing policing functions.[69] However, allegations of misconduct against such contracted personnel highlight some of the problems of employing civilians outside of the military chain of command in peacekeeping operations. The UN itself has very limited authority over civilians attached to a national mission, and where cases of misconduct have occurred, the offending official was simply sent home.[70]

An additional option for the military is indirect participation in peacekeeping. This involves providing transportation for peacekeepers from other nations to and from the conflict area, as was done recently in East Timor. That way the US can show that it is involved without putting its forces in harmful situations (except for landing in hostile places), or risking a long-term deployment without a clear end-state. The Marines and Navy demonstrated another version of indirect peacekeeping when they deployed on ships to East Timor after an attack against UN aid workers by militias. The Marines aboard ship were able to deploy quickly to shore to dispense aid and to protect aid workers while maintaining separation from the actual combatants.[71]

Indirect participation in peacekeeping also involves the provision of funding so that other countries can provide the actual forces. The US military provides such funds under the Defense Security Cooperation

Agency, which distributed some 127 million dollars for fiscal year 2001, with over 46 million dollars going to African peacekeeping operations. Such funding allows the US to claim to support peacekeeping while indigenous armies are actually engaged in the operations.

The State Department

If the State Department marks success as the achievement of long-term elimination of conflict through negotiation, then peacekeeping operations fit well with those objectives. 'Promoting and maintaining peace' has been a part of the State Department's official mission since 1993.[72]

The State Department, though, has no troops of its own, and must depend on the US military to provide forces to enforce State-brokered peace accords. Paradoxically that situation may allow State to take a more 'activist' policy than Defense. State, unlike Defense, tends to avoid direct blame when things go wrong with peacekeeping missions. The US military, for example, found itself roundly criticized when its forces ran into difficulty in Somalia during the early years of the Clinton Administration, with Secretary of Defense Les Aspin taking heat from Congress for not bringing the right equipment to the fight. State, on the other hand, argued in favor of the peacekeeping mission to Somalia, and Clinton's First Secretary of State Warren Christopher backed the continuation of the mission. However, both Christopher and State avoided criticism when the mission withdrew after US soldiers died in a bloody ambush. Moreover, the real costs of peacekeeping came out of the Defense budget rather than the State Department budget, so Defense is understandably more reluctant to enter into long-term missions than is State.

During the Clinton Administration State advocated an activist peacekeeping role for the US. The public preference in State for a strong US interventionist policy was revealed during the Kosovo operations by its head, Madeleine Albright, who told US peacekeepers entering Kosovo that 'This is what America is good at', and that Kosovo was 'simply the most important thing we have done in the world'.[73] Moreover, Albright served as the US Ambassador to the United Nations before assuming the top job at State, and had a reputation as a strong UN supporter. However, State also worked to reduce direct US participation in peacekeeping operations through its Enhanced International Peacekeeping Capabilities (EIPC) Initiative. This program, funded at 2.5 million dollars, was specifically tailored to 'reduce the likelihood and expense of future US involvement in peacekeeping operations ...'[74]

Congress

Congress has involved itself in national security decision-making since the era of the Vietnam War. Since the end of the Cold War, that involvement increasingly focused on US peacekeeping. Across both houses, Congress has been increasingly divided over what role the US should perform in peacekeeping, and how that role should be performed.

Congressional opponents of US participation in UN peacekeeping missions fall into several camps. Some simply oppose US peacekeeping in all its forms, including members from both parties who tend towards neo-isolationism. More commonly, members of Congress believe that they have a constitutional obligation to oversee executive dispatches of military force in a variety of circumstances.[75] The particular case of peacekeeping, though, draws particular congressional attention for a variety of reasons. Some reflect the military concerns about the length and uncertain objectives that most peacekeeping operations carry. Senator Dirk Kempthorne (Republican, Idaho) reflected this position when he asked Defense Secretary William Cohen, 'is it fair to say that there is still no exit strategy in Bosnia?'[76] The same question was posed to the Bush Administration over Somalia when the Democrats held a majority in Congress; said Representative James Oberstar (Democrat, Minnesota) about Somalia, 'How do we get out?'[77] The Somalia débâcle very quickly killed off remaining support for the mission in Congress.[78]

Other members of Congress criticize the details of peacekeeping, for example Senator Gregg, who, in expressing his opposition to UN peacekeeping efforts in Sierra Leone, stated that, 'Because the policy being pursued in Sierra Leone was misdirected from the start, we should not have been making peace. We should not have been bringing into the Government people who acted in such a barbaric way toward their own people. We should have been taking a harder line.'[79] These congressional opponents of UN peacekeeping got a boost when rebel troops took more than 500 African peacekeepers hostage in Sierra Leone in May 2000. In response, Republican Representative Ed Royce of California said, 'I think the whole notion of UN peacekeeping is on the line.'[80]

Yet other members of Congress express an old fear in the US of American troops under a UN commander. Senator Jon Kyle (Republican, Arizona) expressed this concern with a reference to World War I: 'In 1918, during World War I, Gen. John Pershing set a precedent that US soldiers should remain in large units under US command. The historical success of that precedent dictates that we heed this lesson of history.'[81]

Congressional supporters of UN peacekeeping include old-line liberal Democrats who view the global responsibilities of the US through a moral lens. Senator Carl Levin, for example, stated that, 'I believe that it is in the United States national interest to support the United Nations as it seeks to fulfill its primary responsibility to maintain international peace and stability.' Levin did indicate that there were limits on US peacekeeping, though, noting that the US had not, and should not have, committed forces to either the Congo or East Timor, which, he implied, lay outside of US vital national interests.[82]

Other peacekeeping supporters in Congress have more specific interests. The Congressional Black Caucus gave particular emphasis to US participation to UN peacekeeping missions in sub–Saharan Africa. Said Congresswoman Maxine Waters (Democrat, California), 'I am particularly concerned about the situation in the Democratic Republic of the Congo. The war that erupted in the Congo in August of 1998 has been a widespread and destructive conflict, involving forces from several different countries. The peacekeeping efforts of the United Nations are essential to bring peace and stability to the Congo and the entire Great Lakes Region of Africa.'[83] Another Black Caucus member, Congressman Julian Dixon, attempted to increase the funding for peacekeeping activities by 241 billion dollars, back to the original President's request. Some Black Caucus members gave less specific reasons, but still advocated US support for peacekeeping, like Congresswoman Jackson-Lee of Texas, who proclaimed, 'We must re-establish our nation's unwavering commitment to the world's International Peacekeeping efforts, which are designed to bring peace and order in times of strife and chaos.'[84]

Opponents of US participation in UN peacekeeping have the upper hand, at least in the 105th Congress. For fiscal year 2001, The Commerce–Justice–State Appropriations Act cut funding for international peacekeeping efforts by 241 million dollars below the President's request, a 33 percent cut. Congress also restricted money for peacekeeping for fiscal year 2002, capping cost increases for SFOR and KFOR to slightly more than 1 billion dollars apiece.[85]

The public

While most studies on public impact on foreign policy suggest that it is limited at best, the popular notion of the 'CNN' effect rises to suggest that televised images of atrocities against helpless peoples create popular pressure on political leaders to solve the problem through the sending of peacekeepers to the troubled land. This image arose during the starvation in Somalia in 1992–93, and again in both Bosnia and in Kosovo when ethnic cleansing provoked public outrage.

The 'CNN effect', though, needs more examination. A piece in the *New York Times* suggested that, in response to television coverage of Somalia, 'Nearly all of Washington seems to have been converted by the pictures. Members of Congress who opposed the invasion of Iraq now come before the cameras to support the intervention in Somalia ...'[86] However, Lawrence Friedman writes that, 'To an extent, the "CNN effect" – whereby emotive images of suffering are presumed to lead to a near-automatic public demand to "do something" – is overstated.'[87] Moreover, as Ruggie notes, American public support for international engagement has been at an all-time low.[88] Evidence for this is also found in the lack of response to vivid televised pictures of the atrocities in Rwanda and elsewhere. For years, Americans watched pictures of Israeli soldiers gassing and sometimes shooting Palestinians and of Israeli civilians dying at the hands of Palestinian suicide bombers. Yet the US government never really faced public pressure to send in peacekeepers. Finally, the 2000 electoral campaign featured almost no defense of peacekeeping by either Gore (whose administration sent in peacekeepers to Bosnia and Haiti), or Bush (whose father's administration sent peacekeepers to Somalia).

Therefore, which of these actors have the most influence in the decision-making process? The US military appears to have more influence in peacekeeping decisions, largely because it has direct responsibility for operating them. The Clinton Administration, ever mindful of the President's own lack of military experience, appeared unwilling to press the military to expand peacekeeping missions after the Somalia débâcle. The second Bush Administration appears to want to limit its political fights with the military to 'transformation' (away from traditional missions with more emphasis on mobility, for example). As noted above, Bush's Defense department leaders have already limited US involvement in peacekeeping missions, and shifted the military participation to guard and reserve forces, and civilians.

CONCLUSIONS

The United States, as the sole superpower, embraced UN peacekeeping missions reluctantly. Part of the reason for this disinclination lies in the way that the US defines its strategic role in the unipolar era. However, the more robust area for explaining US participation in UN peacekeeping missions lies at the domestic politics levels of explanation. Opponents of peacekeeping in both the US military and in Congress created a climate under which the possible failure of US participation in UN peacekeeping missions has made the administration gun-shy about such commitments. While the US does maintain troops in Bosnia, a place where US interests link more closely to European interests, it quickly withdrew most of its forces from the UN mission to Haiti once the television cameras left. The Clinton Administration eschewed Sierra Leone altogether, agreeing only to train the troops from Nigeria and other African nations scheduled to participate there. The US also avoided Rwanda, with the exception of providing some short-term humanitarian assistance there.

The limited nature of American participation in UN-sanctioned peacekeeping missions indicates a preference for limited engagement and, only then, through multilateral missions. While the US prefers to avoid unilateral participation in peacekeeping efforts, it also prefers to minimize participation in UN missions. This probably reflects the continuing US dissatisfaction with the UN that seems to cross party lines.

NOTES

1. This chapter reflects the views of the author, and does not necessarily represent the positions of the United States Defense Department.
2. See 'Monthly Summary of Military and Civilian Police Contribution to United Nations Operations', May 2002 (New York: United Nations), p. 2.
3. The US initially committed 3,132 troops to SFOR and 6,515 to KFOR under the Clinton Administration, but the second Bush Administration reduced these numbers by over 2,000 in KFOR, with further reductions of 800 in KFOR and 1,200 in SFOR announced in July 2002. Nina M. Serafino, 'Peacekeeping: Issues of US Military Involvement', CRS Issue Brief for Congress (4 February 2002), p. 2; 'Myers: US Reducing Troops in Kosovo as NATO Also Cuts Force', *European Stars and Stripes* (2 July 2002). The US also stations 865 troops to the Multilateral Force (MFO) in the Sinai, although the UN no longer sanctions that operation. The current administration announced plans to curtail this latter operation altogether, though postponed these plans in the face of Israeli concerns. See 'Pentagon Seeks Sinai Cuts', *Washington Post* (30 January 2002).
4. The word 'peacekeeping' does not even appear in the Department of Defense's *Annual Report to the President and Congress* for 2002.
5. See John Gerard Ruggie, 'The United Nations and the Collective Use of Force: Whither or Whether?', in Michael Pugh (ed.), *The UN, Peace and Force* (London: Frank Cass, 1997), pp. 2–3.
6. Ivo Daalder, 'Knowing When to Say No: The Development of US Policy for Peacekeeping', in William J. Durch (ed.), *UN Peacekeeping, American Politics, and the*

Uncivil Wars of the 1990s (A Henry L. Stimson Center Book, New York: St Martin's Press, 1996), pp. 38–9.

7. Ibid., pp. 39–48.
8. Cori Dauber, 'Image as Argument: The Impact of Mogadishu on US Military Intervention', *Armed Forces & Society*, Vol. 27 (winter 2001), pp. 205–30. See also Interview Of The President By David Sanger, Todd Purdum, Marc Lacey, Robin Toner and Jane Perlez of *The New York Times*, The Oval Office (30 November 2000).
9. Michael Hirsh, 'The Fall Guy', *Foreign Affairs*, Vol. 78 (November/December 1999), p. 6.
10. Ibid., pp. 2–3.
11. The text of PDD-25 is Annex 1 in Michael G. MacKinnon, *The Evolution of US Peacekeeping Policy Under Clinton: A Fairweather Friend?* (London: Frank Cass, 2000), pp. 124–39.
12. For an example of this concern, see Clinton Administration Policy on Reforming Multilateral Peace Operations (PDD-25). The Bureau of International Organizational Affairs, US Department of State (22 February 1996). The Clinton Administration listed eleven changes it wanted to strengthen UN peacekeeping operations.
13. 'France Blocks US Bid for Key U.N. Position', *Washington Post* (4 August 2000).
14. 'Leaders Envision Broad New Role for U.N. Council', *New York Times* (8 September 2000).
15. 'US Worries Balkan War Could Spread', *New York Times* (22 August 1992). See also David Yost, *NATO Transformed: The Alliance's New Roles in International Security* (Washington, DC: United States Institute for Peace Press, 1998), pp. 192–204.
16. 'US Links Bosnia Role to Immunity from Court', *New York Times* (28 June 2002).
17. Esther Brimmer, 'Third Time Right: Haiti', in Roderick K. Von Lipsey (ed.), *Breaking the Cycle: A Framework for Conflict Intervention* (New York: St Martin's Press, 1997), pp. 187–8.
18. 'Bush Calls Foreign Leaders for Support on Somalia Force', *Washington Post* (3 December 1992); 'A Few in Congress Advising Caution, or Vote, on Somalia', *New York Times* (7 December 1992).
19. 'Stabilizing Riven Somalia a Monumental Task', *Washington Post* (3 December 1992). The clan leaders referred to were Ali Mahdi Mohamed and General Mohamed Farah Adid.
20. In a strange irony, the US military provided transportation for Adid to attend a peace conference on Somalia, despite the fact that at the time he remained a hunted fugitive.
21. For more on the UN mission in Somalia, see Robert G. Patman, 'The UN Operation in Somalia', in Ramesh Thakur and Carlyle A. Thayer, *A Crisis of Expectations: UN Peacekeeping in the 1990s* (Boulder, CO: Westview Press, 1995), pp. 85–104.
22. The US contribution to Kosovo is not included in this chapter. The US command structure for the Kosovo peacekeeping operation, KFOR, runs through NATO, not the UN. There is a UN peacekeeping mission (United Nations Interim Administration Mission in Kosovo, or UNMIK), authorized by UN Resolution 1244 of June 1999. The deputy director of UNMIK is an American, and the US provides some administrative support (no more than 50 at any given time), but the bulk of US peacekeeping falls under NATO control.
23. 'US Links Peacekeeping to Immunity from New Court', *New York Times* (19 June 2002).
24. 'US Presses Allies on War Crimes Court', *Washington Post* (27 August 2002).

25. For examples of arguments counseling American restraint, see Eugene Gholz, Daryl G. Press, and Harvey M. Sapolsky, 'Come Home, America: The Strategy of Restraint in the Face of Temptation', *International Security*, Vol. 21 (spring 1997), pp. 5–48; Christopher Layne, 'From Preponderance to Offshore Balancing', *International Security*, Vol. 22 (summer 1997), pp. 86–124; Michael Mastanduno, 'Preserving the Unipolar Moment', *International Security*, Vol. 21 (spring 1997), pp. 49–88.

26. See Kenneth Waltz, 'The Emerging Structure of International Politics', *International Security*, Vol. 18 (fall 1993), pp. 45–73; Christopher Layne, 'The Unipolar Illusion: Why New Great Powers Will Rise', *International Security*, Vol. 17 (spring 1993), pp. 5–51.

27. David A. Lake, 'Ulysses's Triumph: American Power and the New World Order', *Security Policy*, Vol. 8 (summer 1999), pp. 44–5.

28. William C. Wohlforth, 'The Stability of a Unipolar World', *International Security*, Vol. 24 (summer 1999), esp. p. 40.

29. Charles A. Kupchan, 'After Pax America: Benign Power, Regional Integration, and the Sources of a Stable Multipolarity', *International Security*, Vol. 23 (fall 1998), p. 41.

30. Jonathan Marcus, 'Kosovo and After: American Primacy in the Twenty-First Century, *Washington Quarterly*, Vol. 23 (winter 2000), p. 80.

31. Ibid., pp. 87–8.

32. Quoted in *United Nations Peacekeeping Missions and Their Proliferation*. Hearing before the Subcommittee on International Operations of the Committee on Foreign Relations, United States Senate, 106th Cong., 2nd Sess., 5 April 2000 (Washington, DC: Government Printing Office, 2000), p. 4.

33. Edward C. Luck, 'The Case for Engagement: American Interests in UN Peace Operations', in Donald C.F. Daniel and Bradd C. Hayes (eds), *Beyond Traditional Peacekeeping* (New York: St Martin's Press, 1995), pp. 76–9.

34. Christopher Layne, 'Minding Our Own Business: The Case for American Non-Participation in International Peacekeeping Operations', in Daniel and Hayes, *Beyond Traditional Peacekeeping*, p. 87.

35. Ibid., pp. 90–1.

36. See Eric A. Nordlinger, *Isolationism Reconfigured: American Foreign Policy for a New Century* (Princeton, NJ: Princeton University Press, 1995), esp. Chapter 3.

37. MacKinnon, *The Evolution of US Peacekeeping Policy Under Clinton*, p. 42.

38. The literature on bureaucratic politics is voluminous, to include the classics such as Graham T. Allison, *Essence of Decision* (Boston, MA: Little, Brown & Co., 1971) and Graham T. Allison and Morton Halperin, 'Bureaucratic Politics: A Paradigm and some Policy Implications', *World Politics*, Vol. 24 (1972), pp. 40–79, the critiques of the model, including Jonathan Bender and Thomas Hammond, 'Rethinking Allison's Models', *The American Political Science Review*, Vol. 86 (1992), pp. 301–22; Steven Krasner, 'Are Bureaucracies Important? (or Allison Wonderland)', *Foreign Policy*, Vol. 7 (1972), pp. 159–79; and Edward Rhodes, 'Do Bureaucratic Politics Matter? Some Disconfirming Findings from the Case of the US Navy', *World Politics*, Vol. 47 (October 1994), pp. 1–41, and applications, including Lauren Holland, 'The US Decision to Launch Operation Desert Storm: A Bureaucratic Politics Analysis', *Armed Forces and Society*, Vol. 25 (winter 2000), pp. 219–42; David S. Sorenson, *Shutting Down the Cold War: The Politics of Military Base Closure* (New York: St Martin's Press, 1998), and James H. Lebovic, *Foregone Conclusions: U.S. Weapons Acquisition in the Post-Cold War Transition* (Boulder, CO: Westview Press, 1996).

39. Stephen Peter Rosen, *Winning the Next War: Innovation and the Modern Military* (Ithaca, NY: Cornell University Press, 1991), p. 2.

40. There are obviously other agencies involved in peacekeeping operations, to include the National Security Council. But State and Defense are the lead agencies and clearly the most influential in the peacekeeping decisional process.

41. For example, Secretary of State John Foster Dulles was more willing to send US military to support the French in Indochina in 1954 than were the Joints Chiefs of Staff, and Chairman of the Joint Chiefs General Colin Powell called for sanctions against Iraq while Secretary of State James Baker argued in favor of combat forces.

42. The Army resisted 'special operations', particularly as national leadership applied then to Vietnam. See Andrew F. Krepinevich, Jr, *The Army and Vietnam* (Baltimore, MD: The Johns Hopkins University Press, 1986).

43. Tonyn Langford, 'Orchestrating Peace Operations: The PDD-56 Process', *Security Dialog*, Vol. 30 (March 1999), p. 144.

44. David C. Hendrickson, *Reforming Defense: The State of Civil–Military Relations.* (Baltimore, MD: The Johns Hopkins University Press, 1988), pp. 35–6.

45. This was aptly demonstrated when the Chairman of the Joint Chiefs of Staff insisted that US peacekeepers in Bosnia should receive protection by hundreds of M1-A1 heavy tanks, although how such tanks might protect peacekeepers from the most likely source of danger, snipers and landmines, was never explained.

46. 'Shinseki: Division Readiness Problems Due to Deployments', *Defense Daily*, 204 (12 November 1999), p. 1.

47. 'US Army, Marines to Gauge Deployment Cost', *Defense News* (17 July 2000).

48. 'Keeping the Balkans Simple', *European Stars and Stripes* (10 July 2000).

49. *Department of Defense Authorization for Appropriations for Fiscal Year 1999 and the Future Years Defense Program.* Hearings before the Committee on Armed Services, US Senate, 105th Congress, 2nd Sess. Washington, GPO (1999), p. 104.

50. Michael M. Green, 'Keeping the Peace Jointly', *Proceedings of the United States Naval Institute*, Vol. 125 (September 1999), p. 90. Critics of this position might argue that peacekeeping missions do resemble low-level combat conditions, and may be the best approximation to realistic training that the military gets in peacetime.

51. 'Differences with U.N. Arise on Part US Will Play in Somalia', *The Wall Street Journal* (14 December 1992); 'U.N. Wants Somalia Disarmed Before US Leaves', *New York Times* (11 December 1992).

52. 'For Marine Corps, Somalia Operation Offers New Esprit', *Washington Post* (6 December 1992).

53. 'Somalia to Impact Debate on Reshaping US Forces', *Aviation Week & Space Technology* (December 1992), pp. 14–21, 23.

54. MacKinnon, *The Evolution of US Peacekeeping Under Clinton*, p. 49.

55. 'Low Morale Saps UN Military Might', *Christian Science Monitor* (8 September 2000), p. 3.

56. See 'A Four-Star Foreign Policy? US Commanders Wield Rising Clout, Autonomy', *Washington Post* (28 September 2000).

57. Deborah D. Avant, 'Are the Reluctant Warriors Out of Control? Why the US Military is Averse to Responding to Post-Cold War Low-Level Threats', *Security Studies*, Vol. 6 (winter 1996/97), p. 67.

58. Message from SecDef, R262216Z, 27 June 2000, Subj: Enhanced International Peacekeeping Capabilities (EIPC), p. 1.

59. Ibid.
60. Seth Appiah-Mensah, 'Lessons from Liberia', *Proceedings of the United States Naval Institute*, Vol. 126 (March 2000), pp. 66–8.
61. 'G.I.'s to be Sent to Train Africans for Sierra Leone', *New York Times* (9 August 2000).
62. 'Special Forces Teach Peace Support Skills', *Jane's Defence Weekly* (23 May 2001).
63. Lyle Goldstein, 'General John Shalikashvili and the Civil–Military Relations of Peacekeeping', *Armed Forces & Society*, Vol. 26 (spring 2000), p. 404.
64. Harold Kennedy, 'Elite Fighters Turn to Peacekeeping', *National Defense*, Vol. 84 (February 2000), pp. 19–21.
65. Chris Maddaloni, 'A Bigger Piece of Peacekeeping', *National Guard*, Vol. 54 (January 2000), pp. 18–20.
66. 'Army will give National Guard the Entire US Role in Bosnia', *New York Times* (5 December 2000).
67. 'National Guard Unit Adds Dimension to a Peacekeeper Role', *New York Times* (18 June 2000). Such missions also bring resource benefits to guard units. Guard commanders previously complained that without specific missions, the Guard fell below regular military units in funding priorities. See 'Army Weighs an Expanded Role For National Guard Combat Units', *New York Times* (4 August 2000).
68. 'Change of Peace', *Dallas Morning News* (9 July 2000).
69. See 'Misconduct, Corruption by US Police Mar Bosnia Mission', *Washington Post* (29 May 2001).
70. See ibid. DynCorp Technical Services, based in Texas, recruited the civilian police. The misconduct included sexual assaults and accepting financial favors from local officials. Some officials believe that the problems occurred partially due to US inexperience in national policing (the US has no national police like the French Gendarmerie or the Italian Carabinieri) and the refusal by US police forces to send regular police officers from their forces.
71. 'U.S. Deploys Warship in East Timor', *New York Times* (15 September 2000). The forces were not a part of the UN peacekeeping force then in East Timor, and operated independently of the UN administration there.
72. Christopher M. Jones, 'The Foreign Policy Bureaucracy in a New Era', in James M. Scott (ed.), *After the End: Making US Foreign Policy in the Post-Cold War World* (Durham, NC: Duke University Press, 1998), p. 59.
73. Michael Mandelbaum, 'A Perfect Failure', *Foreign Affairs*, Vol. 78 (September/ October 1999), p. 7.
74. United States Department of State, Office of Resources, Plans, and Policy, *Congressional Presentation for Foreign Operations, Fiscal Year 2001* (Washington, DC: Government Printing Office, March 2000).
75. See Robert B. Zoellick, 'Congress and the Making of U.S. Foreign Policy', *Survival*, Vol. 41 (winter 1999/2000), pp. 20–41.
76. *Department of Defense Authorization for Appropriations for Fiscal Year 1999 and the Future Years Defense Program*. Hearings before the Committee on Armed Services, United States Senate, Part I, 105th Cong., 2nd Sess. (Washington, DC: 1998), p. 55.
77. 'The Question at the Hearing: How Do We Get Out?', *Congressional Quarterly Weekly Report* (19 December 1992), p. 3890.
78. MacKinnon, *The Evolution of US Peacekeeping Under Clinton*, p. 70.

79. *Congressional Record* (Senate), 23 May 2000, p. S4243. The US has not directly participated in this mission.
80. 'U.N. Debacle in Sierra Leone Reduces Clinton's Leverage for More Peacekeeping Funds', *CQ Weekly*, Vol. 58 (13 May 2000), p. 1132.
81. *United Nations Peacekeeping: The Legal Framework*. Hearing before the Legislation and National Security Subcommittee of the Committee on Government Operations, House of Representatives, 103rd Congress, 2nd Sess., 3 March 1994 (Washington, DC: Government Printing Office, 1994), p. 5.
82. *Congressional Record*, 11 May 2000, p. S3906.
83. Speech of Hon. Maxine Waters of California in the House of Representatives, Monday, 26 June 2000, Congressional Record: 28 June 2000 (Extensions), p. E1137.
84. *Congressional Record* (House), 12 July 2000, p. H5951.
85. Serafino, 'Peacekeeping: Issues of US Military Involvement', p. 6.
86. 'Re Somalia: How Much did TV Shape Policy?' *New York Times* (8 December 1992).
87. Lawrence Freedman, 'The Changing Forms of Military Conflict', *Survival*, Vol. 40 (winter 1998–99), p. 52.
88. John Gerard Ruggie, 'The Past as Prologue: Interests, Identity, and American Foreign Policy', *International Security*, Vol. 21 (spring 1997), p. 91.

SEVEN

Austria

Erwin A. Schmidl[1]

INTRODUCTION

Since 1960 more than 50,000 Austrians have taken part in international peace operations, and politicians and diplomats are quick to point to this proud record as a sign of Austria fulfilling its responsibilities in the international community. For the military, participation in peace operations has become the foremost mission of the Austrian Armed Forces.[2] This chapter illustrates the development of Austrian participation in international missions during these four decades, from the medical contingent in the Congo in 1960–63, to the many and highly diversified missions today.[3] The chapter also discusses the role that internal Austrian politics plays in decisions on peacekeeping.

THE EARLY DAYS OF UN MEMBERSHIP

After World War II, the four Allied Powers occupied Austria until 1955. During these years, maintaining the unity of the country (unlike divided Germany) and regaining its sovereignty were the most important aims of Austrian foreign policy.[4] After this, with Austrian foreign policy formulated for the better part of three decades by Bruno Kreisky (as Deputy Minister, then Minister for Foreign Affairs from 1953 to 1966, and Chancellor from 1970 to 1983), active participation in the international arena was perceived as the best foreign policy option for a small country, especially in an exposed strategic position like Austria, right on the 'Iron Curtain'. Therefore, it is not surprising that Austria, after having sworn to 'neutrality based on the Swiss model' in the spring of 1955 as a precondition of the State Treaty of that year,[5] deviated from that model before Christmas by joining the United Nations Organization.

In 1957 Austria achieved a remarkable success when the new International Atomic Energy Agency (IAEA) accepted Austria's invitation to locate its headquarters in Vienna. This was the first step toward establishing Vienna as the 'third UN city', together with New York and Geneva. In 1961 and 1963, UN conferences dealing with diplomatic and consular relations were held in Vienna, followed in 1968 and 1969 by the UN conferences on space exploration, road transport, and treaty law. In 1966, the new United Nations Industrial Development Organization (UNIDO) also opened its headquarters in Vienna. The Vienna UN Complex (known locally as the 'UN City') was handed over to the UN in 1979 with extraterritorial status and now houses both the IAEA and UNIDO, as well as other UN organizations. It is a visible symbol of Austria's active participation in the UN.

The UN operation in the Congo in 1960 provided Austria with a further opportunity to gain credibility within the organization. This was especially important in the summer of 1960. After Italy rejected Austrian interference in the 'inner Italian' question of the rights of the German-speaking population in South Tyrol, Foreign Minister Bruno Kreisky wanted to 'internationalize' the issue by bringing the matter before the General Assembly in autumn 1960. The ensuing negotiations carried out at the behest of the UN eventually became the basis for the 'package' solution for South Tyrol.[6]

THE CONGO OPERATION

The question of Austrian participation in the Congo operation was first raised in July 1960 in discussions between Austrian diplomats and the Secretariat in New York. Shortly after, the UN formally requested Austria to provide a field post office and a hygiene team, as well as a field hospital with 400 beds. However, although the idea had been initiated by the Austrian Foreign Ministry, it was not clear to what extent Austria as a neutral state could participate in a UN operation, and Austrian laws did not allow units to be sent abroad. Therefore, it was only after lengthy discussions that the Austrian government decided to comply with the United Nations' request. Although the Minister of Transport rejected the request for a field post office, the Ministry of Defence set up the 'UN Medical Contingent of the Republic of Austria'. This contingent was not an existing army unit but was raised on a voluntary basis. Only 15 years after the end of World War II, many Austrians were highly sceptical of such an operation and the 'absolutely voluntary nature' of participation was emphasized to ensure popular acceptance.

Of course, Austria had waited so long before answering the UN request that other states – India and Italy in particular – had also promised medical support in the meantime. The UN therefore reduced its original request to a hospital with 100 beds, and the Austrian contingent eventually consisted only of a 50-strong medical unit, deployed in five rotations from December 1960 to 1963.[7]

The unit's deployment started with a serious incident that was an acid test of Austria's overall willingness to participate in UN operations: in Bukavu, the unit was taken prisoner by Congolese forces who claimed they were Belgians in disguise, and had to be freed by force by a Nigerian UN unit. Fortunately, in the 'battle of Bukavu' no Austrian lives were lost (one Nigerian soldier was killed, however, as were a dozen Congolese), but all equipment was lost, and back home there were even demands that the operation be broken off. But Foreign Minister Kreisky won the day, persuading the reluctant Minister of Defence Ferdinand Graf that the 'serious loss of prestige ... if Austria were now to withdraw its help in Congo ... would be an unimaginable embarrassment for the Austrian Army and for Austria'.[8]

The first Austrian UN medical contingent stayed in the Congo, catering to refugees in Kasai province, and returned to Vienna at the end of May 1961. As the UN Congo operation continued, a new contingent (with new equipment) was dispatched in July 1961 for six months. When its tour ended, new volunteers replaced only about half the personnel while the remainder stayed on. This principle of replacing not the whole unit but only a part was due to a lack of personnel and not the result of planning. All the same, it proved very successful because it allowed greater continuity in the field. In similar form, it is still applied in longer missions today.

After the last Austrian volunteer had returned from the Congo, Foreign Minister Kreisky said in a speech to Parliament on 10 December 1963 that 'this Congo contingent has brought great honour to Austria's name and, what is even more important, has helped tens of thousands of poor people who are plagued by terrible diseases regain their health, in some cases, even saving their lives'.[9] Referring to Austria's membership of the United Nations, Minister of Defence Graf said in 1961, 'it is impossible to conclude agreements and enter into obligations on paper, without being willing to fulfil them. Such action would seriously endanger the prestige that our country has worked so hard to build up abroad.'[10]

CYPRUS AND THE LAW OF 1965

Austrian participation in the Congo operation ended in 1963 and the UN mission there came to an end one year later. However, this was certainly not the end of Austrian peacekeeping. Quite the contrary! Because the Austrians had acquired a good reputation in the Congo, the UN once more approached Austria in 1964 with the request to contribute an infantry battalion of between 700 and 800 men to the new operation that was just beginning on Cyprus. However, Austria was reluctant to deploy an armed battalion, as there was still no legal basis for such a step. Instead, Austria once more offered to send a field hospital with a staff of 54, and also fulfilled another UN request for civilian police.

This shows another important element (again, not planned but developed by chance) of Austrian participation in peace operations. Not only were all personnel volunteers – and are to this day – but the gradual move, from a field hospital (1960) to police (1964), and then military observers (1967) and one (1972), then two, infantry battalions (1973), made it easier for the population to accept this involvement. Acceptance would have been much harder to obtain had a combat unit been sent out at the beginning. The Austrian police contingent remained on Cyprus until 1977.

The conclusion of agreements between the UN and the troop-contributing states concerning the legal status of the contingents on Cyprus in summer 1964 once more raised the question of the status of the Austrian units. As had been the case with the Congo operation, the government had improvised. As the constitution made no provision for the deployment of Austrian military units outside Austria, the volunteers were granted special leave for the duration of their UN mission and simultaneously re-employed with new contracts. This unsatisfactory situation was only remedied by the Foreign Service Act of 30 June 1965 that regulated the secondment of Austrian units to render assistance abroad at the request of international organizations.[11] This remained the legal foundation for Austrian participation in international missions until 1997. According to the 1965 Act, participation in international missions requires the consent of the government as well as the main committee of Parliament (this did not change with the new law of 1997).

What is the standard procedure leading to Austrian participation in a mission? Normally, the UN Secretariat (or whichever authority is organizing a peace operation) informally contacts the Austrian Ministry of Foreign Affairs through the Permanent Mission in New York. After discussions between the ministries concerned (say, Foreign Affairs and Defence, or the Interior Ministry in the case of police, and the Finance

Ministry for the necessary financial arrangements), an informal answer is given to the international organization as to whether and how Austria would be prepared to participate in this operation. Only then comes the formal request, which is, again, discussed on the civil-servant level before being passed on to the government (i.e., the ministers' council) and, usually a week later, to the main committee of Parliament. The same procedure applies for the extension of a mandate, resulting in quite a heavy load of bureaucratic work for all those involved. In most cases, there is little discussion at this stage, as all important arrangements have already been made at civil-servant level before the matter comes up to the ministers' council or Parliament. There were exceptions, however: in the early 1990s, for example, Finance Minister Ferdinand Lacina (a Socialist of the old 68er's mentality, and strictly anti-NATO) opposed the extension of Austria's Cyprus participation at least once out of anti-NATO feelings, necessitating another last-minute round of inter-ministry discussions before the matter could be brought before the ministers' council.[12] In 2001, when the government decided to withdraw the Austrian contingents from Bosnia and from Cyprus for financial reasons, there was an unusually heated debate in the main committee about this decision, but, again, this was the exception rather than the rule.

THE FIRST BATTALIONS

The 1965 Foreign Service Act also formed the basis for the establishment of an Austrian UN battalion to be made available to the United Nations on a stand-by basis on the Scandinavian model. This 600-man reserve battalion was raised by an order issued on 1 September 1965. The first exercises took place in Vienna on 24 and 25 March 1966. The battalion exercised regularly in the years that followed but was never called up for service. There seemed little likelihood of a new UN operation, and the probability that the Austrian battalion would be called upon to replace an existing UN contingent was also low. In addition, the Defence Ministry was hardly unanimous in its enthusiasm for Austrian participation in UN operations. While young officers who had volunteered for UN operations hoped to be deployed soon, General Otto Seitz expressed his concern about personnel shortages in July 1967. In the event of this battalion being deployed, 'some 400 full-time officers and other ranks would have to go too', he said.[13] This would have been particularly difficult in the late 1960s because in 1967 the Austrian army was called upon to help monitor the Italian border to prevent cross-border support for insurgents in South

Tyrol, and in 1968 the Warsaw Pact invasion of Czechoslovakia demonstrated Austria's exposed position at the Iron Curtain.

Although the Austrian battalion remained as a 'stand-by' unit for the UN, the 1967 'Six Day War' in the Middle East led to the increase of the UN Truce Supervision Organization (UNTSO), and Austrian officers served for the first time as military observers.[14]

An Austrian battalion was finally deployed in UN service in 1972 after Ireland reduced the size of its contingent on Cyprus from 400 to 100. Moreover, Kurt Waldheim, the new Secretary General, who took up office on 1 January 1972, was an Austrian. Waldheim immediately enquired whether Austria would agree to send a battalion to Cyprus. While the Ministry of Defence said such a mission was almost irresponsible, considering the personnel shortages in the armed forces, it also recognized the political arguments for the mission. It would have been extremely inappropriate to reject such a request from an Austrian secretary general. At the same time, preparing the UN reserve battalion for seven years and then rejecting an opportunity for deployment when it arose was also inconceivable. On 8 February, the cabinet therefore decided to agree to any request made by the UN, and a week later the formal request was submitted.

The establishment of the new UN battalion began on 2 March 1972, using the personnel who had already undergone training with the stand-by battalion. The advance party reached Cyprus on 24 March, and on 3 May 1972, the 238-man Austrian battalion assumed full responsibility for the Paphos district in the west of the island. In October 1973, after the Yom Kippur War, more than half of this battalion was flown to Egypt as part of the new (Second) UN Emergency Force (UNEF II).[15] Eventually, both units were reinforced,[16] and in 1974 the Austrian battalion in Egypt was transferred to the Golan Heights in Syria as part of the new UN Disengagement Observer Force (UNDOF), where it still serves to this day. Within a few months, Austrian participation in UN operations had doubled to two battalions, and actually increased fourfold within two years from the pre-1972 status.

It was during the build-up phase of these new operations that Austria suffered its first losses in the service of United Nations peacekeeping. Early in 1974, a non-commissioned officer was injured when he drove his Land Rover over a landmine. His lower leg had to be amputated. Shortly after completion of the transfer to the Golan Heights, four young soldiers died in a landmine accident on 25 June 1974. And on 14 August 1974, during the second phase of the Turkish invasion of Cyprus, three Austrian soldiers were killed near Goshi when a Turkish fighter jet mistook their

Land Rover for a Greek Cypriot vehicle, and dropped napalm on them. These events were received as a shock in Austria, but remarkably the determination to continue the engagement in UN operations was never in doubt, despite occasional complaints about the UN in general, and its tardiness in refunding expenses incurred in peace operations in particular.[17] This shows that by then participation in peace operations was already accepted as 'normal' by the population. Altogether, 45 Austrians have lost their lives 'in the service of peace' since 1974.[18]

THE 1970s AND THE 1980s

At the end of 1973, nearly 900 Austrian soldiers were serving in UN operations, so that by the mid-1970s Austria was one of the most important troop-contributing countries. This commitment was certainly a contributing factor to Austria's nomination for a non-permanent seat on the Security Council in 1973–74. Also in 1974 an Austrian was appointed to command a UN force for the very first time.[19] Both on Cyprus and on the Golan Heights, Austrian commissioned and non-commissioned officers were assigned to headquarters in various functions.

One might mention at this point that Austria continued its engagement in the eastern Mediterranean after the end of the Cold War. It also used the operations on Cyprus and the Golan Heights as an opportunity for cooperation with its neighbours. A Hungarian contingent was integrated into the Austrian battalion on Cyprus in 1995 and a Slovenian contingent in 1998. (In 2001, when the Austrians withdrew from Cyprus, the Slovenes withdrew too, but the Hungarian company remains within the Slovak battalion that took over from the Austrians.) On the Golan Heights, a Slovak contingent (a platoon at first, and then a company) was also integrated into the Austrian battalion in 1998.

In the 1970s, Austria was careful not to become involved in operations that were set up under dubious circumstances. A case in point was the UN operation in southern Lebanon authorized by the UN Security Council in 1978. To Secretary General Waldheim's disappointment, the government in Vienna rejected his request for a third UN battalion because there was no clear mandate, the parties to the conflict had only a limited will to enforce the ceasefire, and it was not really possible to control all the factions. Austria insisted that all parties to the conflict agree to the stationing of a UN force. In view of the many local warlords in south Lebanon, this was impossible.

In the early 1980s renewed East–West tensions meant that the UN played less of an active peacekeeping role than in the 1970s. There was no new large-scale UN operation during this period, but two smaller military observer missions were established after 1984 to monitor the ceasefire lines between Iraq and Iran, and the border between Afghanistan and Pakistan, and Austria contributed to both of them. One could describe Austrian 'peacekeeping policy' of this time as the wish to be present in as many operations as possible, although this was not really a formulated policy (apart from a general wish to be present in the international field). Within the Foreign Ministry, some of the diplomats (notably those with experience in the UN context who saw the multilateral field with more open eyes than their colleagues from the bilateral departments) advocated an intensification of Austrian peacekeeping involvement, while others remained sceptical about the *real* benefits of the United Nations in a world still dominated by the Cold War. After the changes of 1989–90, the UN's reputation grew for some time, which rather strengthened the aim to have Austria figuring in the troop contributors' lists of as many operations as possible, even where only with a few observers or police. Indeed, the early 1990s witnessed the 'mushrooming' phase of UN peace operations, with Austrian military or civilian observers, police officers or medics taking part in most missions established after the Cold War.[20]

'DIVERSIFICATION' OR 'MUSHROOMING' OF UN MISSIONS

This phase of increased participation began with Austria contributing 50 police to the UN Transition Assistance Group (UNTAG) to oversee the transfer of the former German colony South West Africa, which was still administered by South Africa under a League of Nations mandate, to attain its independence as Namibia in 1990.

Following Iraq's invasion of Kuwait in 1990, Austria had at first considered sending a medical unit to the Gulf, but the government finally decided not to participate in the Second Gulf War for reasons of 'neutrality'. Not only the Social Democrats, but also their Conservative partners in government (at that time, the Chancellor was Socialist, and both Foreign and Defence Ministers were Conservatives) were still tightly glued to the Cold War ideas of 'neutrality' between the blocs, failing to realize that 'neutrality' had lost its meaning in the case of the world acting as one against Iraq.[21] Apart from the Socialists, the Green Party adamantly opposed any support for the coalition forces, and peace activists tried to block the transport of US armed recovery vehicles across Austrian territory. Many people were shocked that a 'hot' war was being fought just after the end of the Cold War, thus abruptly ending all hopes that Big Peace had finally broken out.

Austria's strange 'neutralist' policy actually contradicted the attitude it adopted in the framework of the UN where Austria was, in 1991–92, for the second time a member of the UN Security Council, and the Austrian permanent representative had taken over the presidency of the sanctions committee monitoring the embargo against Iraq in January 1991. Austria did participate, however, in those UN operations to stabilize the situation after the end of the campaign in 1991. These included the United Nations Iraq–Kuwait Observation Mission (UNIKOM) to monitor the Iraqi-Kuwaiti frontier (an Austrian, Major-General G. Greindl, was the first Chief Observer),[22] the United Nations Special Commission (UNSCOM) to destroy Iraqi nuclear, biological and chemical weapons of mass destruction, the deployment of an Austrian field hospital (under UNHCR auspices) to assist Kurdish refugees in Iran, and the less successful experiment to deploy UN Guards to protect organizations providing aid to refugees in Iraq.

In view of the United Nations' apparently regained strength after the end of the East–West conflict, which was demonstrated in the Kuwait conflict, and because the operation in Namibia was generally considered to have been successful, new and more ambitious UN operations were set up in Western Sahara, Cambodia, Somalia and elsewhere in the early 1990s. To most of these, Austria contributed small numbers of military and police personnel, as well as civilian election monitors. Early proposals to second a larger number of troops to the UN force in Cambodia (Austria had earlier been involved as a mediator in the Cambodian peace process) were rejected, as the climatic conditions would have required a long period of training and special equipment.

TO SOMALIA? OR SOUTHEASTERN EUROPE?

The military at that time had already established a long tradition of taking part in peace operations, and many officers saw international missions in a more positive light than had been the case a generation earlier. There was some agreement among those concerned with international missions, however, that larger missions (involving troop contingents as opposed to a handful of observers) should preferably be not too far away and not in extreme climatic conditions, for obvious logistical reasons. Although this was never advertised as a fixed rule, troop contingents should be limited to theatres within a certain distance, including Europe and the Middle East, as well as parts of Africa, about as far south as Somalia.

Austria considered contributing a battalion of mechanized infantry to the operation there, and had already informally agreed to do so. The operation is now generally regarded as a failure, but in 1993 it was seen as a major challenge, and indeed chance, for the UN. Due to internal political differences between the more active foreign and defence ministers (both of them headed by conservatives in the then 'great coalition' government of the day), and the reluctant and less international-minded chancellor and finance minister (both social democrats), Austrian participation in the Somalia venture was eventually limited to a few military observers.[23] However, that disagreement was not so much about the mission itself (this was discussed mainly at lower levels of the hierarchy, where sound reasons were put forward both for and against participation), but the issue became 'hostage' to the – by then – already strong tensions within the government.[24]

Part of the reasoning behind possible participation in Somalia was that many in the military were less than happy with the fact that two battalions had been 'tied down' in conventional, very static peace operations since the early 1970s. Austria wanted to participate in more active missions as well, but the military realized that it would be difficult to send a third battalion-sized unit out for longer periods. Experience shows that it is hard to find enough qualified personnel, especially for some specialist positions, while relying on volunteers to go on missions.[25] In these circumstances, Somalia was considered a good possibility for taking part in a more active (yet short) mission, at the same time preparing for an eventual withdrawal of the battalion from Cyprus (which could then be justified by pointing to the additional battalion serving in Somalia). More than the Golan mission, the Cyprus operation was always contested for political as well as for military reasons: it was seen as 'freezing' an uneasy armistice rather than contributing to a permanent solution to the conflict, and had gained the reputation of a 'sunshine mission', also referred to as 'Club Med peacekeeping' or 'beach-keeping' rather than peacekeeping. That the Cyprus mission is, in reality, far from easy, and that some soldiers who have taken part in both described Cyprus as more demanding than Kosovo or Bosnia, unfortunately had little influence on negative stereotyping. In UN circles, too, Austrians were sometimes accused of doing only the 'easy missions', so the wish to participate in other operations having more of an 'enforcement' character was understandable. Eventually, though, it was in operations closer to home that the opportunity to do so arose.

When the disintegration of Yugoslavia began in 1991, the war in Slovenia directly affected Austria, and the army was called upon to protect the border and prevent border violations. However, Austria at first refrained from a more active participation in the efforts by the international community to intervene in the conflict. The parties to the conflict considered Austria anything but 'neutral' due to the Habsburgs' historical role there, and to Austria's open support for the secession of Slovenia and Croatia. Austria lent logistical support to the EC/EU and UN observers and troops from the beginning, but only took an active part beginning in 1994, first with observers, and then with a transport unit for the NATO-led peace Implementation Force (IFOR) and its successor SFOR (Stabilization Force) from 1996 to 2001. From 1995, Austria also sent police to the various police missions run by the UN, EU, WEU or OSCE.

THE 1997 LAW

During the 1990s, the new political situation after the end of the Cold War opened the way for a new and long-overdue political debate about Austria's future military and security policies. Mistaking 'neutrality' for a guarantee for peace, many Austrians were sceptical about joining NATO (which had not been possible during the Cold War when the Soviet Union watched closely to prevent any too pro-Western stance), and the social democrats were quick to adopt these ideas for their platform.[26] The conservatives, as well as the 'Freedom Party' (which is not a liberal party as such, but defies traditional right–left stereotypes, being populist with a nationalistic, sometimes openly xenophobic touch), were more open (but still divided) on these issues, and so far Austria had stuck to its traditional 'non-alignment' (a better term than 'neutrality'). Partly because of this political dispute, the social democrats had blocked all attempts to modify the 1965 Foreign Service Act in the early 1990s.[27] Only in 1997 did this position change, when a former Austrian social democratic chancellor, Franz Vranitzky, was appointed as OSCE representative during the Albanian crisis of 1997, when administration and security in Albania broke down in the wake of the fraudulent 'pyramid games' scandal. To support him, Austria contributed a company (ranger-trained) to the Multinational Protection Force (Operation 'Alba') organized by Italy, but this required a new law which was duly passed in early 1997.[28] The new 'Cooperation and Solidarity Act' (KSE-BVG) offers greater flexibility (such as allowing limited participation in disaster relief operations without prior consultation in Parliament), and also includes participation in non-UN multinational peace operations.[29] As the OSCE mission to Albania allowed the former socialist chancellor to 'play a role' in the international arena, the Socialists had a vested interest in agreeing to the new law.

An interesting change of attitude took place in the military in the 1990s. Until then, UN missions were seen as the realm of the few, with participation limited to officers and NCOs who were idealistic and enthusiastic to go on missions abroad. Those who participated were denounced by those who stayed at home as people going on well-paid holidays instead of doing their proper jobs.[30] UN peace operations were seen as hardly compatible with the prime task of the military, i.e. national defence. True, these attitudes had already started to change from the 1970s, but it was only with the new post-Cold War situation and with the new missions of the 1990s that a new enthusiasm for international missions grew. UN peace operations were still considered 'out' by some, but NATO peace support operations were definitely not. Within a few years, participation in international missions became the prime task of the Austrian Armed Forces, with national defence and assistance to the civil power taking second place only.[31] In 1999, the new Austrian International Peace Support Command (brigade level) was established at Götzendorf barracks in lower Austria (southeast of Vienna), and it is probable that with the new army structure this will be upgraded to a two-star command.

In addition, the participation of police officers in peace operations increased to over 100, leading to problems of recruitment and selection. Like the military, the Austrian police – both the grey-uniformed *gendarmerie* which is responsible for organizing the international missions, and the green-uniformed police – have acquired an excellent reputation in peace missions and are involved in training programmes for police in various countries.[32] Austria also was involved in several programmes to (re-)train police from Bosnia and Herzegovina, as well as Albania and Kosovo.

Another feature of the multidimensional missions of the 1990s was the role of civilian specialists, both for election monitoring and for other tasks. Austria contributed personnel, because of different legal arrangements, to many of these missions, and in 1993 started training courses for civilian functions in peace operations at the Peace Institute at Castle Schlaining in the Burgenland. In the second half of 1998, during its EU presidency, Austria contributed the command staff and some 70 personnel to the European Community Monitor Mission in the Balkans (ECMM, since renamed EUMM).[33]

THE KOSOVO OPERATIONS

When the Kosovo crisis erupted in 1999, Austria, invoking 'neutrality' despite its EU membership and its own strong anti–Serb attitude, did not take part in 'Allied Force', the air campaign against Yugoslavia. The paradoxical situation of consenting to the NATO air strikes within the political framework of the EU, while at the same time refusing NATO permission to pass through Austrian air space, was hardly understood abroad. The decision, though, had much more to do with the discussions about Austria's future defence and security policy (with a significant part of the Socialist Party's leadership still advocating neutrality), than it did with peace operations *per se*.

Austria contributed to the international relief efforts in Albania, and then took part in the international peace operations in Kosovo with both a military and a police contingent. As before in the case of the NATO-led missions in Bosnia, public opinion was quite positive, despite more divided response to 'Allied Force'. The Austrian mechanized infantry battalion, equipped with Steyr 'Pandur' armoured personnel carriers (and incorporating a Swiss company as well as a Bulgarian and a Slovak contingent), forms part of the German brigade. Its base in Suva Reka is known as 'Camp Casablanca'.

In order to facilitate preparations for future missions, Austria also participates in the UN system of 'stand-by arrangements', in which states inform the United Nations in advance which units could be deployed at short notice. To ensure faster mobilization, in 1996 Denmark initiated the concept of the Stand-by High Readiness Brigade (SHIRBRIG), in which Austria also participates. This framework was utilized for the first time by the UN in 2000 to help organize the UN Mission in Ethiopia and Eritrea. Along similar lines, to improve troop preparations for peace missions, Austria initiated the Central European Nations' Cooperation in Peace Support (CENCOOP) in 1998. Participating nations include Austria, Hungary, Romania, Slovakia, Slovenia and Switzerland.

In May 1993, the government decided to create an organizational framework for the provision of up to 2,500 soldiers and 50 police officers for international missions. By the end of the 1990s up to 1,500 Austrians were serving in missions abroad at any given time. In November 2000, in the context of preparations for the planned EU crisis reaction forces, Austria expressed its willingness to provide an organizational framework for up to 3,500 soldiers and 110 police officers for such operations. Currently, at any given time, Austria can deploy up to 2,000 soldiers abroad.

Recruiting the necessary number of volunteers for these missions remains a problem. In previous missions, it was not always easy to recruit sufficient personnel, but for the time being, the volunteer principle will be maintained. While this makes planning more difficult and requires greater personnel reserves, it also ensures the high level of motivation among Austrian peacekeepers. Between two-thirds and three-quarters of all Austrian soldiers serving on missions abroad are reservists. Their age and greater civilian experience means that they are more suitable for peace missions than younger professional soldiers whose military training does not always prepare them adequately for the mental stress of peace operations. The difficulties faced by certain states in recent years are clear evidence of this. The high standard of Austrian training has been demonstrated in international operations, even if improvements could still be made in certain areas.

The Austrian Ministry of Defence calls up military personnel to volunteer for international service. In the 1990s, the Austrian military became increasingly involved in international missions, and existing units in Austria serve as parent units for contingents serving abroad. For example, the Austrian battalion sent to Kosovo as part of KFOR was prepared by a Styrian unit, the 17 Rifle Battalion in Strass. To enable it to respond faster when new missions come up, the Austrian Army devised the PREPUN system of pre-established unit modules. PREPUN is now to be replaced by the 'Forces for International Operations' system.

Taking part in international missions has become increasingly important, but it soon became clear that financial resources are far too restricted to fulfil all political and diplomatic wishes. Therefore, in 2000 the Ministry of Defence decided to withdraw Austrian troop contingents from Cyprus and from Bosnia and Herzegovina by 2001.[34] In the case of Cyprus, this meant the end of an Austrian presence going back to 1964. Austrian battalions continue to serve on the Golan Heights (with UNDOF) and in Kosovo (with KFOR), as do military observers in other missions. In 2002, partly to signal commitment to the West after the attacks of September 2001, a platoon was sent to the International Security Assistance Force (ISAF) in Afghanistan, forming part of the German contingent there. For the police, Kosovo and Bosnia and Herzegovina remain the most important operations.

With the international situation as it is, peace operations will remain in demand for a long time. For Austria, active participation in these missions has been an important aspect of its foreign policy – and there is no reason to change this line. Contributing to international solidarity helps to re-establish or preserve stability and is thus of benefit to the contributing countries as well. Over the past years, Austria has increasingly committed itself to the new operations in Southeastern Europe. In the future, Austrian foreign and security policy will have to set priorities for international missions, taking into account the special commitments entailed by EU membership as well as the need to take part in more dangerous operations for reasons of international solidarity. To fulfil these increased tasks, it will also be necessary to provide greater financial, material and personnel resources than hitherto.

NOTES

1. This chapter was written in the author's private capacity as a scholar and does not necessarily represent an official view of the Austrian Government, the Ministry of Defence, or the Austrian National Defence Academy.
2. Austria still has obligatory national service for all males, although only for the comparatively short period of 8.5 months. For a recent study of Austrian participation in peace operations from a military point of view, see also the Ph.D. dissertation written by Colonel Karl Schmidseder, 'Internationale Interventionen und "Peace Support Operations" – Folgerungen und Aufgaben für Österreich' (University of Vienna, 2001).
3. As this is only a summary, footnotes have been kept to a minimum. For more information, the reader is referred to two books by the same author: *In the Service of Peace: Austrian Participation in Peace Operations since 1960* (Graz: austria-medien-service, 2001) [In English and German]; and *Blaue Helme, Rotes Kreuz: Das österreichische UN-Sanitätskontingent im Kongo, 1960 bis 1963*, Innsbrucker Forschungen zur Zeitgeschichte 13 (Innsbruck and Wien: StudienVerlag, 1995) [*The Austrian Medical Contingent in the Congo*, in German].
4. The standard work on this subject is Gerald Stourzh, *Um Einheit und Freiheit: Staatsvertrag, Neutralität und das Ende der Ost-West-Besetzung Österreichs 1945–1955* (Studien zu Politik und Verwaltung 62, Wien, Köln and Graz: Böhlau, 1998).
5. The 'State Treaty' of Vienna, of 15 May 1955, signed by the four Powers and Austria, re-established Austrian sovereignty, although with some restrictions (most of which were declared obsolete after the end of the Cold War).
6. Officially, both countries declared their differences solved in 1992. Three years later, Austria joined the EU.
7. This is not the place to describe this mission in detail. See Erwin A. Schmidl, 'The Austrian Medical Unit in the Congo, 1960–63: Austria's First Participation in a UN Operation', in *Maintien de la Paix de 1815 à aujourd'hui*, Actes 21 (Ottawa: Commission canadienne d'histoire militaire, 1995), pp. 629–35.
8. As noted in the diary of the Austrian Chief of Staff General Erwin Fussenegger, following a discussion between the two ministers on 9 January 1960. Quoted after Manfried Rauchensteiner, 'Landesverteidigung und Außenpolitik – Feindliche Brüder', in Manfried Rauchensteiner and Wolfgang Etschmann (eds), *Schild ohne Schwert: Das österreichische Bundesheer 1955–1970* (Forschungen zur Militärgeschichte

2, Graz, Wien and Köln: Styria, 1991), pp. 129–71, here 150 (translation by the author).

9. Kreisky in Parliament, 10 December 1963 (*Stenographische Protokolle des Nationalrates* X/38), p. 2074.

10. Defence Minister Graf's reply to an article in the Freedom Party's *Neue Front*, 14 January 1961 (Austrian State Archives Vienna: Archiv der Republik, BMLV, Karton 1830, Zl. 802.284-WPol/60).

11. Bundesverfassungsgesetz vom 30. Juni 1965 über die Entsendung österreichischer Einheiten zur Hilfeleistung in das Ausland auf Ersuchen internationaler Organisationen, BGBl. 173/1965. See Wolfgang Strasser, 'Die Beteiligung Österreichs an internationalen Hilfseinsätzen', in *Österreichische Militärische Zeitschrift*, Vol. 12, No. 6 (November/December 1974), pp. 427–33; and Ivo G. Caytas, *Internationale kollektive Friedenssicherung: zwanzig Jahre österreichischer Praxis. Eine juristische, politische und militärische Studie aktiver Neutralität im Rahmen der Vereinten Nationen* (Schriften des Europäischen Arbeitskreises für Internationales Recht Berlin, o.J.), p. 44f.

12. As UN requests for mandate extensions arrive usually at the very last minute, this was no fun!

13. A series of documentation regarding the early years of Austrian UN service has been collected by the Austrian Army Museum's Department of Military History in the 1980s and 1990s, and was later handed over to the Austrian State Archives (Archiv der Republik, Vienna), BMLV collection.

14. The possibility of deploying Austrian UN observers had already been raised in 1965 when the UN established a new mission along the Indian–Pakistani ceasefire line. However, Austria once again delayed its answer to the UN request for so long that the need passed.

15. Christian Clausen, ' "Operation Dove" – die Verlegung von UN-Truppen von Zypern nach Ägypten: Ein Beitrag zur Frage der Luftbeweglichkeit von Einsatzverbänden', in *Österreichische Militärische Zeitschrift*, Vol. 13, No. 2 (March/April 1975), pp. 102–9.

16. The Cyprus battalion was moved from Paphos to Larnaca in the process of UNFICYP's reorganization, and the Austrian field hospital was reduced to a smaller medical centre which operated until 1976. In 1977, the Austrian battalion on Cyprus moved again, to Famagusta in the east, where it remained until its withdrawal in 2001.

17. This 'legend' of the UN not paying its dues stems largely from the Cyprus operation which from 1964 had been financed by the troops' contributors, with possible reimbursements from voluntary contributions (which were never available in sufficient amounts). Only in 1993 was the UNFICYP changed to assessed contributions, albeit on a reduced scale only.

18. This includes those killed in the field as well as traffic accidents and suicides.

19. On 15 December 1974, Major-General Hannes Philipp was appointed commander of the UN force on the Golan Heights. He was later succeeded by Major-General Günther G. Greindl (1979–81; later commander of the UN force in Cyprus from 1981 to 1989 and commander of the UN observer mission between Kuwait and Iraq in 1991–92) and Major-General Adolf Radauer (1988–91). In 1997–99, Brigadier Bernd Lubenig commanded MINURSO, and since 2001 Major-General Hermann K. Loidolt has been Chief Observer of UNMOGIP.

20. This is not the place to list all these missions. For more detailed information, see *In the Service of Peace* mentioned in note 3, which includes a complete list.

21. Recently, the editor of the *Presse* (Vienna), the leading conservative paper, commented on this subject: Andreas Unterberger, 'Spannende Zeitzeugen, hartnäckige Legenden', in *Presse* (29 July 2002), p. 6.

22. At first, the observers were supported by infantry seconded from other UN operations, including 115 Austrian infantry from Cyprus. Later, Austria also contributed a medical platoon (1993–95), and a logistics contingent of 34 men (1996–99).

23. Because of earlier positive signals in New York, Austria's change of mind was seen as an annoying gesture by the UN. It also was an indication of the deadlock into which the coalition government had already manoeuvred itself (eventually leading to the much-commented-on change in government in 2000). Earlier differences between the two coalition parties about participation in peace operations (about continuation in the Cyprus operation, for example) had usually remained hidden both from the public as well as the international community.

24. Those were the days of pre-EU-accession debate (Austria joined the EU in January 1995, together with Finland and Sweden), with very little room left for compromises on any matter between the 'partners' of this government. In general, coalition governments in Austria often suffered from tensions between the chancellor (from the dominating party) and the foreign minister (the second party's leading figure), both trying to conduct their own foreign policy (or, rather, policies).

25. A traditional problem has been the recruitment of medical doctors. This is why recruits undergoing their national service after completing their medical studies were occasionally employed on peace operations as physicians, as were women even before the army was opened to women in 1998.

26. In Austria, the three major parties are known as the Social Democratic Party (SPÖ, used to be the Socialist Party), the conservative People's Party (ÖVP), and the liberal/national Freedom Party (FPÖ). The fourth party represented in government are the Greens, who are much more anti-military and pacifistic than their German counterparts.

27. This law had become dated, as it had never envisaged the need to cater to Austrians sent to a dozen or so missions at one time. It made little provision for alliances outside the UN, and required a very cumbersome procedure for mandate renewals.

28. This *Bundesverfassungsgesetz über Kooperation und Solidarität bei der Entsendung von Einheiten und Einzelpersonen in das Ausland* (KSE-BVG), BGBl. I 38/1997, had already been drafted in 1996, and goes back to several rounds of discussions initiated by the Ministry of Foreign Affairs in 1990, but its passage had been delayed until the new situation enabled rapid approval in April 1997.

29. When Austria decided to take part in the NATO-led IFOR in 1996, this was interpreted as being really a UN mission, as it had a UN mandate.

30. Although it is difficult to generalize, foreign service pay is usually twice as high (or higher) than respective military salaries (which, like public servants' in general, are very low by international standards).

31. This was closely linked to the development of a new Austrian security doctrine, efforts made possible by the untiring efforts of Erich Reiter, a high-ranking civilian in the Ministry of Defence. Still holding the rank of Director-General (four-star equivalent), Erich Reiter is now Director for Security Policy and adviser to the government in security affairs. For further details, the reader is referred to Reiter's numerous publications, including the annual *Jahrbuch für Internationale Sicherheitspolitik* (Hamburg: Mittler, latest edition 2002).

32. Two Austrian police generals held positions as high commissioners in the UN operations in Rwanda (Manfred Bliem, 1993–94), Western Sahara (Walter Fallmann, 1996), and Eastern Slavonia (Walter Fallmann, 1996–98).

33. Although basically a diplomatic mission, and now having no military tasks at all, the ECMM/EUMM is staffed mainly by military officers, with some non-military personnel added. Because of the all-white dress adopted when the mission was established in July 1991, the EU observers are known as the 'ice-cream vendors'.

34. These were the smaller missions of the four, where Austrian withdrawal had the least negative consequences for its international reputation. Also, it meant withdrawal (with the exception of a handful of staff personnel) from a UN and a NATO mission, thus balancing the effects. Although such a move had been contemplated before, as already mentioned in the context of Austria's Somalia ambitions of 1993, and made sense from a recruitment point of view, observers also interpreted the defence minister's decision to withdraw as a signal to the finance minister who (although from the same party) refused funds that the military desperately needed. Since then, relations between the two ministries have improved again in this field.

EIGHT

————◄◦►————

Canada

David Rudd

INTRODUCTION

Although many countries claim to have invented modern peacekeeping, Canadians have always considered this type of military operation to be their own creation. Successive Canadian governments rarely lose the opportunity to remind citizens of the leading role Canada has played in international peacekeeping since the birth of the United Nations (UN). It is often cited as the 'uniquely Canadian' contribution to global peace and security. To be sure, there is evidence to corroborate these claims. However, while the public's appetite for this activity has been fairly consistent, the enthusiasm of governments has waxed and waned over time. In addition, as the rigid bipolarity of the Cold War gave way to an environment characterized by several international systems, Canada's belief in the efficacy of peacekeeping has been put to the test. A new generation of complex and risky operations, the rising cost of training and equipping modern military forces, the concentration of power in the hands of a small number of officials, and the ascendancy of new actors on the domestic policy-making stage have significantly altered Canada's perceptions of and appetite for an endeavor that is considered by many to be a sacred part of the country's self-image.

CANADA'S PEACEKEEPING HISTORY IN BRIEF

As Canada is a founding and enthusiastic member of the United Nations, it should come as no surprise that it would involve itself in international peacekeeping. Canadians have contributed to no fewer than 35 UN operations since 1949, as well as at least six missions approved but not directed by the international body. Deployments have ranged in duration from a few months to three decades. They have involved everything from small numbers of personnel on simple observer missions to more robust force packages charged with enforcing a civil peace. Other roles have included monitoring the disarmament and demobilization of combatants, rendering humanitarian assistance, truce supervision, and landmine clearance. Contributions have been army-centric, as these missions invariably take place on land. But units from the navy and air force have also been called upon to fulfill critical support roles. More recent deployments have also included police officers who are assigned basic law-and-order tasks until local authority can be reconstituted from the ashes of war.

Well over 120,000 members of the Canadian Forces (CF) have rotated through these missions, some many times over. Over 100 service personnel have lost their lives while on peacekeeping duty. By 1992, and for several years thereafter, Canada had deployed a greater proportion of its armed forces on a broader array of missions than many of its allies – 4,000 personnel out of a military establishment of approximately 70,000. This represented 10 percent of the peacekeepers under UN contract.[1] But while the scale of the effort drew praise from domestic and international commentators, the CF lurched under the weight of a commitment which was, in effect, double that which the government had mandated in its last defence policy statement of the Cold War.[2] Meanwhile, post-Cold War defence budget cuts, amounting to 25 to 30 percent, were accompanied by an abrupt rise in the number and risk factor of missions assigned to the CF, and its reduction in size to fewer than 60,000 personnel by 2000. Only recently has the government of Canada realized the risks inherent in not addressing this situation. It has introduced limited corrective measures in the form of more money to sustain individual operations and a cap on the duration of future contributions to future peacekeeping missions.

However, Canada has done more than contribute human and material resources to peacekeeping. It has been a tireless advocate of reforms to enhance the world body's ability to rise to the challenges of modern and complex peacekeeping operations. Frustrated by the inability of Canadian field commanders in Bosnia to communicate with UN Headquarters on weekends, Ottawa pushed for the establishment of a situation room in New York to be manned 24 hours a day. Canadian military officers consistently provide planning guidance to decision-makers in UNHQ. Canada has also been at the forefront of efforts to enhance the organization's ability to respond rapidly to unfolding crises. It tabled an in-depth study on rapid reaction in the General Assembly in 1995[3] and has set aside a battalion of troops for deployment with the UN Standing High Readiness Brigade (SHIRBRIG). The latter was deployed to Africa in early 2001 to monitor the ceasefire between Ethiopia and Eritrea. Having recognized both the complexity of modern peacekeeping operations and the fact that the mandate of deployed military forces would increasingly overlap with those of police services, civilian governmental, and non-governmental organizations (NGOs), the government of Canada created the Pearson Peacekeeping Centre in 1994. The Centre acts as a sort of staff college in which military personnel and civilians learn new trends in peacekeeping and how to bridge the operational and cultural divides which threatened to dilute their effectiveness.[4] In 1996 the Canadian Army established the Peace Support Training Centre (PSTC) in Kingston, Ontario to study and disseminate the lessons learned on peacekeeping missions.

Such activism has its roots in a mixture of national interests and a desire to promote values dear to Canada. Many scholars have noted that Canadians are reluctant, if not embarrassed, to articulate their interests on the international stage.[5] They often underestimate the degree to which interests have brought Canadians into the midst of crises which, on the surface, had little to do with them. Ottawa's decision to participate in UN operations in Cyprus (UNFICYP) in 1964 may have seemed unusual given the island's geographical distance from Canada. On closer inspection, it is clear that the commitment was undertaken in order to prevent two NATO allies – Greece and Turkey – from coming to blows, thereby undermining the political and strategic integrity of the Alliance's southern flank. An infantry battalion would remain on the divided island for the next three decades.

Between the 1950s and the 1970s, Canada deployed troops to various locations in South Asia and the Middle East. They helped monitor ceasefires between, respectively, India and Pakistan, and later between Israel and its Arab neighbours. Contributions to UNMOGIP (UN Military Observer Group in India and Pakistan), UNTSO (UN Truce Supervision Organization) and UNDOF (UN Disengagement Observer Force) involved only a few officers in the observer role. However, the frequency and duration of the deployments showed that policy-makers appreciated the broader international interest in keeping heavily armed belligerents apart. In the Middle East, the re-ignition of war had the capacity to poison relations between key Arab nations and Israel's chief sponsor, the United States. The oil shocks of the early 1970s caused financial chaos from which Canadians were not immune. Another war would do the same, if it did not first draw in the nuclear-armed superpowers onto opposing sides.

This is not to suggest that interests have always been the driving force behind Canadian peacekeeping. Canadians have long been aware of their differences from their powerful southern neighbour, and its tendency to look at the world through utilitarian eyes. Disagreement over Washington's policy in Vietnam heightened these differences, and peacekeeping took on added importance since it was something Canada did outside of the US orbit. Of course there is less substance to this view than meets the eye. Peacekeeping missions invariably depended on the US for logistical support and on both superpowers for their very existence. Still, in a time of war and socio-political change, few would have quibbled with the positive aura that surrounded peacekeeping. Moreover, as Canada approached its hundredth birthday in 1967, it was inevitable that the national character would derive some of its uniqueness from the long commitment to the UN and its peacekeeping brief. This self-perception endures to the present day and has even weathered the arrival of the US (and other countries) on the peacekeeping stage. With its permanent seat on the UN Security Council and considerable diplomatic and military clout, Canada sees US engagement in international conflict resolution as essential.[6] This has worked both ways, however. Mindful of American sensibilities to placing its troops under UN (read foreign) command, Canada will often step into the breach with US encouragement and behind-the-scenes logistical support. It is not uncommon for Canadian troops to be dispatched following a brief phone call from the President of the United States to the Canadian Prime Minister. Such was the case when Canada agreed to lead an abortive mission to Zaire in 1995[7] and when it deployed 400 personnel to the Australian-led mission to East Timor (INTERFET).[8]

Another factor weighing heavily on government decision-making is that Canadians have consistently put the promotion of Canadian values near the top of their list of foreign policy priorities. The last include the peaceful resolution of disputes, the promotion of liberal democracy and the rule of law, the alleviation of suffering, and the creation of conditions which are conducive to global socio-economic development.[9] The latter has spurred Canada to act when poorer and unstable nations have been racked by civil strife. The UN-sponsored mission to bring stability to Haiti in 1995 (UNMIH) is a prime example of liberal internationalism at work, although affinity with a francophone country, and pressure exerted on Canada's foreign minister by his Haitian constituents, also played a substantial role.[10]

By the end of the 1990s, values were more visibly asserting themselves in the policy formulation process. Under the activist Minister of Foreign Affairs Lloyd Axworthy, the term human security became formally entrenched in Canada's foreign policy lexicon. The doctrine received extra support as states began to collapse after the bipolar discipline of the

Cold War had been removed. It postulated that the security of the individual – not that of the state – was of primary concern, and that if the state was negligent in its treatment of its citizens, or if the trappings of government were absent, the international community had the moral obligation to intervene.[11] This worldview explains why Canada agreed to dispatch forces – albeit for the restoration rather than the keeping of an existing peace – to famine-stricken Somalia in 1993 and strife-torn East Timor in 1999. In neither case was the safety of Canada or Canadians under threat. But images of widespread human suffering and the denial of basic democratic rights were sufficient to bring Canada into the field again and again. In the wake of the Kosovo crisis Canada lent its support to the work of the International Commission on State Sovereignty (ICSS). In 2001, the Commission completed a project aimed at hammering out broadly acceptable guidelines for when intervention in the affairs of failed or failing states was justified.[12]

Although many Canadians would assert that a spirit of altruism is the foundation upon which Canada's admirable peacekeeping record is built, this could not be further from the truth. Indeed, Canada's reasons for becoming involved and remaining involved stem as much from hard-headed calculations of the national interest as they do from a desire to be a good international citizen. Party politics has occasionally been a contributing factor, swaying the government toward action. Public opinion has been consistently supportive, if not simply acquiescent, while the influence of the electronic media has grown over time. Three case studies will illustrate this point.

UNITED NATIONS EMERGENCY FORCE I (UNEF I)

Although Canada participated in many UN observer missions in the immediate postwar period, these truce-supervisory tasks were not officially termed 'peacekeeping'; nor were the Canadians who participated in the mission called 'peacekeepers'. Nevertheless, Canada saw clearly the utility of helping newly independent states (and their former overlords) manage the process of de-colonization as peacefully as possible. But neither the government nor the military were under any illusions. Peacekeeping was regarded as a thankless task and a drain on military resources made scarce by postwar demobilization.[13]

Canadian peacekeeping had its primary origins in the Suez Crisis of 1956. After Egyptian President Gamal Abdel Nasser had moved to nationalize the Suez Canal, Britain and France (with Israeli assistance) launched an air/sea-borne attack to punish Nasser and restore Anglo-French prestige. After being subject to fierce condemnation by the United States, the Soviet Union and much of the Third World, London and Paris were obliged to look for a face-saving way out. Eager to help its allies avoid a rift with Washington, Canada moved quickly to find ways to disengage the colonial powers from the Egyptians. When Soviet Premier Nikita Khrushchev threatened to rain down nuclear bombs on London and Paris if they did not withdraw immediately from the Canal Zone, Canada realized that the stakes were infinitely higher; that the survival of the Western camp depended on effective action. At this time, Canada's Secretary of State for External Affairs, Lester B. Pearson, developed an idea that would see a 'police force' under UN control inserted into the Canal Zone to separate the warring parties so that a timetable for withdrawal could be drawn up. Pearson's stage-management of the proposal and the success of the resulting mission – which was organized and commanded by Canadian General E. L. M. Burns – netted him the Nobel Peace Prize in 1957.

There were other, less tangible factors at play in the decision to take the lead in resolving the dispute. At the end of World War II Canada had attained a position of political and economic strength far greater than when it had entered the war. Emerging out of the shadow of Great Britain – to whom Canada had looked to for so long for its defence and security – it longed to demonstrate independence from both London and Washington in foreign affairs. Multilateralism was regarded as the only legitimate approach to fostering international peace and security, and its handmaiden – peacekeeping – was seen as an activity done outside the US or British orbit. It was supported by both elected officials and the powerful mandarins at the Department of External Affairs, who believed that it was the duty of 'middle powers' to occupy the ground between the permanent members of the UN Security Council (in this case, Britain and France) and the countries of the post-colonial Third World which lacked the means to defend their interests on their own.[14] It would also permit Canada cost-effectively to increase its influence on the international stage. Furthermore, the persona that Canada would be cultivating through its participation and, indeed, leadership in peacekeeping was that of a 'helpful fixer' or 'honest broker' motivated neither by self-interest nor by a desire to do the bidding of larger, more powerful allies. The fostering of such a positive self-image could only enhance national unity and self-esteem.[15] In a country perpetually concerned with reconciling the interests and ambitions of its anglophone and francophone communities, this was not an insignificant matter for the government.

While it had a demonstrably positive effect on regional stability and relations between the rival superpowers, the legacy of UNEF I for Canadian peacekeeping was ultimately ambiguous. Its initial success and Pearson's Nobel Prize caused such public enthusiasm for peacekeeping that in 1961 the government felt compelled to swallow its reservations about sending a signals regiment and several transport aircraft to the UN Mission to the Congo (ONUC).[16] But the Suez Crisis did not herald a new, independent direction in Canadian foreign policy. As in many missions to come, the Security Council sanctioned Canada's involvement because it was a member of the Western camp; it balanced the contributions of Eastern Bloc states to the same mission. It was, in effect, a grand attempt to manage Great Power relations, rather than an act of selflessness.[17]

Ultimately the high hopes created by UNEF I would not last. In May of 1967, as momentum built in the Arab world for war with Israel, President Nasser summarily ordered UNEF to vacate the Sinai. Clearly, the mere existence of a peacekeeping force could not ensure, let alone compel, peaceful behavior. Public opinion in Canada was shocked and insulted by the expulsion, although the need for multilateral intervention was never questioned on principle.[18] Still, the government of Pierre Trudeau saw the effort as a grand failure to prevent war and reduced peacekeeping in listed military priorities in its 1971 defence White Paper.

It should not have been surprising that non-participation had been the preferred option when the UN requested Canadian participation in ONUC. There was much disagreement over how the mission should be funded and, despite the goal of helping to manage de-colonization, little appetite for intervening in a civil war. The subsequent contribution was made only when public opinion demanded that the government act, if only to live up to the noble image it had created in the wake of the Suez Crisis. Moral suasion and the ability of domestic actors to influence policy thus became a factor in Canadian peacekeeping. It is perhaps coincidental that they began to assert themselves when faced with a war of secession – a particular type of conflagration that UN members were unprepared to meet, but which would occur with greater frequency in the decades ahead.

THE BALKANS – UNITED NATIONS PROTECTION FORCES I AND II (UNPROFOR I, II); IMPLEMENTATION FORCE (IFOR)

The disciplines of the bipolar system began to loosen at a time when budgetary concerns began to effect Canada's claim to pre-eminence in the field of peacekeeping. Massive cuts to federal expenditures beginning in 1989 saw the defence budget hit hard. The Canadian Forces were subsequently ordered to close their bases in Germany, and many equipment programs were either postponed or cancelled.

Against this backdrop, the government of Canada took an interest in the growing ethnic tensions in what was then the Republic of Yugoslavia. An uneasy peace between ethnic communities had been enforced by the communist regime and by the personality of the country's long-time communist leader, Josip Broz Tito. His death in 1980 gave way to new leadership, which earned the enmity of the regions for its heavy-handedness. Slovenia and later Croatia seceded from the Republic in 1991. Gripped by expansionist nationalism, Bosnian Serb and Croat leaders declared that there were long-lost territories which would soon be returned to the fold.

The initial stages of the crisis saw heated debate in the House of Commons in Ottawa, with Opposition parties advocating immediate and significant Canadian involvement. The government was encouraged to recognize Slovenia and Croatia, to support a sanctions regime against Belgrade, and to participate in a peacekeeping mission. The frequency and intensity of the debate were virtually unprecedented, and may be explained by the number and size of the expatriate communities of Yugoslav origin[19] who encouraged their elected representatives to voice their concerns. Internecine warfare, moreover, was an affront to one of Canada's core values – tolerance and harmony between ethnic communities. Canada was, after all, a cultural mosaic. It could not stand by while people were slaughtered for no reason other than their religion.

In February of 1992 an infantry battle group comprising 1,200 troops was formed and sent to Croatia to serve with UNPROFOR I. Its mandate was unique in the history of UN peacekeeping. Instead of policing a ceasefire and separating armed factions, it was ordered to supervise and facilitate the delivery of humanitarian aid while the civil war raged on. Another 800-man battle group was later dispatched to Bosnia and UNPROFOR II for largely the same reasons. In both cases, Canadian troops were exposed to hostile fire by irregular military forces, and on several occasions small numbers of soldiers were taken hostage by Bosnian Serb forces and used as human shields. Word of these events prompted fierce debate in the House of Commons on how best to ensure the safety of the troops. Opposition parties consistently voiced their support for the missions, although several members of a new right-of-centre party advocated withdrawal.

The government's patience with the mission – given both the risks to Canadian personnel and the seeming unwillingness of the parties to achieve a durable ceasefire – would not be eternal. The pitiless nature of the conflict and scant prospects for resolution coloured a March 1995 debate on the renewal of the Canadian commitment. The Opposition was split on whether to leave the troops in place. In the event, no decision was reached, as NATO air power and a combined Muslim–Croat offensive turned the tables on Bosnian Serb forces. The new balance of forces on the ground, combined with NATO intervention and the exhaustion of the warring parties, opened the door to a political settlement reached in Dayton, Ohio and a new mission to implement it.

The government of Prime Minister Jean Chrétien had always been leery of the mission to the Balkans on political and financial grounds. It was equally uncertain of the wisdom of contributing an infantry battle group to the NATO-led force which would replace UNPROFOR and which would be operating under the peace-enforcing Chapter VII of the UN Charter as opposed to Chapter VI, which specified a more passive observation role. In December of 1995, parliamentarians debated the matter, with the majority accepting the logic of Canada's continuing commitment; it was both a member of the Alliance and one of few countries with a knowledge of the region's geographical and political landscape. In addition, the government had recently tabled a new White Paper on defence after holding broad public consultations. NATO membership and participation in multi-national military operations were high priorities,[20] and each would find expression in the commitment to IFOR. It would also help deflect criticism that the decision to reduce the size of the Canadian military to 60,000 and its budget to 1 per cent of GDP was illustrative of Canada's unwillingness to shoulder its share of the collective defence and security burden.

Canada's involvement in the Balkans was a product of interests and values. Humanitarianism, coupled with the realization that a fire on NATO's doorstep had the capacity to involve the Alliance whether it chose to be involved or not, combined with domestic pressure by politicians and their constituents (and later by allied governments) brought Canada onto the field. The consultation of parliament was notable for its frequency and the surprising quality of the speeches and recommendations of parliamentarians. The government was constructively challenged on issues such as troop safety and the evolution of the mission's mandate from one of peacekeeping to peace enforcement. Some observers went so far as to suggest that the government could no longer assume that parliament or the public would automatically acquiesce to its decisions regarding participation in peacekeeping operations.

RWANDA AND ZAIRE

The mission to the Great Lakes region of Africa is notable in that it never truly came into being. Nevertheless, efforts to alleviate the unprecedented suffering of the peoples of Rwanda represent a short but unique chapter in Canada's peacekeeping history.

When Prime Minister Jean Chrétien announced in November of 1996 that Canada would lead an international force into Zaire, the decision had been neither vetted by the federal cabinet nor discussed in parliament. The Prime Minister confined consultations to the Ministers of Foreign Affairs and Defence, and the UN's Special Emissary for the Great Lakes, who also happened to be his nephew, Raymond Chrétien. The views of the Chief of Defence Staff were not solicited. The input of military planners who would have to assess the situation on the ground were either taken for granted or considered to be of minor significance.[21] But with missions in Bosnia and Haiti ongoing, military leaders soon felt compelled to make clear that another task – particularly one in which the warring parties had not agreed to an international presence – would be impossible. Furthermore, Canadian leadership of the mission would be problematic given the military's modest transport, logistic, and command-and-control capabilities.

The Prime Minister's announcement initially drew praise from newspaper editorialists, while some Opposition parliamentarians touted it as a diplomatic triumph,[22] and proof of Canada's commitment to the alleviation of suffering and tolerance between ethnic communities. In reality it did not involve much in the way of diplomacy; the circle of consultants was inexplicably small, and Canadian. The praise soon turned to caution when word arrived that half a million refugees had returned home, and Canada's military shortcomings became ever more clear. The government tried to portray the exodus as the result of its initial efforts on behalf of the displaced, but many commentators dismissed this as preposterous.[23]

Again, Canada's tradition of humanitarianism and liberal internationalism had the capacity to propel the government into action. There were strong domestic political forces at play, including senior cabinet ministers, as well as French Canada's concerns for a francophone region of Africa. But the plot had been hatched with little public notice, incomplete information on conditions on the ground, and without the knowledge and support of the military. The question of Canadian leadership of the mission was mooted early on, as allied governments balked at Chrétien's haste. A 1998 post-mortem of the stillborn mission revealed that the government had grossly underestimated the operational challenges associated with rapid response, and suggested that it had been unduly influenced by humanitarian aid organizations who had counselled immediate action but lacked any appreciation of the complexities of military operations.[24]

A more recent account of the events in the region alleges that powerful Western (including Canadian) business interests persuaded their governments tacitly to support Zairian rebel leader Laurent Kabila's bid for power in return for mining rights.[25] Robust intervention by the UN would have likely gone some way to stop Kabila's troops from mass killings of Rwandan refugees. That no such pressure was brought to bear, that a Canadian fact-finding team, for reasons still unclear, did not adequately assess the humanitarian situation, indicates a sinister undercurrent to UN and Canadian peacekeeping.[26]

Suffice to say that a mix of interests and values has shaped Canada's commitment to international peacekeeping. Some have postulated a fusion between the two: interests as values. But the ascendancy of a value-based guideline on where and under what set of circumstances to deploy peacekeepers has presented a challenge to policy-makers. While difficult to articulate, their primacy in policy formulation could theoretically place untenable burdens on the nation's resources. With the proliferation of intra-state emergencies after the Cold War, affronts to Canadian values arose from all quarters and continue to do so. As far as Ottawa was concerned, the temptation to go off on moral crusades was not accompanied by an appreciation of what remedial measures entail for the military and the treasury.

ACTORS AND AGENDAS

The deployment of Canadian peacekeepers is a relatively simple matter. Although there are many governmental and non-governmental actors in the policy formulation process, only a few have any real impact. Foremost among these is the prime minister. Canada's parliamentary style of government invests executive power with the governing party, which holds a majority of seats in the House of Commons. (Canada's second legislative chamber, the Senate, is composed of appointed representatives who do not normally challenge decisions made by elected members of the House.) This majority allows for the swift passage of legislation, as well as easier formulation and execution of policy directives, including those relating to national defence. Party discipline is rigid by Western standards, with relatively few opportunities for members of parliament to vote against their own party. As leader of the governing party, the prime minister expects loyalty and consistency in voting patterns. He or she is unlikely to tolerate more than the odd voting transgression, with repeated offenders banished to the back benches.

This concentration of power into what some commentators have called an elected or benign dictatorship, combined with general public apathy towards defence and international security, ensures that the prime minister can, if he or she chooses, make a decision that will stand up not only in parliament, but in the mind of a less-than-attentive public. This is not to suggest that decisions are unilateral. Key cabinet ministers can bring their concerns to the prime minister, encouraging either action or inaction. While former Foreign Minister Lloyd Axworthy's human security agenda was clearly instrumental in operationalizing Canada's interventions in Kosovo and East Timor, the ministers of defence and finance may also assert themselves. The defence minister will report to cabinet on the physical ability of the Canadian Forces to undertake a peacekeeping operation. He/she will convey the concerns of the military leadership with respect to the complexity, risk level, and proposed duration of the mission, and carry back questions from the cabinet to his military chiefs. The supplementary costs of a given operation, including higher pay levels for deployed troops and last-minute purchases of key equipment sets, may require input from the Finance Ministry. Ongoing missions may result in further concerns (if not frustrations) expressed by these two departments as human, material, and financial resources continue to be expended with no end to the mission in sight. The articulation of an 'early in, early out' approach to future peacekeeping deployments by the Department of National Defence (DND) could be regarded as a culmination of concerns from these two departments and their ministers. The fiscal conservatism of recent ministers of finance (a quality shared by the Prime Minister) undoubtedly prevented a larger infusion of cash into the defence budget above what was announced in June of 2000. Morale problems stemming from constant operations also led the Defence Minister to sell to the government the idea that the Canadian army needed time to recover from years of constant deployments and shrinking resources.[27] Thus after the turn of the millennium, the government's enthusiasm for peacekeeping was being constrained, although not by an unwillingness to remain a committed peacekeeper. Indeed, in a private conversation caught on tape, Prime Minister Chrétien was overheard referring to Canadians as boy scouts eager to be seen doing good.[28]

For the Canadian military, the opaqueness with which deliberations and planning take place makes it somewhat difficult to assess the impact of DND on a decision to mount a peacekeeping mission. The service's top officer, the Chief of the Defence Staff, is an advisor to the government, and is bound by dual loyalties: to the government and to those serving under him. Public disagreements between the political and military leadership are almost non-existent. No government craves the embarrassment of being second-guessed and would surely limit the career of any officer who publicly criticized policy. Not surprisingly, there exists a perception that an eagerness on the part of the office of the military leadership to please the government has resulted in the over-commitment of CF personnel to operations which, while otherwise noble, made no allowance for the toll they would eventually take on equipment, service personnel and their families, and morale in general. Many analysts have attributed the difficulties in recruiting and retaining sufficient personnel to a government seemingly blind to the issues facing the CF.[29] Responding to suggestions within the officer corps that the CF was being deployed into situations of marginal interest to Canada, Lloyd Axworthy retorted that anyone who dared challenge the frequency of the contributions made to peacekeeping operations should be 'taken out to the woodshed'.[30]

While the military as a whole can counsel restraint, it is seldom clear whether it is doing so. The military's own culture makes this difficult. The 'can-do' attitude exhibited by any professional force encourages its members to make do with scarce resources. Canadians are widely known to overcome such obstacles. But as personnel levels dropped to 60,000 and below toward the end of the 1990s, one may have expected that frequency of deployments to diminish accordingly. That they have done so only recently indicates either an inability to convince the government of the existence of a 'commitment-capability' gap, or, alarmingly, a desire among senior officers to demonstrate post-Cold War relevance of the CF, albeit to the detriment of their subordinates.[31]

Government committees routinely survey defence and security issues and table reports on their findings. Novel ideas are often put forth, although in the end few of these reports have resulted in major changes to Canada's defence policy or in increased levels of government support for the Canadian Forces. To many observers they are either a public relations effort to maintain the illusion of public input, or exercises in catharsis for organizations seeking to influence policy.[32] Nevertheless, the committees and those invited to appear before them are a way of spreading knowledge of defence issues in general and peacekeeping issues in particular to decision-makers who would otherwise have little incentive to learn about them. The quality of the interventions by parliamentarians during the Balkans debates was enhanced by the work of the committees.

Much has been made of the role of the print and electronic media in influencing decisions to intervene in a far-away land. The much-maligned

'CNN factor' does ensure that the plight of threatencd peoples is publicized, making it less likely that governments will shrug their shoulders and return to their domestic policy agenda. No government is likely to attribute its actions to television images. But pictures of emaciated children in Somalia, of victims of the Sarajevo mortar attack, and of rampaging militias in Rwanda and East Timor could not help but catch the attention of Canadians. These images are said to have played a role in prodding the Chrétien government into action on Rwanda.[33] However, it is worth noting that the interest of much of the Western media is to publicize novelty – that is, not to dwell on stories that lose their sensational edge. The morbid adage 'if it bleeds it leads' is freely adhered to by journalists and is a contributing factor to the breadth and depth of coverage of international crises.[34] Thus while the decision to deploy will receive attention, follow-up coverage of Canadian peacekeeping missions has been sporadic at best. This separates the Canadian public from its soldiers, relieving it of the need to share their hardships, and has diminished the probability that the risks, complexities, and costs of these missions will be learned and internalized.

It would be a truism to state that politics and economics are intertwined. Corporations are constantly (and not without reason) alleged to affect policy choices in a manner consistent with their parochial interests. Theoretically this may result in pressure being brought to bear to stabilize an unstable situation, thereby safeguarding the economic interest from pilferage or destruction. It may also result in pressure to forgo or delay intervention. The crisis in the Great Lakes region of Africa may have revealed some of the 'unseen politics' of Canadian peacekeeping. However, without further study no firm opinion can be offered here.

Rounding out the policy community is the 'attentive public' – those individuals and organizations dealing with international security matters on a more or less ongoing basis, as well as those concerned with specific issues. The former include individuals, research organizations, and academic institutions which attempt to enhance the public's and the government's understanding of complex emergencies. Their insights and advice are enthusiastically sought by government committees and the media, and periodically result in important issues relating to peacekeeping entering public discourse. But due to the closed nature of the policy-making environment, policy changes are seldom the result of their efforts.

Single-issue advocacy organizations are less visible, although some have made use of press conferences to publicize their case and demand action. Publicity generated by the East Timor Action Network is credited with helping to nudge (although some would say shame) the Chrétien government into joining INTERFET.[35] Major international organizations such as the Red Cross and Doctors Without Borders (Médecins sans frontières) have played some role in publicizing the plight of threatened populations. They have been consulted by the Canadian government when the latter has no or insufficient field personnel in the theatre to gather information for the decision-makers.[36]

The various ethnic/expatriate communities that compose the Canadian mosaic have also attempted to insert themselves into the policy formulation process. Some, like groups representing Canadians of Haitian, Albanian, and Serb origin, have made great use of the Internet and other media to either shame the government into acting or to discredit a decision already made. Although the influence of these groups is small due to their size, their concentration in central Canada gives them greater access to major media outlets, which theoretically enhances their ability to conduct successful information/propaganda campaigns.

THE FUTURE

Canada's peacekeeping 'policy' was most recently articulated – albeit obliquely – in the 1994 Defence White Paper. The first document to lay out Canadian security policy objectives since the end of the Cold War, and formulated at a time when UN operations in the Balkans were being roundly criticized for keeping a non-existent peace, the White Paper made infrequent use of the term 'peacekeeping' when it listed the role of the CF. Instead, it grouped peacekeeping under the umbrella of multinational military operations. It made several recommendations for enhancing the UN's ability to deal effectively with complex emergencies, and suggested that the ceiling of 2,000 personnel to be made available to the UN may be too restrictive. However, significantly, there were no criteria that would give direction on when, where, or for how long Canada would deploy its scarce resources. Of course, to governments who would prefer to maintain the highest degree of flexibility possible, criteria are anathema. But without such guidelines, there can be no formal policy; there will only be *ad hocery*. With nothing to impose discipline on its ambitions, it would only be a matter of time before Canada began to will the ends without providing adequate means.

It is difficult to encapsulate Canada's peacekeeping experience through an analysis of only three case studies. Each mission took place in a unique international political context. The development and implementation of an approach to peacekeeping have historically resulted from a mixture of domestic and international considerations, interests and values, not all of which were in play at any given time. Moreover, some of the most significant factors, and some of the most important actors, have made themselves felt in between missions rather than as a direct prelude to them. With the end of the Cold War the probability of general warfare engulfing Canada and its major allies is low. As a result, military operations are increasingly discretionary. It is therefore unsurprising that certain domestic considerations (i.e. financial) are playing a greater role than international ones have in years past. Similarly, the national interests that initially brought Canada into the field and kept it there are increasingly giving way to the promotion of values which Canada professes to hold dear. Thus at the dawn of the new millennium, Canadians find themselves playing the role of a relatively benign intervener. The age of 'enlightened self-interest' is at hand.

This situation has worked to the benefit and to the detriment of the Canadian Forces. The number and variety of missions it has undertaken in the last decade suggest that its overall relevance to the security environment of the late twentieth and early twenty-first centuries is not in doubt. But the tendency of successive governments to view it as a bottomless pit of human, material, and financial resources has clearly brought it to a crossroads from which it knows not how to emerge. The most recent mission undertaken by Canadian troops – to Afghanistan – was closed down only after six months because there were insufficient numbers of troops to replace them. Despite American pressure to stay on and assist in the pacification of the Afghan countryside, Ottawa had to acknowledge that the army's cupboard was bare.

The answer to this dilemma rests firmly in the hands of the Government of Canada. Due to the parliamentary system of government and party discipline, the prime minister and key members of the cabinet are able to set policy with little room for debate or opposition. And why would anyone seriously debate, let alone oppose, peacekeeping or its contemporary iterations? Should not anything relating to 'peace' be uncontroversial? Thus imprecision in the discourse ensures that public acquiescence to whatever the government proposes is virtually assured.

Since the deployment to the Balkans, the Canadian media and the wider public have had to play a game of catch-up. Their understanding of the new strains of 'peacekeeping' (for want of a better word) is limited by their attention span, the complexity of the military and strategic issues at hand, and by competing domestic priorities. True, media attention can be focused on sensational events – either declining military capabilities or an overseas bloodletting – thereby spurring the government to action. But the fact that these actors lack a sense of perspective on what a new generation of peacekeeping operations can and cannot achieve, and at what cost, will relieve pressure on the civilian and military leadership to articulate clearer policy guidelines that will form the foundation of a strategic approach to peacekeeping. The questions of 'when, why, how, and for how long' will go unanswered. It will also be impossible to judge whether defence spending levels will allow Canada to live up to its self-image as 'the world's best peacekeeper'.

NOTES

1. Joseph T. Jockel, *Canada and International Peacekeeping* (Toronto/Washington: CISS/CSIS, 1994), p. 2.
2. Department of National Defence (Canada), *Challenge and Commitment: A Defence White Paper for Canada* (Ottawa: Supply and Services Canada, 1987), p. 34.
3. Albert Legault, *Canada and Peacekeeping: The Major Debates* (Clementsport, Nova Scotia: The Canadian Peacekeeping Press, 1999), p. 81.
4. For more information, see the website of the Pearson Peacekeeping Centre: www.cdnpeacekeeping.ns.ca.
5. D. W. Middlemiss and J. J. Sokolsky, *Canadian Defence: Decisions and Determinants* (Toronto: Harcourt Brace Jovanovich, 1989), p. 117.
6. Minister of National Defence, *The 1994 Defence White Paper* (Ottawa: Government of Canada, 1994), p. 20.
7. Carole Jerome, 'The Unseen Politics of Peacekeeping', in David Rudd (ed.), *Future Peacekeeping: A Canadian Perspective* (Toronto: CISS, 2000), p. 42.
8. Interview with Len Hill, Second Secretary, US Embassy in Ottawa, 14 March 2000.
9. Minister of National Defence, *The 1994 Defence White Paper*, p. 12.
10. James I. Hanson, Canada, Haiti and the UN (CISS unpublished paper, March 1995), p. 8.
11. Lloyd Axworthy, 'Canada and Human Security: The Need for Leadership', *International Journal*, Vol. 52, No. 2 (spring 1997), p. 184.
12. For more information, see the ICSS website, www.iciss-ciise.gc.ca/report-e.asp.
13. J. L. Granatstein and D. J. Bercuson, *War and Peacekeeping: From South Africa to the Gulf – Canada's Limited Wars* (Toronto: Key Porter, 1991), p. 25.
14. Legault, *Canada and Peacekeeping*, p. 67.
15. Jockel, *Canada and International Peacekeeping*, pp. 19–20.
16. Fred Gaffen, *In the Eye of the Storm: A History of Canadian Peacekeeping* (Toronto: Deneau and Wayne, 1987), p. 220.
17. Peter Jones, *Peacekeeping: An Annotated Bibliography* (Kingston, Ontario: Ronald P. Frye, 1989), p. xvi.
18. Legault, *Canada and Peacekeeping*, p. 67.
19. Ibid., p. 84.
20. Minister of National Defence, *1994 Defence White Paper*, p. 20.
21. Legault, *Canada and Peacekeeping*, p. 91.
22. See 'Canada's commitment to Rwanda and Zaire is brave and honourable', *The Globe and Mail* (14 November 1996), A20.

23. See editorial, *Toronto Star* (20 November 1996), A23.

24. J. Appathurai and R. Lysyshyn, 'Lessons learned from the Zaire Mission', *Canadian Foreign Policy*, Vol. 6, No. 2 (winter 1998), p. 100.

25. Jerome, 'The Unseen Politics of Peacekeeping', p. 43.

26. Dispatched to assess the need for humanitarian action, Canadian General Maurice Baril confined his inspections to the route between Goma and Mugunga. Although he had been briefed by officials of Doctors Without Borders that the route was empty only because the refugees had moved on, he proclaimed that they had all gone home and that intervention was therefore unnecessary. See Jerome, 'The Unseen Politics of Peacekeeping', pp. 41–3.

27. Allan Thompson, 'Canada taking troops out of Afghanistan', *Toronto Star* (22 May 2002), A1.

28. See 'Boy Scouts and Proud', *The Globe and Mail* (20 November 1996), A23.

29. Scott Taylor, 'Poor gear, thin ranks hitting military with both barrels', *Halifax Herald* (22 July 2002), A18.

30. David Pugliese, 'Peacekeeping criticism "bunk," Axworthy says', *Ottawa Citizen* (8 June 2001), A1.

31. Hugh Segal, 'The International Environment and Canadian Foreign Policy: A Time for Candor', in David Rudd (ed.), *Vision Into Reality: Toward a New Canadian Defence and Security Concept* (Toronto: CISS, 2002), pp. 18–25. Segal discusses the 'Sokolsky Principle', whereby the Canadian military is viewed as under-equipped and under-funded, but which manages to perform well on any given mission, prompting the government of the day to ask why additional funds should be added to the defence budget.

32. Recent examples include 'Facing our Responsibilities: The state of readiness of the Canadian Forces' (Ottawa: Standing Committee on National Defence and Veterans Affairs, 2002); and 'Canadian Security and Military Preparedness' (Ottawa: Standing Senate Committee on National Security and Defence, 2002).

33. Jerome, 'The Unseen Politics of Peacekeeping', p. 42.

34. Conversation with Marci Ien, CTV Newsnet, 20 February 2002.

35. Nader Hashemi, 'Why Yasser Arafat must go', *The Globe and Mail* (18 July 2002), A17.

36. Jerome, 'The Unseen Politics of Peacekeeping', p. 45.

NINE

◄○►

Nigeria

Herbert M. Howe

INTRODUCTION

The prolonged and devastating conflicts in Liberia and Sierra Leone demonstrate that West Africa needs effective regional peacekeeping and peace-enforcing capability. The international community will not send ground combat forces, and Nigeria, the physical, financial, and military giant of the region, claims some ability, experience, and willingness to act as West Africa's primary peacekeeper and peace enforcer.[1]

However, does Nigeria have sufficient capability to carry out effective peacekeeping and peace-enforcing operations in West Africa? Nigeria suffers from several shortcomings including some thirty years of authoritarian rule until 1999 and ongoing military unprofessionalism, as Nigeria's ten-year stewardship of ECOMOG (Economic Community of West African States Military Observer Group) demonstrates.[2] While the country's nascent democratization since 1999 may heighten military professionalism, voter demands that Nigeria channel its resources to its domestic citizenry may prevent deployment of an improved military for future peacekeeping/enforcing missions. Nigeria's international suppor-ters, especially the US, hope to assist Nigerian regional intervention but they face a range of political obstacles. This case study is not *sui generis* to Nigeria alone; many of the difficulties it faces resemble those of other Third World countries involved in regional peace operations.

WEST AFRICA'S GROWING NEED FOR MILITARY SECURITY

The Cold War stabilized many African regimes whereas its ending facilitated the emergence of failed states, such as Liberia and Sierra Leone in West Africa.³ The Soviet Union supplied about 18.8 billion dollars of military hardware to sub-Saharan Africa while the US gave close to three billion dollars. Stabilization came in other forms.⁴ Non-African patrons discouraged their African clients from invading or subverting their neighbors, as Western or communist states had no desire to become involved in African interstate conflicts. During Africa's first three decades of independence, African states also heeded the Organization of African Unity's charter, which argued for the territorial integrity of sovereign African states.

The West African state of Liberia was an American favorite during much of the Cold War; the United States provided about half a billion dollars between 1980 and 1985 to the despotic Samuel Doe government. Britain retained close ties with Sierra Leone, and both Liberia and Sierra Leone faced no significant conflicts from foreign or domestic foes between 1960 and the end of the 1980s.

The Cold War's ending encouraged domestic and regional conflict within much of Africa. Internationally, the precipitous drop in foreign aid and military assistance from both communist and Western nations undercut rulers' patronage and coercive capabilities beginning in the mid- to late 1980s. The US had stopped aiding Samuel Doe as the perceived Soviet (and Libyan) threat to West Africa faded and as Doe's ineptitude and corruption thoroughly exasperated Washington. The National Patriotic Front of Liberia's (NPFL) 100-man 'invasion' of Liberia on 24 December 1989 failed to persuade the US to aid to the now beleaguered Liberian government. The NPFL's military campaign continued for some six years; in 1997 it gained power through a national election. Britain declined to send troops or greatly enhanced military aid programs to Sierra Leone in the early and mid-1990s, even as the Revolutionary United Front guerrillas gained increasing influence.

Military supplies to insurgents, usually *gratis* from Warsaw Pact countries or the People's Republic of China, also plummeted, but this drop of weaponry surprisingly *worsened* African security. During the 1970s and 1980s, superpowers exercised some control over combatants' behavior by conditioning their support upon their patrons' behavior. None of the insurgencies backed by the superpowers had emphasized the selling of natural resources (diamonds, gold, and timber) for military supplies or the wide-scale brutalizing of defenseless groups.

After the end of the Cold War, rebels could free themselves from such conditions – if they could purchase weaponry. This occurred in both Liberia and Sierra Leone. Charles Taylor's National Patriotic Front of Liberia (NPFL), already emboldened by the absence of US military

H. M. Howe

support for the Liberian government, became a modern warlord to support his military ambitions. He supplied various Asian and French companies with high-grade lumber, for example. Sierra Leone, which sits on Liberia's western border, saw the insurgent RUF (Revolutionary United Front) make somewhere between 20 and 80 million dollars yearly from diamond sales.

These new insurgencies went after the civilian population: the RUF chopped off the arms of some 30,000 rural Sierra Leoneans between 1996 and 2000 and Liberia's various insurgencies gained an odious human rights reputation. International relief groups were no longer immune, and the rebels attacked them to seize foreign exchange and hostages as well as communications and transportation equipment. Insurgents in Liberia seized some 20 million dollars of equipment (including some 480 vehicles) over a three-day period in April 1996.

African states now also have to worry about their neighbors more than they did before 1990. Drops in foreign assistance lessened previous conditions upon behavior and increased the need to find alternative resources. 'Military mercantilism' grew in the 1990s, as some states militarily crossed international borders for financial gain: some seven states fought in the Democratic Republic of Congo (Zaïre), and money was often a major motive.

West Africa has seen an upsurge of bad neighbor behavior since the late 1980s. Côte d'Ivoire served as the springboard for the NPFL's 1989 Liberian invasion. When Taylor gained control of Liberia in 1997, he continued assisting the RUF (as he had done during his rebel years) against the Sierra Leonean government as well as apparently aiding Guinean dissidents as they fought to undermine their own government.

The wars' costs to fragile states and unprotected civilians have proven immense. Damaged infrastructure, the loss of foreign investment and exports, the rise of internally displaced citizens and unwanted foreign refugees, the drop in state legitimacy, the intensification of group animosities within each country, the growth of several uneducated generations, and alarming surges in serious diseases such as AIDS and tuberculosis will severely constrain future domestic development.

WESTERN TEMERITY TO INTERVENE

The need for effective peacekeeping is obvious but the West will continue refraining from dispatching troops to virtually any of Africa's post-Cold War conflicts.[5] The end of communism diluted the West's already weak national interests in the continent. America's (and the UN's) retreat from Somalia further underlined foreign unwillingness to serve as foreign military stabilizers. That Somalia is not in West Africa is largely irrelevant; its embarrassment of the US and the UN involvements between 1992 and 1995 led to the 'Somalia Syndrome' and the subsequent US government's Presidential Decision Directive 25 of 1994, both of which essentially constrained the US from committing ground troops in countries relatively unimportant to the US.[6]

Although the US had been a virtual colonial power in Liberia since the mid-1800s and had strongly supported Doe until the mid- to late 1980s, Washington refused to supply troops when the NPFL was threatening Doe in early 1990. Equally, former colonial ruler Britain refused to send troops or significant supplies to Sierra Leone throughout the 1990s as the RUF continued its destructive campaign.

WHAT ROLE FOR NIGERIA?

Nigeria as the region's policeman

Since the threat to West African stability has grown, and since non-African states refuse to intervene, then Africa must assume major responsibility for its own security. Numerous military and non-military reasons suggest Nigeria as the policeman of the region.

On paper, Nigeria certainly shows the ability. Its Order of Battle is daunting by regional standards. Its military of perhaps 90,000 men surpasses the combined total of all of its neighbors, and its equipment includes MiG fighters, eight MI-24 helicopter gunships, 150 Vickers MK3, and 50 T-55 main battle tanks. Nigerian soldiers served ably in several peacekeeping missions, most notably with the UN's mission to the Congo in the 1960s. Nigeria was the main contributor of men, materiel and money to ECOMOG's ten years of peacekeeping (1990–2000), first in Liberia and then in Sierra Leone. Nigeria also has the biggest economic base among West African states to support foreign military operations – the country produces 75 percent of West Africa's GNP – and it has 50 percent of the region's total population.

This West African giant has long sought the role of regional leader. Shehu Shagari, Nigeria's president between 1979 and 1983, argued that 'Just as ... President Monroe proclaimed the American hemisphere free from the military incursions of European empire builders and adventurers, so also do we ... in Nigeria and in Africa insist that African affairs be left to

Africa to settle.'[7] A former Nigerian ambassador to Nigeria proclaimed, 'We have to be recognized as a regional power in West Africa. This is our region and we have a right to go to war. It is a Monroe Doctrine of a sort.'[8]

Nigeria essentially created ECOMOG and quickly assumed most of the responsibilities of this peacekeeping force. President Ibrahim Babangida's close personal friendship with President Doe, a fear that the Liberian conflict could destabilize neighboring states, and concern for Nigerian nationals trapped in Liberia help explain Nigeria's leadership. By mid-1990, Charles Taylor's NPFL had spread rapidly throughout Liberia and was posed to participate in a firefight for Monrovia, Liberia's capital. The government of Ibrahim Babangida seized the diplomatic lead by persuading four other nations (Gambia, Ghana, Guinea, and Sierra Leone) in early August 1990 to contribute troop units to a largely Nigerian operation; in late August, ECOMOG's 2,700 soldiers departed their staging base in Sierra Leone and entered Liberia's capital of Monrovia, where they encountered armed opposition from the NPFL. ECOMOG pushed the NPFL out of Monrovia but it declined to mount significant counter-insurgency operations in Liberia's heavily vegetated interior, and for most of the next six years it primarily garrisoned Monrovia and several other cities while providing materiel and intelligence to several anti-Taylor factions.

Nigeria began wearying of its ECOMOG commitment by the mid-1990s. It had been providing at least 70 percent of ECOMOG's continuing costs in an apparently unwinnable war against Charles Taylor. Nigeria initially thought that ECOMOG would serve as peacekeepers for a six-month maximum period. Instead, ECOMOG fluctuated between peace-keeping and peace enforcement for some five years, at which point President Abacha began negotiations with Taylor to end an unwinnable war. Two years later, in May 1997, Taylor won election as President of Liberia.

Peace in Liberia did not end ECOMOG's regional intervention. ECOMOG entered Sierra Leone, Liberia's western neighbor, in 1997, following the toppling of President Ahmed Tejan Kabbah by the Armed Forces Revolutionary Council, a coalition of the RUF and rebellious army officers. A bloodied ECOMOG left Sierra Leone in early 2000, although it would contribute several battalions to its successor, UNAMSIL (United Nations Assistance Mission in Sierra Leone).

Nigeria in ECOMOG

Nigeria's motives for, and support of, ECOMOG appear positive at first glance. ECOMOG agreed to enter where superpowers feared to tread, the failed states of Liberia and then Sierra Leone. The government of Ibrahim Babangida understandably worried that (1) conflict in Liberia could jump the country's arbitrary boundaries and destabilize the neighboring fragile states, (2) foreign nationals trapped in Liberia could suffer, (3) more innocent Liberians would suffer, and (4) neither the US (a historically close ally of Liberia) nor the UN showed any inclination to intervene. Each of these justifications had a basis in fact. Charles Taylor soon began sponsoring the RUF, which undermined Sierra Leone throughout the 1990s and Guinea in 2000. Taylor's NPFL may have killed up to a thousand Nigerians in 1990, and the war itself claimed over 40,000 dead, mostly civilian, Liberians. The ending of the Cold War and the decline in Africa's strategic importance coupled with the Gulf War help explain the world's inattention to Liberia.

Nigeria provided about 75 percent of ECOMOG's men, materiel, and money in Liberia and some 90 percent in Sierra Leone. Despite significant costs – perhaps four billion dollars and 600 fatalities in Liberia alone – Nigeria 'stayed the course' and contrasted favorably with the international timidity displayed towards Somalia, Rwanda, and elsewhere. ECOMOG undoubtedly saved thousands of Monrovians who may have otherwise been killed during two punishing attacks by the NPFL in 1990 and 1992. The US government (which over ten years contributed about 100 million dollars to ECOMOG)[9] has praised the largely Nigerian force's 'patient determination and commitment ... to bring peace and security to Liberia'.[10] In 1997, shortly before leaving Liberia, ECOMOG entered Sierra Leone, eventually overthrowing the tyrannical and universally unrecognized Armed Forces Revolutionary Council (AFRC) government. Nigeria's manpower costs were even higher in Sierra Leone despite the shorter time period: Nigeria lost about 1,000 soldiers over a three-year period.

But Nigeria's political motives and military methods cast doubts on Nigeria's achievements and raise questions about Nigeria's future peace-making/enforcing role. Critics note that some of Nigeria's motives and methods for supporting ECOMOG appear less than exemplary. They contend that anglophone–francophone rivalries, rather than regional protection, encouraged Nigeria's championing of ECOMOG. Robert Mortimer contends that 'the multilateral, but Nigerian-dominated, force is more a classic study of competing national interests in the West African subregion than ... a case study in regional peacekeeping'.[11] A former English colony, Nigeria has seen France and its former colonies as its primary rival for regional influence. Paris's exceptionally strong political, economic, and military ties with most of its former West African colonies had thwarted Nigeria's drive to impose its own Monroe Doctrine upon the region (France also had militarily supported the breakaway state of Biafra during the Nigerian civil war). Côte d'Ivoire and Burkina Faso, two former French colonies, assisted the NPFL with equipment and training and it was from Côte d'Ivoire that Taylor staged his 1990 invasion of anglophone Liberia. Not surprisingly, four of ECOMOG's five initial members were anglophone.

The hypocrisy of a manifestly undemocratic government fighting for overseas democratization was not lost on many African observers and undoubtedly diminished ECOMOG's legitimacy. ECOMOG's mandate included 'creat[ing] the necessary conditions for free and fair elections', yet Stephen Stedman writes that 'Nigeria, led by a regime that came to power through a military coup and in existence as a state because it triumphed in a civil war, had no credibility when it came to urging parties to resolve their conflict peacefully.'[12]

The repressive authoritarianism of Nigeria may have facilitated its ability to deploy troops overseas. Personal rule, in which individual rulers control the institutions of state (rather than vice versa), has been Nigeria's prevailing form of government since the mid-1960s. Babangida never consulted institutions such as parliament about forming ECOMOG because Nigeria had no parliament to approve and then monitor the deployment – Babangida and then Abacha largely ruled by personal fiat. These rulers increasingly cowed a traditionally feisty media and withheld basic information about ECOMOG: manpower levels, financial costs, news from the front, and casualty figures. The papers lacked foreign exchange required for serious coverage of the war (housing, transportation, and communication for correspondents; even wire photo costs were prohibitive for some papers). The public may not have paid much attention to such information anyway, given its preoccupation with domestic necessities – the authoritarian government was cracking down increasingly upon most forms of political protest and per capital income was dropping rapidly, from 1,250 dollars in the mid-1980s to about 230 dollars in 1993.

Nigeria attempted to fight a counter-insurgency (COIN) campaign without the requisite equipment. The absence of an accountable political system and the abundance of corruption resulted in Nigeria lacking necessary COIN equipment, such as spotter planes and adequate radios (ECOMOG's forward checkpoints could not notify headquarters about the start of a major Taylor offensive in October 1992 – two years after ECOMOG's arrival). Main battle tanks and surface-to-air missiles were basically useless against small guerrilla units that had few economic targets, which did not fight in fixed-line positions, but which did live and operate under double- or triple-canopy jungle. This author was in Liberia in 1995 and saw ECOMOG's *sole* helicopter at that time, which was used to transport the Force Commander rather than to move cargo or troops, or to act as a weapons platform.

Nigeria and the other ECOMOG countries lacked knowledge of Liberia and Sierra Leone, despite the geographic proximity. The force obtained a tourist map of Monrovia about a day before it deployed on that city's beaches and it lacked suitable topographic maps until the US supplied them. Few, if any, of the ECOMOG troops had trained in Liberia or spoke Liberian dialects.

Lack of political knowledge had military consequences. Nigeria and the other contingents had ECOMOG deploy with a peacekeeping, rather than a peace-enforcing, mandate since they assumed that Charles Taylor and the other combatants would stop fighting once the conventionally equipped ECOMOG arrived. They misread Taylor, who opened fire upon ECOMOG and then continued to oppose ECOMOG's presence. ECOMOG planners had also underestimated the actual and potential business connections of Taylor's that would supply him with military materiel in exchange for natural resources.

The appreciation that Nigeria garnered for 'staying the course' in both countries must be qualified. Nigeria built up anti-Taylor factions with some free equipment, intelligence, and transit so that they could relieve ECOMOG from carrying the fight to Taylor. This policy worked in the short run but it later empowered future 'Frankensteins', who turned against their benefactor. By early 1996, Nigeria had reached a political accommodation with Taylor, but when Nigeria told the anti-Taylor units about the peace settlement, several factions turned their anger and their ECOMOG-supplied firepower against ECOMOG units. One of the factions killed about a hundred Nigerian soldiers in one of the firefights, outside of Tubmanberg in early 1996.[13]

A permissive Nigerian view towards corruption saw ECOMOG – and especially the Nigerian contingents – receive a derivative ECOMOG appellation: 'Everything Covered Or Moveable or Gone'.[14] Officers' economic pursuits curtailed already-limited military capabilities. Financial gain distracted units as some officers spent time managing their own financial affairs or by delegating their soldiers to gather local resources. Lagos's *This Day* claimed, 'Nigerian troops contributed immensely in the looting of that country to the extent that almost every soldier has something to send back home like automobiles, electronics, etc.'[15] A Nigerian colonel exchanged timber rights in his command sector and received 500 dollars monthly in return, for example.

A high-ranking Sierra Leonean diplomat, while expressing appreciation for ECOMOG, told this author in 1999 that some Nigerian officers commanded their soldiers to dig for diamonds, rather than to pursue the RUF.[16] Some battalion commanders 'parked' their units' money in the officers' private interest-bearing accounts or else skimmed off some of the pay before distributing the rest to its rightful owner. The result was that Nigerian enlistees at times extorted money or food, drink, and cigarettes (often courteously) at the ECOMOG checkpoints and, by so doing, weakened civilian support of ECOMOG and probably their willingness to provide local intelligence. Corruption sometimes directly threatened the lives of Nigerian soldiers: officers responsible for securing ballistic helmets reportedly purchased cheaper, and less protective, motorcycle helmets and pocketed the difference.

Corruption continued over ECOMOG's ten years, apparently even at its highest command levels. Major-General Vijay Jetley, the Indian commander of UNAMSIL in 2000, wrote a report stating that 'The Nigerian army was interested in staying in Sierra Leone due to the massive benefits they [*sic*] were getting from illegal diamond mining ... it is understood that a tacit understanding was reached between the RUF and [the Nigerians] of non-interference in each other's activities. Protecting Nigerian interests was paramount even if it meant scuttling the [peace process]'.[17] Jetley claimed that Nigerian General Maxwell Khobe had received ten million dollars to allow RUF's economic activities and that the Nigerian Force Commander of ECOMOG had the cooperation of RUF's leader, Foday Sankoh, to mine diamonds.

Importantly, the Nigerian military did not significantly reform itself during the 1990s, despite the obvious – and sometimes painful – learning opportunities. The Nigerian-controlled ECOMOG did not acquire relevant COIN material. Although ECOMOG did push the RUF from Freetown in February 1998, it insisted upon conventional infantry tactics in rural Sierra Leone against an increasingly capable RUF insurgency. General Timothy Shelpedi, the Nigerian commander of ECOMOG, expressed confidence in imminent victory during late 1998, but the RUF brazenly entered Freetown in January 1999 and departed only after three weeks of battle and perhaps 500 Nigerian deaths. The Nigerian military reportedly has not significantly upgraded its domestic training capabilities.

Logistics remains another Achilles' Heel. Following some five years of not being able to move equipment and men efficiently, ECOMOG in the mid-1990s began relying upon two American-financed private security companies for ground and air logistics, rather than strengthening an indigenous capability. ECOMOG also had to depend upon a motley but effective group of white, mostly South African, combat helicopter pilots. The London *Times* in January 1999 reported that 'ECOMOG officers admit that they would have lost Freetown last month without Mr. [Fred] Marafuno and his comrades, "Juba" Joubert and Neil Ellis, both South Africans, and their Ethiopian engineer, Sindaba. "Without these guys, we would have run out of food and ammo and fled the front. They are amazingly brave. I know they do it for money, but I wouldn't do it for anything," said a Nigerian lieutenant colonel.'[18]

THE EFFECT OF PERSONAL RULE UPON NIGERIA'S MILITARY

Personal rule played a major role in undermining Nigeria's military capabilities.[19] A succession of Nigerian rulers saw the armed forces as threatening to their regimes – a quite understandable concern, given that Nigeria has experienced five successful and at least two unsuccessful military seizures of power. While authoritarianism has given way, at least temporarily, to Obasanjo's present democratization, its effects upon the military will not leave so easily.

These authoritarian rulers, most of whom were military officers themselves, deliberately emasculated their security forces. Rulers crossed over the presumed civil–military divide to interfere in strictly military responsibilities as maintenance, promotions, and training. They mothballed military assets and promoted political sycophants while demoting or firing politically undesirable officers. A few examples: President Babangida, who ruled from 1985 to 1994, ordered Nigeria's MiG-21 fleet not to fly after he viewed it impressively performing aerial maneuvers. Babangida issued that order in 1989; the MiGs have not flown since then. Maintenance of much of the equipment, including all of the MiGs, became largely non-existent after the early 1990s.

President Sani Abacha, who ruled from 1994 to 1998, continued Babangida's emasculation of the armed forces. He forbade any combined field-training exercises by units larger than a company, from at least 1996 to 1998. Since a company numbers approximately 100 men and Nigeria claims an army of about 80,000, the absence of training diluted whatever capability the army once may have had.

Politically determined promotions and demotions hurt military professionalism. Jimi Peters, in his *The Nigerian Military*, writes that such decisions, which had begun in at least the 1970s, 'liquidated the senior ranks of [the Nigerian military's] professional cadre. The remaining officer corps became understandably reticent – to give professional military advice necessary for the improvement of the organization.'[20] Babangida reportedly removed from the air force over thirty officers with the rank of air commodore or above, following a failed *coup* in April 1990. Political meddling weakened the chain of command by elevating the rulers' personal favorites. Babangida and Abacha provided Captain Hamza al-Mustapha with unusual powers, to the extent that three generals at different times actually had to bow in front of this junior officer to receive their requests. Abacha continued this interference in promotion process.

Political fears of *coups* encouraged fiefdoms within the military. Successive chief of army staffs possessed more power than suggested by organizational flow charts. Given the predilection for army *coups* (neither the air force nor the navy played any significant role in Nigeria's successful and unsuccessful *coups*), the chief of army staff acquired wide latitude in defense matters and rarely had to answer to the Chief of Defense Staff or the Minister of Defense.

Successive presidents undermined the military's operational capabilities while granting unusual non-military powers to active-duty officers. Almost one hundred officers served as state governors whereas more served in other, secondary political positions. The lack of official or civic society oversight of authoritarian system encouraged many of these officers to pass state-controlled munificence to themselves and their own ethnic–regional–religious groups. These still active-duty officers often paid more attention to civil activities rather than such mundane military responsibilities as training. Chances for economic gain also caused competition and resentment among officers.

Officers benefited from the *enrichissez-vous* permissiveness of authoritarian rule, especially in the areas of procurement and payroll, and often this resulted in irrelevant or inferior equipment. 'Backhander' is a Nigerian term for 'kickback', and successive regimes permitted a wide range of officers to purchase weapons and other materiel, in part, to maintain their support. J. Kayode Fayemi and other Nigerian observers believe that backhanders encouraged the purchase of expensive, and often highly sophisticated, weaponry since the kickback would be higher.[21] Nigerian officers received 3.6 million dollars in backhanders when they purchased from the Lockheed Corporation six Hercules C-130 transport planes valued at 45 million dollars.

Such procurement paid more attention to the cost and the status of the item rather than to its applicability to Nigerian defense. Nigeria had no national defense plan to establish procurement priorities, and the country probably faced no conventional threat following independence. This did not stop it from purchasing the Vickers and T-55 battle tanks or the MiG and Alpha fighter jets or Roland surface-to-air missiles. Yet Nigeria needed a highly mobile light-infantry capability. US intelligence sources maintain that Nigeria in the late 1980s turned down offers to develop a local airborne, as well as riverene, capability. One long-serving African specialist speculates that the lack of significant backhander was a major reason for the rejection, along with a possible fear that dissident officers could turn such specialized capability against the regime.

Corruption increased manpower costs. Nigeria claims that its military numbers about 90,000, with the army claiming perhaps 80,000, yet Nigerians acknowledge that these are guesses – no accurate figures exist. Some Western military observers claim that the armed forces number between 35,000 and 60,000,[22] with 'ghost soldiers' accounting for the difference. Unit commanders may claim an exaggerated number of soldiers in order to secure a larger payroll.

Corruption each month hurt many actual army enlistees and lowered morale. Army battalion commanders traditionally have responsibility for paying the approximately eight hundred men in each of their units. Some of these colonels deposited, or 'park', these bulk monthly allotments in private banks to accrue interest. After one or more months, the officers pocketed the interest before passing the salaries (in whole or in part) to the soldiers. Drops in morale and the 'requisitioning' of food and other supplies from angry civilians resulted. Substandard barracks and mediocre medical care – sometimes a result of corruption – also lessened the attractiveness of the military as a career option.[23]

CORRUPTION'S EFFECT UPON FOREIGN DEPLOYMENT

Nigeria's corruption undermined its peacekeeping and peace-enforcing capabilities. Placing loyalty over effectiveness in officer selection and promotion lessened leadership effectiveness. Procurement of major weapons systems, e.g. main battle tanks, that were unsuitable in dense terrain and that required significant maintenance weakened ECOMOG's firepower. The allowing of officers to engage in economic pursuits distracted the Nigerians from their primary military responsibilities. Parking of soldiers' pay forced, or at least encouraged, enlistees to steal from Liberians and thereby lose some of their initial public support.

By the mid-1990s, Nigeria was reconsidering its role as the pre-eminent peacekeeper of the region. The Abacha government brokered the Abuja agreements that led to Liberia's 1997 elections. Tom Ikimi, Nigeria's Foreign Minister, admitted in 1996, 'we are concerned that Nigerian soldiers should continue to lose their lives over a matter [Liberia] that docs not necessarily concern us'.[24] The RUF's increasingly successful small unit operations and then its entry into Freetown in late 1998 debilitated Nigerian morale, especially following General Shelpedi's confident predictions. *Tempo* magazine wrote:

> Many Nigerian officers who are supposed to lead troops are said to have gone into hiding, not [because of] cowardice but because they felt the Nigerian participation in the war was senseless. The question on the lips of many now is what is Nigeria still doing in Sierra Leone.[25]

Tempo complained about 'the continued humiliation of the ECOMOG [*sic*] by undisciplined, rag-tag Revolutionary Front rebels',[26] a point also mentioned by the BBC: 'Though well trained and fully armed with air and artillery support, ECOMOG troops have been made to look foolish by motley groups of rebels.'[27] Nigeria's inadequate medical care of its enlistees suffered significant public embarrassment when 26 wounded soldiers protested that in Nigeria they 'were made to rot in bed without drugs and medical care' and had to spend their own money for whatever drugs they could find.[28]

The growing unpopularity of the Babangida and especially the Abacha governments – both champions of ECOMOG – undermined remaining domestic support for Nigeria's regional peacekeeping. Nigeria's failing economy, eviscerated especially by now-endemic corruption, persuaded citizens that the state should concentrate its resources domestically.

Olusegun Obasanjo, Nigeria's current president (and a retired major-general), summarized a widespread view about ECOMOG when he complained in 1998:

> Nigeria can go to Liberia and make a mess up there and spend and waste our money because what we got after five years of ECOMOG in Liberia, we would have got without sending one single troop to Liberia, because it's the same thing we got at the end. Taylor would have been there if we hadn't sent one single soldier. Taylor was there after five years – we have the same difference.[29]

In May 1999, the anti-ECOMOG Obasanjo won election as Nigeria's President amidst overwhelming public sentiment that the state needed to focus its resources domestically. Nigeria presently has a demoralized, poorly equipped and poorly trained military that will be hard to reform within the next several years – even if the armed forces and the Nigerian populace want such improvement.

NIGERIA'S PEACEKEEPING–ENFORCING FUTURE

Since personal rule encouraged unprofessional militaries, will Nigeria's nascent democratization improve operational capability of the country's armed forces? The answer could be no, and this helps explain why Nigeria will probably not regain its pre-eminent peacekeeping role.

President Obasanjo clearly wants a more capable armed force. He spoke movingly about the military in his inaugural speech and stated that he wanted to 're-professionalize' it: 'a great deal of re-orientation has to be undertaken and a redefinition of roles, retraining, and re-education will have to be done to ensure that the military submits to civil authority and regains its pride, professionalism and tradition'.[30]

Most analysts believe the President's sincerity but wonder whether the obstacles are too great. Reform of his armed forces may benefit Obasanjo in the long run but, like any ruler, he realizes the immediate importance of security – and a relatively content military – for the short run. By late 2001, soldiers were patrolling in at least six of Nigeria's 36 states and issues of religion (especially the implementation of *sharia* by thirteen states), ethnicity, and revenue allocation had led to the killing of some six thousand civilians since Obasanjo's election. Changes in training and other areas have angered some high-ranking officers and could weaken the country's security.

Foreign military training and advising has proven especially difficult. President Obasanjo and the US government implemented two programs, one short and one longer-run, to raise the armed forces' overall capabilities. 'Operation Restore Hope' supplied US Special Forces (Green Berets) to train five Nigerian (and two other West African) battalions in combat skills for Sierra Leone. Military Professional Resources Incorporated (MPRI) has suggested measures to reform military administration, including systematized payroll dispersal.

Opposition was quick in coming. General Victor Malu, the Chief of Army Staff until May 2001, publicly objected to US training and advising programs, including the Special Forces and the MPRI programs. Malu instituted several measures to derail Operation Restore Hope, and he claimed that an already professional Nigerian military did not need foreign advice; Nigeria had conducted more peacekeeping than had the US. Other

officers questioned the credentials of a force that departed Somalia because
of a firefight that killed only eighteen American soldiers. Some Nigerians
felt that Malu and his followers feared that an outside competent force
might reveal the military's corruption and inefficiency.

Obasanjo fired Malu, and the two other service chiefs, in late April 2001
for such public criticism: Obasanjo had previously fired several hundred
officers for ineptitude or public criticism. These officers have apparently
taken their forced retirement gracefully but the threat remains that officers
embittered by Obasanjo's plans for greater transparency and accountability
may link up with powerful ethnic, religious, or regional groups and turn
forcibly against the Obasanjo government. No civilian government has
successfully conducted democratic elections in Nigeria's history and
probably all observers anticipate increasing and sometimes armed tension
preceding the 2003 elections.

A prime paradox is that while a more capable military may result from a
relatively transparent and accountable Nigerian government, such an
armed force may not act as foreign peacekeepers as often as it might under
an authoritarian government. Any future foreign deployment by a
democratizing Nigeria will face public criticism if it requires domestic
funding, if its mission is other than defending Nigeria's borders, and if it
involves significant combat. Indignation over ECOMOG's various costs
with few benefits has prompted leading Nigerian security officials to soft-
peddle possible Nigerian peacekeeping/enforcing in the future. Minister of
Defense Theophilus Danjuma has stated, 'Right now, we are becoming the
United States of ECOWAS at very great cost to us. We think this is
unaffordable to us now.'[31]

ECOMOG's future appears uncertain, given the likelihood of heightened differences about whether to deploy and the diminution of Nigerian
backing. Several West African countries opposed the creation of
ECOMOG for various political reasons and several ECOMOG contributors still smart from what they perceived as Nigerian arrogance or
incompetence.[32] Any future ECOMOG will probably feature a wider base
of decision-making – which may lessen the chance of deployment, given
the various political allegiances of West Africa's sixteen states. In addition,
a domestically focused Nigeria may be reticent to provide 70 to 90 percent
of future ECOMOG needs, especially if it cannot exercise as much control
as it did previously. Regional concerns and distrust about Nigeria acting as
West Africa's hegemon may also restrict that country's unilateral military
insertions.

Having said that, Nigeria may still become a significant peacekeeping,
but not peace-enforcing, power. Should re-professionalization succeed,

and by mid-2002 the military had improved somewhat,[33] the United Nations would jump at the chance to hire these newly competent African peacekeepers. Nigeria would be willing to dispatch company- and perhaps battalion-sized units for peacekeeping if other nations or organizations provide financing and if the mission is likely not to slide into peace enforcement, complete with higher political, financial, and political costs. The United Nations provides some inducements, including international prestige and about one thousand dollars monthly per soldier to the supplying country. Ghana's small army regularly has one of its six battalions serving with the UN and the soldiers reportedly enjoy the chance for travel, to work with other militaries, and to earn more pay (usually at least an extra 5 dollars per day). In mid-2001, Minister Danjuma indicated that Nigeria and South Africa had agreed that Nigeria would send troops to Burundi.[34] As of mid-2002, the deployment had not occurred.

Nigeria's peacekeeping record since 1990 provides several possible lessons to regional powers. First, insertion of an unprofessional force may prove worse than not intervening at all. While the Nigerian-based ECOMOG did save thousands of Liberian lives in August 1990, the military subsequently helped to plunder Liberia and then Sierra Leone as well as helping to militarize local forces who sometimes turned against their foreign benefactors and who might pose a destabilizing presence years after the peacekeepers have left. Taylor became Liberia's president after some seven years of fighting, the ruination of Liberia's already weak economy, and the deaths of at least 40,000 Liberians, and about 600 ECOMOG (mostly Nigerian) soldiers. ECOMOG's record during the 1990s may dissuade the region from future peacekeeping/enforcing missions, even should the specific situation deserve intervention.

Second, peacekeeping can quickly become peace-enforcing, which will usually increase the political, military, and economic expenses of the interveners, as ECOMOG discovered when it first entered Monrovia in 1990. Countries attempting regional peacekeeping should have adequate military capability and political support to shift into the more costly peace-enforcing, if necessary.

Third, an avowedly neutral peacekeeping force from within the region may not enjoy special acceptance from the combatants. The NPFL and the RUF resented Nigeria and other countries positioning themselves between the capital city and the rebels. Even the recipients of military supplies from the peacekeepers may eventually turn against their benefactors. Local forces use the foreign troops just as much as if not more than the peacekeepers used them.

Fourth, even a regional hegemon may not possess especially relevant military capabilities. Nigeria relied too much on conventional strategy and tactics and on often non-operational equipment. Rulers' fears about a capable military and their acquiescence in widespread corruption contributed to military ineffectiveness. Supporters of a proposed intervention should look behind a country's Order of Battle and ascertain actual operational effectiveness.

Fifth, a regional intervener may have unstated agendas that differ from its public mission. Some West African analysts wonder whether Obasanjo and Abacha may have been content (at least until the mid-1990s) for the Liberian and Sierra Leonean conflicts to continue. Foreign deployment allowed the rulers to send possibly mutinous officers overseas, to gain economic wealth via theft and illegal mining, and to secure some international goodwill as 'peacekeepers' that could counterbalance widespread criticism of domestic authoritarianism.

NOTES

1. Peacekeeping is the positioning of a force between two or more combatant units who have agreed to a ceasefire and political negotiations, as well as the presence of the neutral, foreign military force. Essentially, there is a peace to keep and peacekeepers will fight only in self-defense. Peace-enforcing is the use of might to force active belligerents to comply with agreed-upon conditions, e.g. a ceasefire and negotiations.
2. As elaborated upon later, Nigeria and four other members of ECOWAS (Economic Community of West African States) created ECOMOG (Economic Community of West African States Military Observer Group) in August 1990 as a peacekeeping force for strife-torn Liberia. ECOMOG later entered Sierra Leone to reinstall the ousted government of Ahmed Tejan Kabbah.
3. The Cold War did destabilize specific African countries, most notably Ethiopia and Angola, into which the superpowers poured significant military supplies. Stability, by itself, was not necessarily desirable, since superpower support of some despots only postponed needed political reform. See the author's *Ambiguous Order: Military Forces in African States* (Boulder, CO: Lynne Rienner, 2001).
4. Material and political assistance, by implying possible military intervention by the patrons if necessary, might have solidified public support for the ruler while dissuading potential insurgents.
5. The West usually did not insert ground troops into troubled African areas between 1960 and 1990. France was the major exception, given its still strong commitment to former francophone colonies. France had five military bases in Africa and a rapid response force in France, and the country dispatched troops on some twenty different occasions during this time period. Britain did send a combat force to Sierra Leone in 2000, ten years after the conflict had begun there.

6. Nothing demonstrated the universality of the Somalia syndrome more poignantly than the world's unwillingness to halt Rwanda's 1994 genocide. Various sources vividly document the determination of the UN, the US, and other countries not to acknowledge the Hutu-led genocide which killed Tutsis at a rate some five times faster than German death camps annihilated Jews and other prisoners.
7. Adekeye Adebayo, 'Nigeria: Africa's New Gendarme?' *Security Dialogue*, Vol. 31, No. 2 (March 2000), p. 186.
8. Ibid.
9. Critics of the US involvement note that much of this aid came only after 1995 (and the two punishing assaults by the NPFL upon Monrovia in 1990 and 1992) and that the aid's bilateral nature fostered resentment between national contingents since the US especially supported the latter ECOMOG arrivals, Senegal, Tanzania, and Uganda. The US conducted bilateral assistance, rather than support the centralized ECOMOG, because Washington had 'decertified' the Nigerian government from receiving aid. The US strongly believed that the Obasanjo and Abacha governments were heavily involved in the international drug trade.
10. 'US Congratulates ECOWAS on Liberia Election', 8 August 1997. US Information Service Archives, gopher://198.80.36.82:70/OR4493575444937917-range/archives/1997/pdq97.
11. Robert Mortimer, 'From ECOMOG to ECOMOG II', in John Harbeson and Donald Rothchild (eds), *African World Politics: The African State in Flux* (Boulder, CO: Westview, 1991), p. 203.
12. Stephen Stedman, 'Conflict and Conciliation in Sub-Saharan Africa', in Michael Brown (ed.), *The International Dimensions of Internal Conflict* (Cambridge: Cambridge University Press, 1996), p. 253.
13. Ulimo–J (the United Liberation Movement of Liberians for Democracy–Johnson) battled ECOMOG over ownership of a diamond mine. ECOMOG had been supporting Ulimo–J and other anti-Taylor factions, but the relationship turned hostile when Nigeria tried to broker a peace settlement with Taylor while the Liberian factions remain unalterably opposed to Taylor. All forces in Nigeria, including ECOMOG, engaged in economic activities which financially helped underwrite their continued military presence, but which distracted them from conducting even basic operations.
14. 'Every Car or Moveable Object Gone' is a common variation.
15. 'Jetley's Allegations and Nigeria's Image', *This Day* (6 October 2000).
16. Interview with author, spring 2000.
17. Jetley, *Perspective* (11 September 2000).
18. 'Mercenaries' Rage Kindled By Atrocities', *London Times* (24 January 1999).
19. Robert Jackson and Carl Rosberg, while underlining major differences among personal rulers, wrote that 'politics in most black African states do not conform to an institutionalized system', and Michael Bratton and Nicolas van de Walle define personal rule, or 'neo-patrimonialism', as when 'authority is entirely personalized, shaped by the ruler's preferences rather than any codified system of laws'. Jackson and Rosberg, *Personal Rule in Black Africa: Prince, Prophet, Autocrat, Tyrant* (Berkeley, CA: University of California Press, 1982), p. 1, and Michael Bratton and Nicholas van de Walle, *Democratic Experiments in Africa: Regime Transitions in Comparative Perspective* (Cambridge: Cambridge University Press, 1997), p. 61.

20. Jimi Peters, *The Nigerian Military and the State* (International Library of African Studies, 4; New York: St Martin's Press, 1997), p. 215.
21. J. Kayode Fayemi, *Threats, Military Expenditure and National Security: Analysis of Trends in Post-Civil War Defense Planning in Nigeria – 1970–1990*. Ph.D. dissertation, University of London, 1993.
22. Interviews, August 2001.
23. Falling pension benefits, not necessarily stemming from corruption, also hurt morale. In the late 1970s, the monthly pension was 110 naira, which then corresponded to 250 dollars. By 1989, the pension was still 100 naira but was now worth only 3 dollars, given the rise of inflation. By 2001, widespread press reports of retirees queuing for up to three weeks to receive pension payments undoubtedly worried active-duty soldiers and may have persuaded some to use their present military status to acquire wealth in preparation for their eventual retirement.
24. Ikimi, quoted in J. Kayode Fayemi, 'Nigeria's Military Politricks: Maniacal Tyrant Repositions Himself', Nigerian Democratic Movement, *NDM On-Line Magazine*, Vol. 1, No. 3 (27 April 1996), p. 4, http://www.cldc.Howard.edu/~ndmorg/ndmpage.html.
25. Ibid. General Jetley referred to Nigerian public sentiment when he wrote: 'It is well known that public opinion in Nigeria was against the continued deploying of Nigerian troops as part of ECOMOG in Sierra Leone.' Jetley, 'Report on the Crisis in Sierra Leone', http://www.Sierra-leone/jetley0500.html.
26. 'Unending Massacre', *Tempo* (4 February 1999).
27. Blunt quoted. Ibid.
28. The courts martial occurred because the soldiers publicly complained by refusing to leave their plane upon arrival in Cairo and by demanding to speak to Egyptian and American authorities. In Egypt, the soldiers complained that their superior officers had embezzled their allowances. A court martial in December 2000 sentenced the 26 to life imprisonment for mutiny. The decision provoked criticism from civilians and some military officers. Nigeria's Civil Liberties Organization wrote that 'it is evidently clear that the Nigeria Army's intention is to punish the servicemen rather than investigate their complaints, which is basically about the misappropriation of their estacode, lack of adequate medical attention [and] lack of care and sympathy by the army high command'. 'Don't Court-martial Wounded ECOMOG Troops-CLO', *Vanguard Daily* (16 October 2000).
29. Transcript of President Obasanjo's speech in Washington, DC, sponsored by the Center for Strategic and International Studies, 4 August 1998. Taylor won the election after seven, not five, years of ECOMOG's presence.
30. President Obasanjo's inauguration speech reprinted as an advertising supplement in the *Washington Times* (30 September 1999), p. 3.
31. *Vanguard* (18 August 1999). Quoted in Ebenezer Okpokpo, 'The Challenges Facing Nigeria's Foreign Policy in the Next Millennium', http://web.africa.ufl.edu/asq/v3/v313a16.htm.
32. See Christopher Tuck, ' "Every Car Or Moving Object Gone:" The ECOMOG Intervention In Liberia', http://www.africa.ufl.edu/asq,v4/v4ilal.htm.
33. Combat capability had increased within some units. The US 3rd Special Forces trained five battalions (about 3,500 men) in light infantry skills by late 2001 and the American trainers were reportedly impressed by the Nigerians' improvement. Professionalism has also risen somewhat because many officers, looking back on the

devastation caused by military rule, accept for now the concept of civilian political rule. Yet old habits die hard and resistance to civilian oversight remains strong. The US private security company Military Professional Resources, Incorporated (MPRI) has been trying to assist the military's administrative effectiveness, e.g. payroll dispersal, but success has been limited, in part because many Nigerian officers resent an outside group questioning basic doctrine – as well as examining financial records.

34. 'Nigeria, South Africa To Send Troops to Burundi', *This Day* (31 July 2001).

TEN

——◄◇►——

India

Alan James Bullion

INTRODUCTION

Of all the developing world countries, India is the most consistent and active supporter of United Nations (UN) peacekeeping operations. Over the past 50 years or so it has contributed to some 35 missions.[1] India's significant contribution to and former leadership of the recent UN Assistance Mission in Sierra Leone (UNAMSIL) represented a prime example of its continuing commitment to peacekeeping missions.[2] However, there are strong indications that India's future role in UN operations may be contingent on a range of other factors, such as the dynamics of its fraught relationship with neighbouring Pakistan, growing concerns about domestic security amid rising Hindu–Muslim tensions and the attack on key parliamentary buildings in December 2001, as well as the impact of continuing the 'global war against terrorism'. In these changed circumstances, India's foreign policy priorities have inevitably undergone a radical reappraisal. One of India's main strategic goals in participating in such missions has been to secure a permanent seat on the UN Security Council (UNSC). Despite this, expansion of the UNSC looks highly unlikely for the foreseeable future.[3] India will therefore review any force contribution to future operations very carefully, taking into account salient domestic, regional and global configurations.

The Sierra Leone case study well illustrates the various tensions between these factors. Following continuing conflict with the regional power Nigeria, which together with India and Jordan contributed the bulk of troops to UNAMSIL, force commander Major-General V. K. Jetley suddenly returned to New Delhi in early September 2000, reportedly suffering from malaria. India subsequently announced on 20 September that it would withdraw its entire force from Sierra Leone by the end of the year. India officially announced in a blandly worded statement that it was part of a 'routine rotation so as to give other member states a chance to participate in the mission'.[4] However, there was little doubt that India was primarily pre-empting a move from Nigeria and others to replace Jetley with a non-Indian general of higher rank to lead the expanded mission. In the event, a Kenyan, General Daniel Opende, finally replaced him. The decision to pull out the Indian troops was taken personally by Prime Minister Atal Behari Vajpayee, who was facing increasing criticism from members of parliament and some leading armed forces personnel for India's continuing involvement in the mission. There was also the factor to consider that since the British intervention in May 2000 the operation had taken a qualitative shift. With UN Secretary-General Kofi Annan's commitment to expand the total force to over 20,500 troops by early 2001, India would have almost inevitably become even more deeply committed to an indefinite mission.[5]

Although India had become involved in a more 'muscular' mission in Sierra Leone after the release of its captives in June 2000, which some commentators compared favourably with its assertive role taken in the Congo during the early 1960s, it should also be noted that since then India has hesitated to participate in peace enforcement missions governed by Chapter VII of the UN Charter. Indian Army Chief, General V. P. Malik, has issued a forceful critique of such peacekeeping operations. In a thinly veiled reference to the operation in Sierra Leone, Malik said that the UN should ensure that troops were not 'compromised due to political leverages'.[6] This demonstrates a major difference between India and most other developing countries that contribute to such operations. Although the responsibility for sending and withdrawing Indian troops lies ultimately with the prime minister, in a vibrant democracy such as India he or she can be influenced by lively criticism from opposition parties, the national press, and particularly both serving and retired generals, who have never been slow since the loss of 36 lives in the Congo mission to voice disapproval of key policy decisions or the direction of UN peacekeeping operations. For example, following overt criticism of his role, Lieutenant General Satish Nambiar angrily resigned as mission head of the UN Protection Force in the Former Yugoslavia (UNPROFOR).

Similarly, in Sierra Leone, Jetley's increasing differences with army officials and diplomats from Nigeria came into the open after the international press published several official documents he had submitted to UN headquarters in New York, which had allegedly been stolen from his computer in Freetown.[7] However, an embarrassed Jetley subsequently denied the existence of these reports, in which he informed the UN that some Nigerian officials were directly linked to the lucrative diamond trade in Sierra Leone and neighbouring Liberia, and that this was undermining the position of the peacekeeping mission.[8] Furthermore, Jetley confirmed rumours that he was having difficulties with insubordinate Nigerian officials disobeying his commands. He specifically named his Nigerian second-in-command General Mohammed Garba, as well as the UN Secretary-General's Special Envoy, Oluyemi Adeniji. Nigeria vehemently denied all these charges, and officials responded that Jetley had been high-handed and aloof, often acting without consultation with close colleagues.

MOTIVATIONS AND RATIONALE FOR PEACEKEEPING

Since the end of the Cold War, India has been engaged in most UN missions, providing military observers in the Iran–Iraq (1988–91) and Iraq–Kuwait border disputes (1991 onwards), Namibia (1989–91), Angola (1989–91), Central America (1988–92), El Salvador (1991–95), Liberia (1993–97), the Congo (1999 onwards), and Ethiopia–Eritrea (2000 onwards). Additionally, sizeable military contingents participated in operations in Cambodia (1992–93), Mozambique (1992–94), Somalia (1993–94), Rwanda (1993–96), Haiti (1994–2000), Angola (1995–99), Lebanon (1998 onwards), and Sierra Leone (1999–end of 2000).

In India's case, the reasons for this involvement in UN peacekeeping operations have been analysed by various commentators, including several eminent Indian generals who have served on UN missions. First, some argue that Indian participation has served its geo-strategic interests. This is most notable in the case of various East and Southeast Asian missions in Korea, Indo-China, Indonesia (west Irian) and Cambodia, which were all perceived in India to be vital to its conception of both regional stability and international order. The continued stability of the Middle East is also considered to be of vital strategic importance and India has thus participated in several missions in the region (Egypt, Iran–Iraq, Kuwait and Yemen). The free flow of energy (oil and gas) supplies and the openness of international waterways (the Suez Canal, the Persian Gulf) are other important factors here. In this context, Somalia, with its pivotal position on the Horn of Africa and close political and economic connections with West Asia, can also be considered of geo-strategic importance. It is less clear, however, what direct strategic purpose participation in African missions such as the Congo, Angola, Mozambique, Rwanda, Liberia and Sierra Leone has served.

Participation in these operations is explained by Parakatil and others as an expression of solidarity with non-aligned countries.[9] Allied to this, India has often taken a stridently anti-colonial stance, as in the Congo and Indonesia, when it regarded the conflict as one of aggression primarily perpetrated by a colonial power, such as Belgium or the Netherlands. India still perceives most of the recent African wars as the continuing legacy of the colonial era.

India possesses the fourth largest army in the world (over 1,400,000 troops), and arguably one of the most professionally trained, having served in two world wars, including in Africa. It is thus well suited to serve in a wide variety of conflict situations. In turn, these operations provide Indian troops with valuable experience which some commentators have more controversially suggested could also be utilized for domestic conflict resolution, in divided states such as Assam, the Punjab and Kashmir.[10] Other cogent reasons for participation include humanitarian concern, such as in Rwanda and Somalia, and the revenue to be earned by participation in such missions. In this regard, it is also acknowledged by fellow South Asian nations Pakistan, Bangladesh and Nepal, which likewise make sizeable contributions to UN missions, that payment by the UN helps them offset the large standing armies they wish to maintain for local strategic reasons. Following from this, it appears that inter-regional rivalry plays a part in India's wish to retain a major peacekeeping role and there is clearly an element of sub-continental competition about such deployments from South Asia. Finally, the wider desire for international *kudos* as a major power is a significant factor. There has been considerable lobbying by India in recent years to become a permanent member of the Security Council, in the face of competition not only from Pakistan, but also from Egypt, Brazil, Argentina, Nigeria, Kenya and South Africa among other Third World states.[11]

India suffered a significant setback to this ambition when it was beaten by Japan to the Asian non-permanent Security Council seat nomination on 26 October 1996. This was attributable in part to India's intransigence over the Comprehensive Test Ban Treaty (CTBT) negotiations of June–September 1996. Nevertheless, although pressure for reform of the UN system has since somewhat diminished largely due to a reassertion of the interests of the Permanent Five (P5) members in the wake of the terrorist attacks of 11 September 2001, any future expansion of the Security Council membership should lead to serious consideration of India's candidacy. In this respect, India's peacekeeping operations would theoretically stand it in good stead. UN Secretary-General Kofi Annan has previously voiced his support for India's candidature for a permanent seat. In an interview with

Doordarshan's *Worldview India* program, Annan said one of the proposals to reform the Council was to have five new members – two from the industrialized countries and three from the developing world.[12] 'When it comes to the Indian seat, even though the decision will have to be taken by the members, I think there is a sense among a large number of members that India will be natural for consideration of such a seat,' Annan said.

Indian journalist Jayachandran asked in an interview: 'Do you think that India will become a permanent member of the UN Security Council in due course?' Prime Minister A. B. Vajpayee replied, 'India has a legitimate right to become a member of the UN Security Council. India is gaining support on this front.'[13] India and Germany have both affirmed their claim to become permanent members of the UNSC, and agreed to work together for an early revamping of the UN system. The two countries, which have already announced their candidature, emphasized 'the need for reform and balanced enlargement' of the UNSC in order 'to make it more representative'. At a joint press conference in New Delhi on 17 May 2000 with Indian External Affairs Minister Jaswant Singh, German Foreign Minister Joschka Fischer said India 'is on its way to becoming one of the most important powers in the 21st century'.[14] Suggesting that this reality must be reflected in a reformed Security Council for the new century, Fischer indirectly backed India's case for a permanent seat in the UNSC. Declaring India as a 'force for regional stability', Fischer praised India's restraint during the Kargil conflict in 1999. Further discussions on international security were held when Indian Prime Minister Vajpayee attended his first ever summit of European Union (EU) leaders in Portugal at the end of June 2000. Similar talks were held with UNSC permanent member China, when Indian President K. R. Narayanan visited Beijing at the end of May 2000. Utilizing the Chinese interest in greater cooperation on global issues, Narayanan sought support from Chinese Prime Minister Zhu Rongji for India's bid for a permanent seat on the UNSC, in order to counter 'unipolarity'.[15]

Academic Amitabh Mattoo has offered India some cogent advice on how to improve its chances of getting a permanent seat on the UNSC: (a) bilaterally engaging with the permanent members on a sustained basis (for example, the visits of Indian President K. R. Narayanan to Beijing in May 2000 and Foreign Minister Jaswant Singh to Moscow from 21 to 24 June 2000, where such matters were raised); (b) making common cause with Germany and Japan (for example, the visit of German Foreign Minister Joschka Fischer to New Delhi in May 2000, where India's UNSC candidacy was discussed); and (c) retaining flexibility on the criteria for permanent membership.[16] Margaret Thatcher, a former British prime minister who adopts a traditional realist view of world politics, has also recently suggested that it might now be time for India's 'great power' status to be recognized with permanent membership on the UNSC.[17]

INDIAN CRITIQUES OF THE SIERRA LEONE OPERATION

The conflict in Sierra Leone commenced in March 1991, when fighters of the Revolutionary United Front (RUF) launched attacks to overthrow the government. In spite of joint peace efforts by a UN Special Envoy, the Organization of African States (OAU) and Economic Community of West African States (ECOWAS), armed hostilities continued. Despite the unrest, a peace agreement known as the Abidjan accord took place between the RUF and the government. These peace efforts were derailed due to a military *coup* in May 1997. In October 1997, the UN Security Council (UNSC) imposed an oil and arms embargo against the country and authorized ECOWAS, primarily under the auspices of Nigeria, to ensure strict implementation. In late October, negotiations culminated in a second peace plan to be monitored by the ECOWAS military observer group, commonly known as ECOMOG. Having subsequently ensured the security of most of Sierra Leone through military action, the UN lifted the oil and arms embargo, and established an observer mission (UNOMSIL) in July 1998. India contributed several military observers and medical personnel to this mission, under Brigadier S. C. Joshi.

However, the peace process soon broke down and rebels entered the capital Freetown on 6 January 1999 when the rebels targeted the UNOMSIL premises. Indian military observers stationed there volunteered to stay behind until all the others escaped or were evacuated. Joshi led the planning and execution of the evacuation of civilian staff while under attack. In October 1999, the UNSC passed Resolution 1270 creating a peacekeeping mission in Sierra Leone, the United Nations Assistance Mission in Sierra Leone (UNAMSIL) and charging it with a range of tasks: helping to carry out the government's 'disarmament, demobilisation and reintegration' plan; monitoring adherence to the ceasefire agreement; and protecting UN personnel and establishing 'a presence at key locations'.

The Security Council initially authorized 6,000 troops for the operation, and then the UN's Department of Peacekeeping Operations (DPKO) set about canvassing the countries that might contribute them. Certain countries, such as Canada, Australia, the Netherlands, Poland and Fiji, are regular contributors to international peacekeeping and it has been argued that a peacekeeping mission needs at least some of them in order to be successful. None of them, however, wanted to send their soldiers to Sierra Leone. India was the only country with a genuinely professional army that was willing to send troops. The other contributors came from African forces already on the ground – Nigeria, Ghana, Guinea and Kenya.

There is a certain persuasiveness to the argument that the 3,000 or so Indian soldiers stationed as part of UNAMSIL had no business being in Sierra Leone. For instance, there is a domestic consensus that the Indian Army should not be sent again to neighbouring Sri Lanka to fight the separatist Liberation Tigers of Eelam (LTTE). Critics therefore ask why Indian lives should be put at risk in a remote African country that does not figure on Delhi's diplomatic radar. However, a country that has ambitions for great power status and aspires to a permanent seat in the UN Security Council (UNSC) cannot forego its associated responsibilities. Supporters therefore argue that a leading role in a UN mission is certainly one such prime example of how to curry international favour.

A signed editorial in the influential weekly magazine *India Today* cogently argued that

> rather than take alarmist postures, the critics of the Indian presence in Sierra Leone should consider what makes the Indian *jawan* (soldier) such a model peacekeeper, a valuable servant of the UN from the Congo to Somalia. Defence analysts refer to the Indian Army as a 'developmental army', not just an aggressive unit but a force equipped for larger community service. The army, warts and all, has done such duty in the Northeast, taking medical care to remote villages. This is what makes valiant men India's ambassadors to the land they hope to calm. They represent the best India has to offer – in terms of protocol and manpower. The battalions serving in Sierra Leone include soldiers who won the Kargil war in 1999. They did not go there expecting to be ambushed by a treacherous militia. No doubt they will fight back the challenge. India must keep its faith in them – and in its obligations to the world.[18]

According to a media interview with retired Lieutenant General Satish Nambiar, former force commander of UNPROFOR,

> India has no immediate interests in Sierra Leone. But that is not the point. We have to look beyond our immediate interests.

As a great country we have certain commitments; if we aspire to be permanent members of the UN Security Council it cannot come on a platter – we must develop a stake in strengthening the Security Council set-up and such missions help do just that. But what has gone wrong? The assessment of the topography in Sierra Leone and understanding of the strength of the RUF was clearly inadequate. I am afraid the whole operation reeks of premature deployment and half-baked tactics. In cases of such conflict it is always best to go prepared for the worst-case scenario. But sometimes quick-reaction requirements demand that you take these sort of chances ... Unfortunately when Sierra Leone is not news-worthy even in India how can we expect it to be newsworthy abroad? I mean, how many journalists from India are in Sierra Leone today?[19]

However, others, for example Lieutenant Colonel (retired) A. K. Sharma, argued that from a regional security perspective,

India has no stakes in Sierra Leone, yet a large contingent of Indian troops has been committed there as part of UNAMSIL on the wooly-headed premise of a peacekeeping role. ... This in itself is not bad considering the handsome UN largesse paid out to the troops, the exposure to a multinational, multicultural and multifaceted operational environment and so on. But is it a wise decision? Why have Indian troops been put in a predicament, where they may be required to put their life on the line; a situation where even the basic tenets of humanitarian con-siderations, international convention and law are flouted by the protagonists?

Sharma also voiced concerns about domestic security and imperial over-stretch: 'Besides, it is not as if the Indian Army is sitting idle in the barracks ... it is also heavily engaged in defending our borders in Srinagar, Kargil etc.' He concluded that

If India needs to flex its muscles, pretensions to which it is credited with, or our diplomacy wants to strut and do its stuff, it should be done in the immediate neighbourhood where its writ is likely to run, where it will be of some benefit to at least a portion of its citizenry. Not half way round the world in some remote corner of Africa.[20]

SOMALIAN OPERATION COMES UNDER PARLIAMENTARY FIRE

UN operations in Somalia started in April 1992 with efforts to help provide humanitarian and food aid to those most affected by civil war and famine. From this initial mandate, the mission was widened to help stop the conflict and rebuild the basic institutions of a viable society. In December 1992, the UN established a Unified Task Force (UNITAF), led by the United States. For UNITAF, India contributed a naval task force under Commodore Sampat Pillai, consisting of three ships – *INS Deepak*, *INS Kuthar* and *INS Cheetah* – for carrying out relief and humanitarian aid to the people of Somalia. This was the first-ever Indian naval participation in a UN mission. In May 1993, following the establishment of UNISOM II, India contributed an extensive contingent for the mission. This comprised HQ66 (I) infantry brigade group; 1 Bihar; 5 Mahar; 3 Jammu and Kashmir Light Infantry; 3 Mechanized Infantry Battalion; Squadron Ex 7 Cavalry; 8722 Light Battery; 6 Reconnaissance and Observation Flight; Cheetah Armed Helicopters from the Indian Air Force (IAF); Detachment Remount & Veterinary Corps; and a logistics unit. Brigadier M. P. Bhagat commanded the Indian infantry brigade group in Somalia, with Colonel D. P. Merchant as Deputy Brigade Commander.

As with the US and other leading participants, Indian experience in Somalia led to a radical reappraisal of the future of UN peacekeeping within domestic political and military circles. On 23 August 1994, several opposition members of the Rajya Sabha (Upper House of the Indian parliament) tabled a motion demanding the withdrawal of Indian troops, following the loss of seven Indian lives the previous day.[21] Lieutenant Colonel Daljit Singh (retired), a veteran of the Indian Peacekeeping Force (IPKF) operation in Sri Lanka, was also severely critical of the lack of preparation of Indian troops for possible attack in Somalia. He argued that the Indian contingent was handicapped by poor intelligence and being too trusting of the local populace. He concluded: 'had we learnt the lessons of our experiences in the *Indian Peacekeeping Force (IPKF)* in Sri Lanka we could have put those to good use in Somalia. But we are bad students of history.'[22] However, India in turn was highly critical of the lack of US resolve in Somalia following its well-publicized casualties in Mogadishu.[23] The consensus of opinion was that the US had reneged on its responsibilities in the region and that India, Pakistan and other developing countries were left to pick up the pieces.[24]

THE FUTURE OF INDIAN PEACEKEEPING

India has traditionally been keen to contribute peacekeeping troops to new situations as they arise.[25] The former Indian prime minister, Narasimha Rao, was reported to have firmly supported India's continuing participation, with the comment that 'international peacekeeping forces should be selected from regions and areas far removed from where they are to be sent for undertaking credible operations'.[26] This could certainly be regarded as a vindication of Indian participation in Central American peacekeeping operations (ONUCA – UN Observer Group in Central America, ONUSAL – UN Observer Mission in El Salvador, UNMIH – UN Mission in Haiti), as well as in Africa, for instance. It also helps to explain the avoidance of military involvement in missions in other parts of Asia, such as East Timor (UNTAET).

However, some of the criticisms raised against recent UN missions have filtered through into Indian policy-making circles.[27] For instance, given the rapid escalation of conflicts, such as Rwanda, Bosnia and Sierra Leone, it is generally felt that the UN should be able to respond much more rapidly to these situations.[28] Some Indian commentators have also questioned whether the UN has a sufficiently wide mandate to cope effectively with the increasingly complex ethnic conflicts that are very much on the contemporary agenda, which implies that India has already moved towards accepting concepts developed in the 1990s such as 'wider peacekeeping'.[29] For instance, it has been suggested that given India's considerable experience of UN operations, it could usefully perform the function of training other potential peacekeepers in the future.[30] One such proposal is for a Centre for UN Peacekeeping in New Delhi. It is envisaged that this would be modelled on lines similar to other training schemes that already exist in Austria, Canada, Ireland and the Nordic states.[31]

According to a report by the Henry L. Stimson Center, Washington, India has a 'low' overall level of specialized training for peacekeeping purposes, despite conducting pre-deployment orientation and unit training.[32] One suggestion that might go some way to redress this lacuna is that a comprehensive questionnaire should be carried out among experienced peacekeepers, to create a database that can be drawn upon for further training.[33] As a further demonstration of its commitment to the evolving doctrine of UN peacekeeping, in September 1994 India announced that it had promised to keep at least one standby brigade, ready to fly to any part of the world when it was called upon to serve by the UN Secretary-General.[34] This indicated a significant change of policy, as traditionally the general consensus of Indian opinion was against having a contingent of standby troops ready at short notice, which might siphon off troops urgently required for quelling domestic conflicts.[35]

Recent seminars and conferences have included the UN International Seminar on Peacekeeping, in New Delhi, from 17 to 19 March 1999, organized by the Ministry of External Affairs and the Ministry of Defence. A total of 126 delegates from 71 countries attended the seminar. The United Service Institution of India (USI) also held an international conference in New Delhi on Peacekeeping and Peace Support in the 21st Century from 13 to 15 September 2000. An Asia-Pacific Regional Training Workshop was held in New Delhi from 20 to 26 January 1996, while an Indo-UK Defence Cooperation Seminar on UN Peacekeeping was also held in the Indian capital during October 1997.

According to Major-General V. K. Shrivastava, as one of the founder members of the UN,

> India has been aware of her responsibilities and has consistently contributed to some 30 UN peacekeeping efforts. An emerging power gives indications of aspirations in many ways. Strong presence in UN missions is one of them. The activity, besides being noble, signifies a nation's destiny and capacity, to play its part in world affairs. To start with India needs to fine tune our procedures, between the Ministry of External Affairs, Ministry of Defence and the Service Headquarters, to swiftly process the pros and cons of the intended mission(s) as also to train, equip, launch and sustain the mission(s) abroad ... We should establish a permanent Peace Centre to systematically attend to the training of peacekeepers, conduct of mission specific capsules and courses, prepare and update training manuals, carry out case studies, create data bank and so on – all this for our own peacekeepers and also for those from friendly foreign countries ... Austria and Sweden have such institutions. Malaysia has already stolen a march on us while we were 'actively examining' the proposal. We also need to hold international workshops and seminars on UNPKO more often. There is much to share.[36]

Furthermore, another General, V. P. Malik, has argued:

> We believe peacekeeping operations are an international endeavour. For our part, our contribution to peacekeeping operations reflects our commitment to the UN Charter and to international peace and security. India supports and will continue to participate in peacekeeping operations in the coming millennium. Our soldiers' vast experience in varying terrain and in extreme climatic conditions gives them easy adaptability to operate anywhere in the world. They possess a wide range of human and technological skills that are so important for peacekeeping operations . . . India can sustain long-term deployment in UN peacekeeping missions. Our contingents also have stand alone capability in terms of organizational structure, assets, equipment and logistics which was amply displayed in Somalia. De-mining is another facet in which India has contributed significantly over the years. Our sappers have been employed in Rwanda, Mozambique, Somalia, Angola and Cambodia for de-mining operations, generating mine awareness, training locals in undertaking mine clearance and rehabilitation programmes. We continue to believe a well trained, dedicated and disciplined soldier is the backbone of any peacekeeping operation.[37]

Soldiers from developing states such as India, Pakistan, Bangladesh, Nepal, Fiji, Thailand and Malaysia should continue to make vital military contributions to UN peacekeeping operations, based upon the mutual benefits such participation brings. However, there is also a perception that India's contribution has been undervalued and it would like to share in a greater share of decision-making processes of the UN. Most Indian critics now concede that winning a permanent UN seat is a long-term struggle and some even argue that it is not worth the price. The accession of Japan to the Security Council as a non-permanent member in November 1996, joining another US ally, South Korea, swung the balance of this forum away from non-alignment and still more decisively in favour of the United States. In a tersely worded statement, India attributed Japan's success to 'Yen Diplomacy', implying that Japan had used the possible withdrawal of loans to some African states as leverage.[38] At the time, this potentially significant event seemed highly likely to influence India's future participation in UN peacekeeping operations. For instance, N. Nanporia contended that 'New Delhi's rather overweening pride in its peacekeeping credentials has clearly played into the West's hands. Flattered by the attention it has

received on this count, New Delhi has been uncritically overeager to make
its presence felt in places like Somalia, Haiti and Rwanda.'[39] As another
observer of UN affairs pointed out after the killing of Indian soldiers in
Mogadishu and the humiliating US retreat from Haiti: 'Anyone wanting to
provoke trouble knows that attacking American troops is the best way to go
about it. If, say, India sees its peacekeepers killed, there is not a lot it can
do. But because the United States can react, it must, either by retreating or
retaliating.'[40]

CONCLUSION

On Sierra Leone and other recent missions, Lieutenant Colonel (retired)
A. K. Sharma has argued: 'It's good for Indian troops to get a multinational
experience and earn UN salaries, but if the situation degenerates into war,
they will be embroiled in a regional conflict that is of no concern to them.'[41]
Unlike most previous occasions when India sent troops for peacekeeping
operations, its soldiers and the commander were subject to significant
controversy and physical pressures in Sierra Leone. Parallel to this drama
was the unwarranted concern created by Kofi Annan and West African
governments about the Indian peacekeeping force. The Secretary-General
made statements which were obliquely critical of the manner in which
Major-General Jetley was performing his duties and conducting operations. The heads of state and governments of West African countries in a
resolution adopted by ECOWAS asserted that Jetley, not being familiar
with West African conditions, had mismanaged the operations and that he
should be replaced by a commander from the West African region. Even
more importantly, this resolution suggested that the multinational peacekeeping force should be replaced by a regional West African peacekeeping
force. Kofi Annan subsequently amended his initial criticism in the face of
very strong protests from the Indian government and military establishment. But the combined opposition of West African governments to India's
leadership nevertheless continued until the announcement of its troop
withdrawal in September 2000.

In conclusion, it was patently clear that the UN Secretariat did not
clearly define the terms of reference for UNAMSIL. According to Indian
former Foreign Minister J. N. Dixit,

> Major-General Jetley has acted with consummate tact and
> restraint despite the Indian forces being in danger. He has

sufficient coercive force at his command to take corrective action against the RUF. However, he has chosen the more rational path of negotiations. It is the responsibility of the UN Secretary General to ensure that the regional forces of West Africa do not question the credibility, the impartiality, under-standing, and motivations of the Indian commander of the peacekeeping force. Most importantly, despite India's long-standing commitment to be a participant in UN peacekeeping operations, our Sierra Leone experience should make us pause to re-examine the criteria and conditions under which India should participate in UN peacekeeping operations in the future, especially when no tangible interest of India is affected by situations into which India is invited.[42]

India's army is also undergoing a more introspective phase following the adverse reactions to its involvement in Sierra Leone, as well as in the regional arena after the Kargil conflict in 1999 with Pakistan. These ongoing tensions with its neighbour are exacerbated by the fallout from the terrorist attacks of 11 September 2001, the attack on parliamentary buildings in New Delhi on 13 December 2001 and heightened concerns about Hindu–Muslim relations following the Gujarat riots in late February, March and April 2002. There are crucial questions as to whether South Asian countries will in the future be so keen to contribute to UN missions in Africa and other parts of the world. For instance, Nepal has recently recalled some of its peacekeeping troops to deal with the rising tide of Maoist-style guerrilla attacks on its soil, and Pakistan also said that it will be withdrawing its 4,000 troops from the UNAMSIL mission in Sierra Leone. 'We cannot participate in a peacekeeping mission at a time when we are facing a threat of war,' said a Pakistani official.[43]

Although it can be concluded that India will continue its traditional policy of support for UN peacekeeping operations, it is likely to adopt a more critical and reflective stance, judging each new operation on its relative merits and demerits. For instance, Indian policy-makers studiously avoided any military involvement in the UN Transitional Administration in East Timor (UNTAET), neither wishing to upset good relations with Indonesia nor stoke the fires of separatism at home.[44] New Delhi will also continue to demand a more extensive policy input by those developing countries that contribute the bulk of the troops which comprise contemporary peacekeeping missions. However, with US President George W. Bush seemingly intent on spreading his 'war on terror' to other parts of Asia and the Middle East, any significant reform to existing UN institutions and decision-making processes is likely to remain a low priority for the next few years.

NOTES

1. A. Bullion, 'India and United Nations Peacekeeping Operations', *International Peacekeeping*, Vol. 4, No. 2 (spring 1997), pp. 98–114.
2. A. Bullion, 'India in Sierra Leone: A Case of Muscular Peacekeeping?', *International Peacekeeping*, Vol. 8, No. 4 (winter 2001), pp. 77–91.
3. Private conversation on the prospects for reform of the UN Security Council (UNSC) with UK Liberal Democrat parliamentary spokesman on defence, Menzies Campbell. He indicated that it was likely that US President George W. Bush would veto any proposal to expand the permanent membership of the UNSC.
4. 'India pulls out of Sierra Leone', *The Hindu International* (Madras) (30 September 2000), p. 1.
5. C. Hoyos et al., 'UN struggles to replace Indian peacekeepers in Sierra Leone', *Financial Times*, London (22 September 2000), p. 12.
6. Malik cited in R. Laskar, 'India pulls out force from Sierra Leone', *Indiaweekly*, London (29 September 2000), p. 34.
7. E. MacAskill, 'UN gets warning shot on peacekeeping', *The Guardian*, London (9 September 2000), p. 16.
8. Jetley cited in C. McGreal and E. MacAskill, 'UN to bolster peacekeeping force by 5,000', *The Guardian*, London (13 September 2000), p. 14.
9. F. Parakatil, *India and the United Nations Peace-Keeping Operations* (New Delhi: S. Chand & Co., 1975), pp. 16–21.
10. H. K. Srivastava, 'Indian Defence and Peacekeeping: Are the Two Competitive or Supplementary?', *Indian Defence Review*, New Delhi, Vol. 9, No. 4 (October–December 1994), pp. 16–21.
11. See articles in *The Hindu*, international edn, Madras: 'Germany wants India on U.N. Council' (6 August 1994), p. 3; 'Rao for Restructuring UN Security Council' (30 September 1995), p. 12; Former Indian Foreign Secretary J. N. Dixit is also highly revealing on the backroom dealings with the P5 on this issue: 'During my bilateral exchanges with my counterparts in the US State Department, the British Foreign Office and the Japanese Foreign Office, hints were dropped that if New Delhi were to sign the Non-Proliferation Treaty (NPT) and fall in line with various discriminatory regimes being put in place regarding issues such as missile development and transfer of technology and if India were to show an accommodating attitude on the Kashmir issue, India's chances of becoming a permanent member of the expanded Security Council would distinctly increase with support from important powers of the organization. I had clear instructions to reject such overt or covert suggestions.' Cited in J. N. Dixit, *Across Borders: Fifty Years of India's Foreign Policy* (New Delhi: Picus Books, 1998), p. 273. See also R. Drifte, *Japan's Quest for a Permanent Security Council Seat* (New York: St Martin's Press in association with St Antony's College, Oxford, 2000), p. 185.
12. 'Annan backs India on U.N. seat', *The Hindu International*, Madras (27 May 2000), p. 1.

13. E-parliament with the PM, 25 May 2000 (www.india-today.com/chat/20005/vajpayee.html).

14. C. Raja Mohan, 'Indo-German agenda on UN reforms', *The Hindu International*, Madras (27 May 2000), p. 12. Interestingly enough, the Czech Republic has also endorsed India's claim, see 'Czech Republic backs Indian claim for a UNSC permanent seat' (5 July 2000), www.india-today.com/ntoday/newsarchives/100/7/5/n63.shtml. On a trip to New Delhi in October 2000, Russian President Vladimir Putin also commented 'As one of the world's leading nations and as one of our leading partners, India is a prime candidate for a place in the Security Council', in R. Chengappa, 'More Than a Bear Hug', *India Today*, New Delhi (9 October 2000), p. 21.

15. B. Gill and J. Reilly, 'Sovereignty, Intervention and Peacekeeping: The View from Beijing', *Survival* (summer 2000), pp. 43–4.

16. A. Mattoo, 'India and the United Nations', in Foreign Service Institute (eds), *Indian Foreign Policy: Agenda for the 21st Century* (Konark: New Delhi, 1997), pp. 255–6.

17. M. Thatcher, *Statecraft: Strategies for a changing world* (London: HarperCollins, 2002), p. 205.

18. Ashok Malik, 'Keeping the Peace: Sierra Leone is a test of India's great power aspirations', *India Today International*, New Delhi (19 June 2000), p. 9.

19. Lieutenant General (retired) S. Nambiar, 'The whole operation reeks of premature deployment and half-baked tactics', *India Today Online*, New Delhi (14 June 2000), p. 4.

20. Lieutenant Colonel (retired) A. K. Sharma, 'Indian Troops Have No Business to be in Sierra Leone', *India Today Online* (www.india-today.co ...extra/sierraleone/opinion/opinion2.html). See also Lieutenant General (retired) R. Sharma, 'UN Peacekeeping on the Brink in Sierra Leone', *USI Journal*, New Delhi (July–September 2000), pp. 390–402.

21. 'Pull out troops, demands Opposition', *Asian Age*, London (24 August 1994), p. 1.

22. Lieutenant Colonel (retired) D. Singh, 'Complacency responsible for loss of seven lives in Somalia', *Asian Age* (1 September 1994), p. 9.

23. J. Cherian, 'Somalian Realities: After a Failed U.N.–US Mission', *Frontline* (11 March 1994), pp. 45–7.

24. M. Sommer, 'The Price of Peace: US undermining U.N. efforts', *Frontline* (29 July 1994), pp. 52–3.

25. Personal interview with Dr L. Singhvi, former Indian High Commissioner (UK), 17 May 1995, London, where he confirmed India's commitment to UN peacekeeping.

26. Cited in *Hindustan Times*, New Delhi (12 August 1994).

27. J. Singh, 'To Cope with the Times: Indian Security in a Time of Global Change', *Frontline*, Madras (28 August 1992), pp. 84–7.

28. Lieutenant General S. Nambiar (retired), 'India's Role in United Nations Peacekeeping', paper given at Seminar on India's Role in UN peacekeeping, New Delhi, 16 January 1995, p. 2; see also Major-General I. Rikhye, 'The United Nations in the 1990s and International Peacekeeping Operations', Southampton: Southampton Papers on International Policy, No. 3, 1992.

29. Nambiar, 'India's Role', comments: 'waiting for three months for troops to arrive in an area of operations is too ridiculous to be funny' (p. 5).

30. Ibid., pp. 5–6.

31. Srivastava, 'Indian Defence and Peacekeeping', p. 58.

32. Speech by Indian Army Chief V. P. Malik reported in 'Malik opposes regional arrangement for peacekeeping', *The Hindu*, Madras (14 September 2000). In his talk, Malik also opposed regional peacekeeping operations, based upon the missions in Sierra Leone and Somalia.

33. S. Rangarajan, 'The Perils of Peacekeeping: Training United Nations Forces', *Frontline* (30 June 1995), pp. 53–5.

34. Srivastava, 'Indian Defence and Peacekeeping', p. 58, provides details of this idea.

35. Nambiar, 'India's Role', pp. 9–10, discusses training and the proposals and practicalities of operating a standby force for rapid response to new conflicts. The long-running debate over the proposal for a UN Permanent Force is also addressed in Parakatil, *India and the United Nations Peace-Keeping Operations*, pp. 184–90, where various problems with such a contingency force are raised, including what they would do when not engaged on UN operations; whether, if they were kept apart from other national military units, they would become incompetent and outmoded; their acceptability in host countries, i.e. whether Indian troops would be more acceptable in some situations than others, such as South Asian states. As long ago as 1958, UN Representative Krishna Menon presciently stated: 'It is not possible to put by a number of soldiers and officers and say you are there to go out when there is trouble in the world', cited in ibid., p. 187. One possible solution would be to adopt the suggestion by Srivastava, 'Indian Defence and Peacekeeping', p. 59, where such contingents would have a dual role as in training other peacekeepers, and also be utilized for domestic conflict situations.

36. V. K. Shrivastava, Major-General (retired), Executive Editor, *Indian Defence Review*, New Delhi, Vol. 14, No. 1 (January–March 1999), pp. 8–9.

37. Excerpts from the address by General V. P. Malik to the delegates attending the UN International Seminar on Peacekeeping, New Delhi, 17–19 March 1999, reprinted in *Indian Defence Review*, New Delhi, Vol. 14, No. 1 (January–March 1999), pp. 8–9. See also General V. P. Malik, 'The Challenges of Peacekeeping and Peace Support', *USI Journal*, New Delhi (July–September 2000), pp. 379–83.

38. 'UN duel will not affect ties with Tokyo', *Asian Age* (23 October 1996), p. 4.

39. N. Nanporia, 'New Delhi's starry-eyed aspirations at the UN', *Asian Age* (23 May 1995), p. 8. In the same article, it is stated that the US has made consideration of a permanent Indian seat on the UN Security Council dependent upon 'improving relations with Pakistan' and settling the Kashmir dispute.

40. J. Leyne, 'From our own correspondent' (Transcript), BBC World Service, London (13 October 1995).

41. A. K. Sharma, 'Indian Troops Have No Business to Be in Sierra Leone', Opinion 2, *India Today Online* (www.india-today.co...extra/sierraleone/opinion/opinion2.html).

42. J. N. Dixit, 'Re-examine peacekeeping when no tangible Indian interest is involved', Opinion 1, *India Today Online* (www.india-today.co...extra/sierraleone/opinion/opinion1.html).

43. 'Pakistan's new front hits war on terror', *The Times*, London (29 December 2001), p. 17.

44. However, L. L. Mehrorta did serve as Director of the Jakarta office of UN Transition Assistance Mission in East Timor (UNTAET) from October 1999 onwards.

Index